Eric Rohmer

Manchester University Press

French Film Directors

DIANA HOLMES and ROBERT INGRAM *series editors*
DUDLEY ANDREW *series consultant*

Jean-Jacques Beineix PHIL POWRIE
Luc Besson SUSAN HAYWARD
Bertrand Blier SUE HARRIS
Robert Bresson KEITH READER
Leos Carax GARIN DOWD AND FERGUS DALEY
Claude Chabrol GUY AUSTIN
Henri-Georges Clouzot CHRISTOPHER LLOYD
Jean Cocteau JAMES WILLIAMS
Claire Denis MARTINE BEUGNET
Marguerite Duras RENATE GÜNTHER
Georges Franju KATE INCE
Jean-Luc Godard DOUGLAS MORREY
Mathieu Kassovitz WILL HIGBEE
Diane Kurys CARRIE TARR
Patrice Leconte LISA DOWNING
Louis Malle HUGO FREY
Georges Méliès ELIZABETH EZRA
Maurice Pialat MARJA WAREHIME
Jean Renoir MARTIN O'SHAUGHNESSY
Alain Resnais EMMA WILSON
Coline Serreau BRIGITTE ROLLET
André Téchiné BILL MARSHALL
François Truffaut DIANA HOLMES AND ROBERT INGRAM
Agnès Varda ALISON SMITH
Jean Vigo MICHAEL TEMPLE

FRENCH FILM DIRECTORS

Eric Rohmer

DEREK SCHILLING

Manchester University Press
MANCHESTER AND NEW YORK

distributed exclusively in the USA by Palgrave

Published by Manchester University Press
Oxford Road, Manchester M13 9NR, UK
and Room 400, 175 Fifth Avenue, New York, NY 10010, USA
www.manchesteruniversitypress.co.uk

Distributed exclusively in the USA by
Palgrave, 175 Fifth Avenue, New York, NY 10010, USA

Distributed exclusively in Canada by
UBC Press, University of British Columbia, 2029 West Mall, Vancouver, BC, Canada V6T 1Z2

British Library Cataloguing-in-Publication Data
A catalogue record for this book is available from the British Library

Library of Congress Cataloging-in-Publication Data applied for

ISBN 978 0 7190 7234 5 *hardback*
ISBN 978 0 7190 7235 2 *paperback*

First published 2007

16 15 14 13 12 11 10 09 08 07 10 9 8 7 6 5 4 3 2 1

Typeset in Scala with Meta display
by Koinonia, Manchester
Printed in Great Britain
by Biddles Ltd, King's Lynn

Contents

List of figures

Series editors' foreword

To an anglophone audience, the combination of the words 'French' and 'cinema' evokes a particular kind of film: elegant and wordy, sexy but serious – an image as dependent on national stereotypes as is that of the crudely commercial Hollywood blockbuster, which is not to say that either image is without foundation. Over the past two decades, this generalised sense of a significant relationship between French identity and film has been explored in scholarly books and articles, and has entered the curriculum at university level and, in Britain, at A-level. The study of film as an art-form and (to a lesser extent) as industry, has become a popular and widespread element of French Studies, and French cinema has acquired an important place within Film Studies. Meanwhile, the growth in multi-screen and 'art-house' cinemas, together with the development of the video industry, has led to the greater availability of foreign-language films to an English-speaking audience. Responding to these developments, this series is designed for students and teachers seeking information and accessible but rigorous critical study of French cinema, and for the enthusiastic filmgoer who wants to know more.

The adoption of a director-based approach raises questions about auteurism. A series that categorises films not according to period or to genre (for example), but to the person who directed them, runs the risk of espousing a romantic view of film as the product of solitary inspiration. On this model, the critic's role might seem to be that of discovering continuities, revealing a necessarily coherent set of themes and motifs which correspond to the particular genius of the individual. This is not our aim: the auteur perspective on film, itself most clearly articulated in France in the early 1950s, will be interrogated in certain volumes of the series, and, throughout, the director will be treated as one highly significant element in a complex process of film production and reception which includes socio-economic and political determinants, the work of a large and highly skilled team of artists and technicians, the mechanisms of production and distribution, and the complex and multiply determined responses of spectators.

The work of some of the directors in the series is already known outside France, that of others is less so – the aim is both to provide informative and original English-language studies of established figures, and to extend the range of French directors known to anglophone students of cinema. We intend the series to contribute to the promotion of the informal and formal study of French films, and to the pleasure of those who watch them.

DIANA HOLMES
ROBERT INGRAM

Acknowledgements

This project owes its existence to Sue Harris, to whom I am most grateful. In Paris, I wish to thank the staffs of the Bibliothèque du Film and the Institut national de l'audiovisuel, where research for this project was completed. For their insights and advice, I want to express my gratitude to Eric Macé, Nicholas Paige, Sam DiIorio, Alan Williams, and series editors Diana Holmes and Robert Ingram.

This book is for Ana and Adrian. You are always in my thoughts, even when my eyes are turned toward the screen.

Introduction

Upon release in September 2001 of Eric Rohmer's twenty-third feature, the exquisite Revolutionary costume drama *L'Anglaise et le Duc*, the Parisian daily *Le Figaro* coyly asked its readers, 'Faut-il guillotiner Rohmer?' (Must Rohmer be guillotined?) (Macé-Scaron 2001). At age eighty-one, the reclusive director found himself in the glare of a spotlight he had long fled. That Rohmer, born Jean-Marie Maurice Schérer in 1920, had little patience for the institutional French Left and its rigidly Jacobin conception of the national past was no secret: 'Je ne sais pas si je suis de droite, mais ce qui est sûr, c'est que *je ne suis pas de gauche*' (I don't know if I'm a man of the right, but what is certain is that *I'm not of the left*), he famously remarked in the pages of *Cahiers du cinéma* (Biette 1965: 58). That the director of *L'Anglaise et le Duc* was a bona fide royalist nostalgic for the Old Regime, and hence deserving of the same fate as his aristocratic protagonists, however, was hardly a sure thing. No doubt it was the filmmaker's critics who lost their heads in the end. For in their attempts to stir up controversy, these self-appointed guardians of Republican ideology neglected the artistic merits of what was, as the first all-digital French feature (shortly followed by the Gérard Depardieu vehicle *Vidocq*), a signal achievement in the history of film style, and the capstone of Rohmer's half-century career.

It is fitting that an intimist cinema devoted to the analysis of sentiment should have so aroused critics' passions, however late in the director's life course. Political considerations aside, judgements of Rohmer's work have not been uniformly kind. It has been qualified as elitist, coldly intellectual, repetitive in its situations and themes, and downright exasperating in its garrulousness and often precious tone.

While some of these criticisms can be levelled against the director-based French cinema as a whole, others seem to dog Rohmer specifically, who has long drawn inspiration from such 'literary' sources as the short story and stage play and who, in later works like *Les Rendez-vous de Paris* (1995), has pushed his style to the limits of mannerism, at the risk of self-parody. Yet even the most conservative estimates acknowledge the profound originality that Rohmer brings to his filmic universe, idiosyncrasies and all (Thomson 2004: 771–3), and few would contest that he has crafted not a mere collection of features with the habitual number of hits and misses, but an œuvre of single-minded coherence. The six *Contes moraux* (*Moral Tales*, 1962–72), six *Comédies et proverbes* (*Comedies and Proverbs*, 1981–1987), and four *Contes des quatre saisons* (*Tales of the Four Seasons*, 1990–98), together with sketch films (*4 Aventures de Reinette et Mirabelle*, 1987), literary adaptations (*Die Marquise von O...*, 1976; *Perceval le Gallois*, 1979), and costume dramas (*Triple agent*, 2004) present a stylistic and thematic unity all but unparalleled in the contemporary French cinema. Along with Jacques Rivette and Jean-Luc Godard, Rohmer exemplifies auteurism – in Pascal Bonitzer's words, a cinema

> qui ne se moule pas dans les standards exigés: une vedette, un 'sujet', une situation émotionnelle forte, une ligne d'action simple, une positivité immanente du héros.[1] (Bonitzer 1983: 10)

Arguably, the auteurism at hand is a conservative one: in Rohmer's view, the duty of the filmmaker is to explore human interaction through neatly drawn narratives which avoid the traps of introspection, symbol, or experiment.

What these films portray are moments of transition and availability, when characters caught between two or more objects of desire attempt to invent rules of conduct by which to engage to their advantage in the game of love and chance. In the prime of adulthood, they value the abstract freedom to choose among romantic partners in accordance with moral or practical principles, over and above the likelihood of attaining real-world results. Put simply, they find themselves talking about love far more than making it. This elision of sex in favour of discourse reflects not simply a debt to the classical French theatre, with its doctrine of *bienséances* (decorum), and to

1 'which doesn't fit the standard mould: a star, a "subject", a strong emotional situation, a simple plot line, an unfailingly positive hero'.

Hollywood 'sophistication' of the 1930s and 1940s, but the recognition that desire symptomatically must fail to attain its object. A gentle irony, sustained by an unemphatic, respectful camera, contrasts with the numbing physicality of many contemporary films, which tend to confuse emotional truth with extreme situations viewed in close-up. Historical pictures excepted, no one dies in Rohmer's universe, no pistols are drawn, no cars chased. Nothing much in fact will take place on screen, outside the exacting verbal confrontations through which characters of both sexes position themselves as intensely rational human beings who take intention and act, thought and speech to be one and the same – and who deceive themselves in the process. Launching themselves into intense debates and vaudeville-like plots as they seek out kindred spirits with whom to pass the time, only too rarely do they find, aided by chance, the transcendence they have been seeking all along, like Delphine in *Le Rayon vert* or Félicie in *Conte d'hiver*.

This is a cinema of visual understatement and, admittedly, verbal excess, where actors must scrupulously adhere to a text that determines their character's very being. *Je parle, donc je suis*: I speak, therefore I am, such is their motto. Rohmer takes to the letter the 'talking picture', making conversation the dominant form of screen action. But there is always more to a Rohmer film than meets the ear. Endings favour ambiguity over closure, asking spectators to revisit the narrative the better to expose characters' hidden motives and conflicting points of view (Magny 1995). And despite their straightforward, linear design, these fictions are not without what Bonitzer calls their 'secret compartments', their enigmas and their false trails (Bonitzer 1991: 69). Like Hitchcock's narratives, whose influence they bear, they can aspire to chiselled artistic perfection even as they invite us to contemplate the exterior, world-bound beauty which it is, in Rohmer's theologically inflected view, cinema's privilege alone to capture. 'A humbly documentary presentation of reality inevitably reveals an inherent order, which speaks of God', writes to this effect Colin Crisp (Crisp 1988: 5).

In spite of its recurrent narrative patterns and virtually unchanging treatment of image and *mise en scène*, Rohmer's work at the margins of French industry remains difficult to categorise. This is true in no small part for reasons of chronology. While his first completed shorts date to the early 1950s and his feature debut, *Le Signe du Lion*, to

1959 (released 1962), public recognition came late for Rohmer, with the successes of the mildly risqué *La Collectionneuse* (1967) and the international art-house hit *Ma Nuit chez Maud* (1969), which was nominated for two Academy Awards. Though his notoriety postdates the French New Wave's beginnings by nearly a decade, many historians have grouped Rohmer, who was editor-in-chief of *Cahiers du cinéma* from 1958 to 1963, with that journal's younger contributors, the 'Young Turks' Truffaut, Godard, Rivette, and Chabrol, all of whom made the transition to professional directing in 1958–59. Hence, in her influential survey of French film since 1968, Jill Forbes excludes Rohmer, together with Chabrol, Rivette, and Resnais, maintaining that

> although all these directors continued to make films in the 1970s their period of influence was over. This was clearly true of Chabrol, who has devoted himself primarily to making commercial films, and of Rohmer, whose work is based on a deliberate and stylised continuity. (Forbes 1992: 2)

While one may agree with Forbes's premise, her conclusion begs the question as to the ways influence exerts itself over time. The films Rohmer released in the 1980s and 1990s – arguably the apogee of his classicism – may seem less innovative or less beautiful to look at than his *Contes moraux*, but they cannot be dismissed out of hand on the assumption that 'deliberate' variations on a theme are less compelling than bold essays in political filmmaking (Godard) or exercises in stylistic and generic virtuosity (Truffaut).

There is, indeed, a danger in classifying Rohmer based on the contacts he made in the heyday of *Cahiers*, during which he illustrated himself above all as a theorist of the seventh art after the manner of his mentor, André Bazin. As Richard Neupert has written,

> Not every *Cahiers* critic who made a movie in 1959 was catapulted to fame, and just because historians by the late 1960s heralded Rohmer as a major figure of the New Wave does not mean that he was a vital member during its core years. (Neupert 2002: 271)

Whether the director should be considered central to the New Wave, then, depends on the definition given that entity as (1) an historical phenomenon predicated on changes in the economics of film production and confined to the years 1958–1962; (2) a generation of young, independent filmmakers who rejected the industry's rigid hierarchies and standardised notions of professionalism; or (3) a way of seeing that questions the relationship between fiction and documentary, set and location, director and subject, screenplay and *mise en scène* (Marie 1997). By the first criterion, only the financially disastrous *Le Signe du Lion* and, if one stretches things a bit, the shorts of 1962–65 (*La Boulangère de Monceau*; *La Carrière de Suzanne*; *Place de l'Etoile*) are in any significant way New Wave films; by the second and third definitions, in contrast, any number of projects might qualify. With few exceptions, Rohmer has always worked from his own scripts, employed little- or lesser-known actors, and kept technical collaborators to a minimum, even when this has meant violating industry regulations. At the turn of the 1980s, when Truffaut had long accommodated his subjects to robust budgets and passably star-studded casts, when Godard had only just returned to fiction filmmaking after his foray into video, when Chabrol had arguably deserted innovation for tested formulas, Rohmer was virtually alone among his coterie of onetime *Cahiers* critics in making works consonant with New Wave ideals. The rough-edged location shooting of *La Femme de l'aviateur* (1981) and the improvisations of *Le Rayon vert* (1986), each produced on a shoestring in 16mm, attest to the do-it-yourself spirit that perhaps only Rivette, in *Le Pont du Nord* (1980), and Jacques Rozier, in his *Maine Océan* (1986), had managed to preserve intact. It's no accident that as Rohmer entered each new decade in life, the popular press persisted in calling him the most youthful of French directors, and one of few who, owing to a privileged relationship with a single production company – Les Films du Losange – had managed commercial viability without bowing to commercialism.

Film historians have not unduly insisted on sticking Rohmer with the New Wave label. One telling connection is suggested by Susan Hayward, who in addressing the 'moral discourses' of the 1960s and 1970s associates Chabrol's critique of bourgeois morality, Jean-Pierre Mocky's trenchant anti-authoritarianism, and Rohmer's 'intellectually intimist' depiction of 'the social mores of a certain intellectual middle class' and of female subjectivity in particular (Hayward 1993: 262). Despite the obvious differences that set off Rohmer's rather prudish rationalisations from the brash exposés and secret-sharing of a Mocky or a Chabrol, one should not discount the potential of Rohmer's pictures for social critique. This critique, however, would necessarily be of a second order, since a description of French class society is not the rhetorical aim of the films themselves. Rémi Fourier Lanzoni thus quite appositely casts Rohmer as an heir to the humanistic tradition of Jean Renoir. Like Claude Sautet, who came to attention around 1970 with the ensemble picture *César et Rosalie*, Rohmer makes no secret of his affinities for popular romantic comedy. Yet where Sautet defers to dramatic convention, Rohmer betrays his penchant for formal rigour, producing films that appeal to a class of spectators concerned less with identification and catharsis than with the intricacies of discourse. As Lanzoni writes, Rohmer's narratives

> usually overlooked [*sic*] a possible contact with the spectator's deeper mental universe, and, as a result, the presence of unremitting melancholy in Rohmer's films has always had a limited impact on French popular audiences. (Lanzoni 2002: 285)

Box-office figures confirm the modest appeal of the director's concerns: only *Ma Nuit chez Maud* topped one million tickets sold in France, while most of his pictures have hovered in the 200,000–400,000 range during their year of release, pushing the half million mark thanks to frequent revivals.[2]

In France and abroad, critics have largely neglected the extent to which Rohmer's quintessentially French fictions, seductive and contemporary as they may be, are insulated from social and demographic change. No speaking parts are held by actors of African or Maghrebi origin – a fact that may attest as much to the closed state of the country's drama schools and motion picture industry as to the old ways of a director born shortly after the signing of the Treaty of Versailles. All the same, form and content in Rohmer's cinema reproduce the world view of a segment of the white European intelligentsia for which language is prized over action and social privilege is enjoyed uncritically. We do not find activists striving for a better world or workers engaged in struggle (compare with the equally personal universe of Robert Guédiguian, the director of *Marius et Jeannette* and *La Ville est tranquille*), but men and women who, equipped with better-than-average physical and mental characteristics and, one suspects, deep pocketbooks, compensate for their insecurities by speaking their piece. Whether it is worth the trouble to extract social critique from this portrayal remains to be seen. At the very least, readings such as those of Alain Hertay, who brings to bear philosopher Gilles Lipovetsky's

2 For full attendance figures, see the Filmography.

theses on individualism and emptiness on the *Comédies et proverbes* (Hertay 1998), or of Marion Vidal, in her study of the *Contes moraux*'s ambiguous heroines (Vidal 1977), can motivate spectators to delve into the relationship of class and ideology to film form. The same can surely be said of gender. Against the popular clichés that would paint Rohmer as a mild-mannered fetishist with a thing for teenage girls' knees (Claire) or posteriors (Pauline), critic Bérénice Reynaud has argued that female characters are not objects of the director's desire, but abstract figurations of the workings of cinematic desire itself. If the heroines of the *Comédies et proverbes* consistently fail to make themselves loved, it is because the *desire* which motivates them to act cannot, unlike Lacan's principle of *demand*, be fulfilled. The sexual impasse in which they are caught becomes an aesthetic object in its own right, made concrete in the act of waiting for a grace which, most often, will simply not arrive (Reynaud 2000: 262–4).

One gets the impression that, had he but world enough and time, Rohmer, who varies plot structures slightly from film to film, would end up exhausting all the permutations of heterosexual romantic involvement, or how – given a woman and three men, or a man and three women, or two men and two women, and so on – things move from the disorder of freely desiring individuals to a state of order, however provisional. While works like *Pauline à la plage* bring to human relationships an exacting geometry that leaves some spectators cold, they embody at the same time the positive virtues of clarity, concision, and balance that characterise all classical achievements. The range of information they deploy fosters spectatorial engagement while preventing easy psychological identification; exclusion of such industry formulas as the subjective camera and extradiegetic film music reinforce emotional distance. Actors are asked to walk a fine line between naturalness and artifice in a procedure that Maria Tortajada has described as a 'third way' between Diderot's transparency of role and Brechtian demystification. An 'ambiguous' form of seduction results, destabilising the film narrative and the workings of spectatorial desire (Tortajada 1999: 6). If this cinema is so seductive, it is, in the end, due less to its represented content (the amorous games of a well-heeled social set) than to the allure of form itself. Literary models from the classical stage comedy to the eighteenth-century tale and psychological novel inform the dual search for narrative economy and discursive complexity that is the director's trademark. Indeed, as

Rohmer long argued in *Cahiers du cinéma*, tropes that we associate with 'literature' belong to the cinema too, an art which thrives on a constitutive impurity. It is hence all the more essential that the director's work be reclaimed from the province of literature, where it is all too quickly laid to rest, and that we ask ourselves how it resonates with the history and ontology of the medium. Rohmer's predecessors are not only Marivaux, Musset, and Dostoyevsky, but Murnau, Renoir, Rossellini, and Hitchcock, to name but a few.

The goal of this volume is to provide a balanced appraisal of Rohmer's œuvre in historical context. Although interpretation of individual films will not be its main objective (see Magny 1995 and Crisp 1988), representative examples from the director's twenty-five features and fiction shorts will be presented throughout. As I have chosen to privilege questions of theory, style, and form relevant to films of all periods over strict chronology, Chapter 1 will present a full career overview. Its focus is on production history and reception in the mainstream French press. My hope is that the reader will find within that opening chapter reliable information (other than biographical) and a convenient framework for grasping what is an extensive, but by no means unmanageable, body of work.

Paradoxically, among the most significant obstacles faced by Rohmer's viewer is the apparent transparency of the films themselves, or the effacement of the camera's presence through editing. This key stylistic trait cannot be appreciated without reference to André Bazin's concept of ontological realism, of which Rohmer was a major exponent at *Cahiers du cinéma*. To establish the intertexts and artistic principles his films put into play, Chapter 2 reviews the abundant critical writings Rohmer published in France from the late 1940s to the early 1960s. That exploration leads up to the discussion in Chapter 3 of the interdependence of film style and technique in the director's pursuit of cinematographic realism: how are sound and image configured, and to what effect? How is the production process envisaged from screenplay to shoot?

The two remaining chapters broach issues central to the director's finest work for the screen. 'Seriality and theme', devoted to the *Contes moraux*, *Comédies et proverbes*, and *Contes des quatre saisons*, looks at how Rohmer's decision to work by thematic series forces the viewer to intuit, beyond the data of any given film, relations of complementarity, identity, and opposition that lend each cycle a complex, musical texture. The art or, rather, the difficulty of representing the past is the subject of Chapter 5, 'Literature and history', which pays close attention to four of the director's costume films, each of which rethinks the cinema in relation to the artistic imaginary of past epochs. The volume concludes with a brief excursus on *le rohmérien* – that inimitable, instantly recognisable variant of the French language that spectators come to love or to hate.

References

Biette, Jean-Claude, Jacques Bontemps and Pascal Bonitzer (1965), 'L'ancien et le nouveau', *Cahiers du cinéma* 172, November: 33–41; 56–9.

Bonitzer, Pascal (1983), 'Standards d'émotion', *Cahiers du cinéma* 353, November: 9–13.

Bonitzer, Pascal (1991), *Eric Rohmer*, Paris, Editions de l'Etoile/Cahiers du cinéma.

Crisp, C.G. (1988), *Eric Rohmer: Realist and Moralist*, Bloomington and Indianapolis, Indiana University Press.

Forbes, Jill (1992), *The Cinema in France: After the New Wave*, Bloomington and Indianapolis, Indiana University Press.

Hayward, Susan (1993), *French National Cinema*, London and New York, Routledge.

Hertay, Alain (1998), *Eric Rohmer: Comédies et proverbes*, Liège, Editions de Céfal.

Lanzoni, Rémi Fourier (2002), *French Cinema: From its Beginnings to the Present*, New York and London, Continuum.

Macé-Scaron, Joseph (2001), 'Faut-il guillotiner Rohmer?', *Le Figaro*, 12 September.

Magny, Joël (1995), *Eric Rohmer*, 2nd ed., Paris, Payot & Rivages.

Marie, Michel (1997), *La Nouvelle Vague: une école artistique*, Paris, Nathan.

Neupert, Richard (2002), *A History of the French New Wave Cinema*, Madison, University of Wisconsin Press.

Reynaud, Bérénice (2000), 'Representing the sexual impasse: Eric Rohmer's *Les Nuits de la pleine lune*', in *French Film: Texts and Contexts*, ed. Susan Hayward and Ginette Vincendeau, 2nd ed., London and New York, Routledge: 253–68.

Thomson, David (2004), *A Biographical Dictionary of Film*, 3rd ed., New York, Knopf.

Tortajada, Maria (1999), *Le Spectateur séduit: le libertinage dans le cinéma d'Eric Rohmer*, Paris, Kimé.

Vidal, Marion (1977), *Les* Contes moraux *d'Eric Rohmer*, Paris, Pierre Lherminier Editeur.

1

Career overview

Eric Rohmer was born Jean-Marie Maurice Schérer in 1920 in Tulle (Corrèze), a provincial backwater in south-western France, halfway between Bordeaux and Clermont-Ferrand. The fact that many sources give his birthplace as the north-eastern city of Nancy or furnish alternate dates of birth reflects the director's onetime habit of leading those who would pry into his private affairs down false trails. Alhough he has long given up wearing fake beards and dark glasses in public, and even consents to attend the odd festival, Rohmer has neatly separated his professional activities, centred on the Right Bank offices of Paris' Les Films du Losange, from his quiet family life in a Left Bank neighbourhood abutting the Luxembourg Garden. Few artistic collaborators have joined his circle of intimates, and journalists have learned to stick to questions of filmmaking alone, leaving their cameras at the door.

The upshot of this secretive posturing is that little of certainty is known of the director's past. Though presumed to be a 'Catholic filmmaker' (Lopate 2003: 170), Rohmer shares the surname Schérer (pronounced 'shayr-air') with Alsatian Jews, many of whom converted or left the border province. He has shielded from the public eye his spouse, whom he married in the late 1950s, their children and grandchildren. He has never spoken publicly of his brother, the philosopher René Schérer (b. 1924) – who taught alongside Gilles Deleuze at the experimental university Paris VIII and, in the 1970s, co-wrote works on homosexual liberation with gay activist Guy Hoquenghem – or of his son Denis (born 1958), a journalist who, working under the pseudonym René Monzat, helped to found in 1990 the anti-right-wing activist group Ras le Front and has written widely on the history of right-wing movements. Whether the filmmaker's discretion is designed to conceal untold secrets, or simply to give lustre to an otherwise unremarkable existence, is for future biographers to decide. The fact remains that by showing healthy disdain for the industry's star-system, Rohmer has styled himself as a fiercely independent creator, a *cinéaste du dimanche*, or Sunday filmmaker, whose energies are entirely given to the pleasures of creation, as distinguished from the pursuit of public recognition.

Maurice Schérer's initial vocation was not cinema, to which he had limited exposure as an adolescent in the provinces: 'Quelques Charlot Pathé-Baby, *L'Aiglon*, et autres *Tartarin de Tarascon* constituaient tout mon bagage',[1] he noted in 1955 in *Cahiers du cinéma* (Rohmer 1955: 11). Coming from a major film critic, this admission undoubtedly took readers by surprise. But surely they had not been to Tulle, which Schérer left in 1937 to study letters at the Lycée Henri-IV in Paris, a training school for the academic elite. After failing twice the second part of the dreaded *agrégation* examination, Schérer taught French grammar and literature during the war years in various secondary schools outside Paris. Under German occupation, he chose, as did the majority of his compatriots, the middle ground between active resistance and collaboration: 'Je suis resté sans rien faire, sans participer à rien' (I got by without doing or taking part in anything) (Goudet 2004: 26). Germany's creation in February 1943 of the Service du Travail Obligatoire, the compulsory labour service required of all able-bodied French men born between 1920 and 1922, forced Schérer to lie low and even to procure false identity papers. He escaped – narrowly in one instance, in a Métro station – the habitual round-ups of STO-dodgers by the collaborationist Milice (Goudet 2004: 26). Whatever spare moments he had in these uncertain times were presumably spent composing short stories, some of which laid the groundwork for future screenplays.

In 1946, under the pseudonym Gilbert Cordier, Schérer published *Elisabeth* with the venerable Parisian house Gallimard. Written in July and August 1944 and set during the summer vacation just before the war, the novel treats the escapades of young men whose

1 'A few Chaplin pictures for home viewing, *L'Aiglon*, and things like *Tartarin de Tarascon* were the extent of my film culture'. The former is a 1931 historical melodrama set under Napoleon, after Edmond Rostand's play, the latter an adventure story from a novel by Alphonse Daudet.

primary occupation is flirting with the women they encounter along the banks of the Marne and at get-togethers in comfortable suburban villas. The women are prone to fits of pouting and their would-be suitors are listless and uncertain: very Rohmerian indeed. Themes of romantic insecurity, feminine beauty, and changes in the weather as a correlative of emotion likewise prefigure Rohmer's many 'outdoor' films, from *Le Genou de Claire* and *Pauline à la plage* to *L'Ami de mon amie*. Unremarkable in style, the dialogue-heavy *Elisabeth* went all but unnoticed.

For the war-weary French, the years following the Liberation were a time of reawakening, signalled by the arrival on French screens of the countless American films that had been banned under German occupation. As popular film-going entered its boom years, with a record 424 million tickets sold in 1947 (Crisp 1993: 67), a new, self-aware film culture took hold around the *ciné-club* movement, dedicated to the study of film history and aesthetics. As the chief programmer of Le Ciné-Club du Quartier Latin, Schérer came into contact in the late 1940s with younger and often intemperate film enthusiasts like Truffaut and Rivette. He attended *Objectif 49*'s Festival du Film Maudit in Biarritz, which featured premieres of Renoir's *The Southerner* and Vigo's restored *L'Atalante*, and began writing pieces on cinema aesthetics that led to his tenure with *Cahiers du cinéma*, the magazine founded in 1951 by Jacques Doniol-Valcroze, André Bazin, and Joseph-Marie Lo Duca. Influenced by Bazin's own theories of the photographic image, Schérer crafted throughout the 1950s arguments concerning cinema's classicism, its relationship to the other arts, and the notion of film authorship. This activity established him as a prominent critical voice in France, as we will see in Chapter 2.

First steps

From the start, film comment was for Schérer connected to the practice of filmmaking. Aided and abetted by the core group of cinephiles who, on account of their antics and verbal sallies, became known as the 'Young Turks', he began work on his first 16mm shorts as early as 1950. There was at the time considerable demand for short subjects, both as part of standard cinema programmes, since the abolishment in 1941 of the double and triple bills (Crisp 1993: 52), and thanks to an extensive 16mm exhibition circuit. These projects Schérer signed under the pseudonym Eric Rohmer, a rather approximate anagram of his given name. Whether his intent, as critics once speculated, was to hide his directorial pursuits from his mother, who thought teaching literature a far nobler career path, is beside the point. In film circles, the practice was common enough: witness F.W. Murnau, born 'Plumpe'.

Rohmer's first steps as a director, while hesitant, were far from uninspired. Shot with borrowed equipment and on borrowed time (Schérer was not released from his teaching duties until 1957), the short subjects were as often as not to remain unfinished, since ideas and leftover scraps of film came easier than funds for postproduction. Such was the case of the silent *Journal d'un scélérat* (reported lost), inspired by the unlikely bedfellows Kierkegaard and the Stroheim of *Merry Wives*; the same fate initially befell *Présentation, ou Charlotte et son steack*, which sat for ten years in storage before Rohmer and a trio of voice actors postsynchronised it. Shot in the French Jura mountains and in a photographer's studio (Magny 1995a: 101), the wintertime short turns on a simple triangle: Walter (Jean-Luc Godard) is introduced by a girlfriend to her friend Charlotte, whom he tries to seduce as she cooks a steak in her frigid chalet kitchenette. Far more ambitious was Rohmer's subsequent project, *Les Petites Filles modèles*, long one of the murkiest episodes of his career. Thanks to researcher François Thomas, we now have proof that Rohmer was the first among the future core of the New Wave to direct professionally (Thomas 2005: 33). In summer 1952, Rohmer and producer Guy de Ray convinced Dahomey national Joseph Kéké, a student who happened to be the son of a palm-tree plantation owner, to finance an adaptation of the Comtesse de Ségur's well-loved children's novel, first published in 1858. Budgeted at just over 22,000,000 old francs, or one-third the average cost for a feature, the 35mm film did not have a distributor when the crew and a mixed cast of professionals and child non-professionals set off for Normandy in September 1952. Conditions were tense due to the difficulty of using location sound and because crew members saw the first-time director as an aesthete unschooled in the realities of getting usable takes (Thomas 2005: 41–2). Isolated and demoralised, he returned to his teaching post before the shoot's end. Though Rohmer completed a one-hour edit with added voiceover narration, Kéké refused to spend the small sums needed to finish postproduction, to the effect that of the 102 French features made in 1953, *Les Petites Filles modèles* was the only one not to find domestic or foreign distribution (Thomas 2005: 42). The experience proved the gulf between the guild-like state of the French industry and the independent cinema of 'authors' that Rohmer and his combative cohort writing for *Cahiers du cinéma* wished to defend.

The results of subsequent projects that Rohmer undertook in the 1950s were anything but amateurish. As Truffaut noted in 1961, based on his recollections of the short *Bérénice* (1954), after the Edgar Allan Poe story, and of the featurette *La Sonate à Kreutzer* (1956), a Tolstoy adaptation featuring Jean-Claude Brialy, 'le maître du 16mm était, sans conteste, Eric Rohmer' (The master of 16mm filmmaking was Eric Rohmer beyond any argument) (Truffaut 1975: 335/1978: 321). Much like the generation of the 1920s that counted among its ranks Jean Vigo and René Clair, the group that had formed around Rivette, Rohmer, Godard, and Truffaut found in 16mm a ground to test out ideas and techniques before turning to the feature format. Collaboration remained the rule. Thus, in the four-part series *Charlotte et Véronique*, Rohmer and Godard each directed two shorts with input from the other, while Rohmer and Chabrol joined forces to write *Hitchcock* (1957), the first comprehensive treatment of the British director's work in any language. This spirit of cooperation extended to financing as well. As the back-to-back successes in spring 1958 of *Le Beau Serge* and *Les Cousins* had left his fledgling production company, AJYM, flush with funds, Chabrol advanced the moneys for Rohmer's 35mm *Véronique et son cancre* (1958), an off-the-wall vignette about a fidgety dunce who exasperates his private mathematics tutor. Confident in his friend's abilities, Chabrol then bankrolled what was in effect Rohmer's second attempt at feature filmmaking.

Shot in the streets of Paris in summer 1959 by veteran cinematographer Nicolas Hayer, who had spent a decade in French Indochina as a news reporter and had seventy films to his credit (Crisp 1993: 163), *Le Signe du Lion* was co-written by Rohmer with Chabrol's habitual screenwriter, the novelist Paul Gégauff. The narrative traces the downward trajectory of an out-of-work American composer, Pierre Wesserlin (Jess Hahn), who, after losing out on a family inheritance, slides from precariousness into misery in the heat of an insufferable August. His attempts to borrow money from friends around Saint-Germain-des-Prés fall flat, and soon Wesserlin finds himself slumming on the banks of the Seine with a clownish tramp, who carts about the hulking musician in a pram. Salvation comes in extremis, much as it does for the hotel porter in Murnau's *The Last Laugh* (1924), when Wesserlin discovers that because of a cousin's death in a motorcar accident the inheritance is his after all (see figure 1). Grim in subject and verist in detail, the picture, which is reminiscent of Rossellini in its description of solitude, desperation, and redemption, had difficulty attracting a distributor. Asked to re-edit the picture, Rohmer did not cave in, thanks to an insistent Henri Langlois, the director of the Cinémathèque Française. After languishing thirty months in postproduction, the film was released in May 1962 on just one Paris screen, only to close after two weeks; a glowing review in Rohmer's own *Cahiers* appeared too late to make a difference (Beylie 1962: 57). With fewer than five thousand tickets sold, *Le Signe du Lion* met a fate no less cruel than Chabrol's own *L'Œil du malin*, a box-office disaster which netted 8,032 entries in its first run in the capital; only Godard's slapdash *Les Carabiniers* fared worse that year. But whereas Godard, given *carte blanche* by producer Georges de Beauregard, next geared up for the full-colour Franco-Italian 'superproduction' *Le Mépris* starring Brigitte Bardot, Rohmer, unable to secure funding, had no choice but to hole up in the offices of *Cahiers du cinéma* and pursue his work as editor-in-chief. He had missed the crest of the New Wave by a good two years.

Les Films du Losange and the 16mm *Contes moraux*

Early commercial failure was perversely to enable long-term viability for Rohmer at the margins of the French motion picture industry. If he wished to continue directing, budgetary austerity and a keener sense of subject matter were clearly in order (Williams 1992: 376). As generous state subventions (*primes à la qualité*) dried up and producers shied away from projects they saw as financial risks, would-be *auteurs* like Rohmer had to devise self-sustaining modes of production, as had Truffaut with Les Films du Carrosse.

The production company behind nearly all of Rohmer's features from the early 1960s to the close of the 1990s is Les Films du Losange. Founded in late 1962 by the Tehran-born Barbet Schroeder, who hocked a family painting by Emil Nolde for startup capital, the company set out to promote a low-budget art cinema based on the flexibility of 16mm and on new techniques for adapting substandard negatives for 35mm projection (Smith 1995: 74). Using lightweight cameras like the Eclair-Coutant ACL 16, fast film stocks, and the portable audiotape recorders showcased by the *cinéma vérité* movement of Jean Rouch, filmmakers could shoot quickly and on the cheap. These objectives would coalesce in the six-part portmanteau film *Paris vu par...* (1965). Yet before that project got off the ground, Schroeder, himself an aspiring actor, put up funds to complete the first two *Contes moraux*, which Rohmer had originally drafted as short stories and had intended to publish as such. Since there was no discernable market for the genre in France, the author of *Elisabeth* saw fit to adapt these first-person tales to the screen.

The twenty-minute *La Boulangère de Monceau* (1962) is the more accomplished of the two. The opening description of Paris's Monceau neighbourhood, which coordinates fixed shots of city streets and voiceover identifications, grounds the fiction in a locale whose layout proves essential to the unfolding action. The body of the film traces the comings and goings of the narrator-protagonist (played by Schroeder), a law student who first pursues an attractive blonde, and then, when the latter disappears from circulation, begins an elaborate courtship ritual with a brunette pastry shop employee. The very day he has agreed to meet the brunette for a date, he runs across the blonde, Sylvie, who had been convalescing from an injury. It is she whom the narrator will later marry. The short closes on an ambiguous note: we discover that Sylvie, whose apartment faces the corner bakery, may have been aware of the protagonist's puerile games all the while. Each of the male heroes of the subsequent *Contes moraux* will follow a similar moral trajectory: an initial romantic commitment is complicated by the arrival of a second woman or temptress, whom the hero ultimately rejects in favour of the first woman.

In comparison with the compact *Boulangère*, which employs well-chosen camera angles, assertive 180-degree jump cuts, and tight editing, *La Carrière de Suzanne* (1963) is somewhat lacking in dramatic purpose and stylistic polish. Co-written with Paul Gégauff whose misogynistic stamp is on its depiction of Donjuanism, the story revolves around café terraces, jazz clubs, and villas frequented by bourgeois youth who resemble those of Chabrol's *Les Cousins*, minus the Wagnerian bravado. Tensions develop between the narrator–witness Bertrand

and his outgoing friend Guillaume, who shamelessly takes advantage of Suzanne's apparent naïveté and meagre income. Aware that Suzanne may be beyond his reach where romance is concerned, the narrator–protagonist proves equally unable to win the graces of the sophisticated Sophie. But in the closing poolside sequence, Bertrand, who has failed his exams just as he has failed in love, is forced to revisit his opinion of Suzanne, whose 'career' has not ended so badly after all (she is shortly to marry). The use of counterpoint between first-person voiceover and image gives events a double temporality, that of being perceived and remembered at once. In contrast to *La Boulangère de Monceau*, however, the conceit works to marginal effect, so laborious is the set-up. While neither of the first two *Contes moraux* was screened commercially until 1974, they did slowly make their rounds on the *ciné-club* and university circuit, consolidating their director's reputation as well as boosting the profile of Les Films du Losange. By ceding rights over both works, Rohmer gained partnership status in the company. This amounted to guaranteed self-production, provided he could keep budgets down and bring in acceptable returns.

Rohmer's next directing project, and his first foray into colour, was *Place de l'Etoile*, one of six shorts comprising *Paris vu par...*, the group film Schroeder began producing in 1964 with the intent of launching a 16mm 'parallel cinema' movement. Schroeder requested that each director – Rouch, Godard, Chabrol, Jean-Daniel Pollet, Rohmer and his close friend Jean Douchet – apply individually for support from the national film board, the Centre National de la Cinématographie (CNC), since by cobbling together six separate advances they could afford to shoot in colour. If the sketches of *Paris vu par...*, each set in a distinct neighbourhood of the capital, are sometimes innovative, only Rouch's segment, which splices together two shot-sequences to resemble a continuous, twenty-five minute take, takes full advantage of the ease of handling of 16mm. In Jean Douchet's words, *Paris vu par...* was at once 'le manifeste de la N.V. et son testament' (the New Wave's manifesto and last will and testament), a bold statement of intent followed by little effect, as each director would go his separate way (Douchet 1996: 72).

For Rohmer, who in *Place de l'Etoile* indulges his taste for physical comedy à la Buster Keaton and for colour as narrative device (stoplights around the famed eleven-point traffic circle govern the hero's movements), *Paris vu par...* marked the beginning of a long collaboration. When Rohmer's cameraman stormed off on the first day of shooting, a Cuban exile who was milling about on the set taking photographs, Nestor Almendros, volunteered his services. The Barcelona-born cinematographer, who had directed and shot numerous documentaries for the Cuban culture ministry (*Gente de la playa*, 1960), was all too happy to finish *Paris vu par...* for Schroeder, though for legal reasons his work went uncredited. He would go on to make seven full-length pictures with Rohmer, in addition to nine of Truffaut's features, from *L'Enfant sauvage* (1969) to *Vivement dimanche!* (1982).

Film as pedagogy

The 16mm revolution hoped for by Schroeder was not to take place, not least, in Almendros' view, because the available emulsions were less sensitive than those for 35mm (Almendros 1984: 52). Rohmer nevertheless continued to work frequently in 16mm, shooting not fiction, as he might have preferred, but pedagogical documentaries for the state-run Radio-Télévision Scolaire (RTS), significantly expanded under De Gaulle's Ministry of Information. First undertaken after he was ousted from the editorship of *Cahiers du cinéma*, this activity provided Rohmer with a steady, if modest income from 1964 to 1970. The range of topics treated reflects the broad mandate given RTS contributors: literature (*Perceval ou le Conte du Graal*, 1964; *Entretien avec Mallarmé*, 1968), art history (*Les Salons de Diderot*, 1964), philosophy and religion (*Entretien sur Pascal*, 1965), social studies and history (*L'Homme et les gouvernements*, 1968; *La Sorcière de Michelet*, 1969). Quality ranges from slipshod to highly accomplished: whereas *Paysages urbains* (1963) flatly sets views of drawings to seventeenth-century music, *Les Métamorphoses du paysage: l'ère industrielle* (1964), shot by Pierre Lhomme, is a masterful montage piece that pushes the spectator to think critically about the aesthetic potential of industrial architecture, from the premodern windmill to the rail bridge and ring-road. In the mid-1960s Rohmer also prepared two programmes for the prestigious 'Cinéastes de notre temps' television series, the first on Danish master Carl Dreyer (1965), the second, *Le Celluloïd et le marbre* (1966), featuring interviews with contemporary thinkers and artists who address film's relationship to architecture, serial music, kinetic art, and philosophy.

Never one to close off film from worldly concerns, Rohmer later integrated many themes broached in his work for RTS into his fiction features, from the Pascalian meditations of *Ma Nuit chez Maud* to the discourse on town planning in the *Comédies et proverbes*. Equally influential on projects to come were the three 16mm documentary shorts made with Almendros, *Nadja à Paris* (1964), *Une étudiante aujourd'hui* (1966), and the colour *Fermière à Montfaucon* (1968). Commissioned by the spouse of a government minister from Georges Pompidou's cabinet and produced by Les Films du Losange, all three focus on independent young women in a France that is rapidly shedding its traditional character. *Nadja à Paris* is notable for its depiction of everyday life in the Cité Universitaire, Paris' campus for international students, and in the popular neighbourhoods where its subject, a Romanian exchange student, feels herself to be most at home. It marks the first time that Rohmer used tape-recorded conversations to generate content, such that the actress/subject herself becomes the co-author of the screenplay. *Une étudiante aujourd'hui* similarly invites the spectator into its subject's home and workplace, a modern laboratory where the young woman conducts experiments on the neural activity of cats. The third short, *Fermière à Montfaucon*, demythologises the idyllic view of country living by pointing to the difficulties faced by women farmers. While it would be exaggerated to call any of these works feminist, each subject is given a voice of her own and is shown in a respectfully sympathetic light. Almendros' camera discovers a quiet beauty and orderliness in even the most unforgiving locales, while the editing, neither hurried nor leisurely, creates an impression of oneness with the subject. As Jacques Bontemps wrote in *Cahiers*, 'pedagogical' films such as these deal a mortal blow to 'la ruineuse distinction établie entre "film de commande" and "film d'auteur"' (the debilitating distinction established between the 'commission piece' and the '*auteur* film') (Bontemps 1965: 65).

Recognition: the full-length *Contes moraux*

Rohmer's breakthrough came in March 1967 with the surprise success of *La Collectionneuse*. Officially the fourth instalment of the *Contes moraux* series, it was third in order of shooting and theatrical release, since *La Fille à bicyclette* – the future *Ma Nuit chez Maud* – had to be postponed due to funding troubles and to Jean-Louis Trintignant's reluctance to take on the project. Modelled after Agnès Varda's cooperative venture *La Pointe courte* (1954), the film's production embodied the principles of economy that were to become Rohmer's signature. The cast of three non-professional actors agreed to work without a fee and lent their real-life personalities to the dandyish art-world characters they portrayed, with Rohmer transposing bits of their tape-recorded conversations into his original screenplay. During the shoot, actors, director, and reduced crew shared a villa near Saint-Tropez, in Ramatuelle, where the film's action transpires. Budget was impossibly tight. The 35mm Eastmancolor stock that Schroeder had purchased was in such limited supply that, when the negatives were sent for development, lab technicians assumed they were dealing with a short: the ratio of footage shot to footage edited was a jaw-dropping 1.5:1 (Almendros 1984: 56). This was proof of Almendros's resourcefulness – 'covering' scenes from multiple camera angles was excluded – and a pay-off for Rohmer's insistence on copious rehearsals. Finished with help from maverick producer Georges de Beauregard (Demy, Varda, Godard, Melville...), the cooperative venture yielded more than acceptable returns, with over 50,000 tickets sold during its first run in Paris, the majority of them at a single Left Bank art cinema, Studio-Gît-le-Coeur. That figure would rise to almost 300,000 in all runs.

Provocative and up-to-date, *La Collectionneuse* put the French public face-to-face with the erotic games of contemporary youth. The beauty of suntanned bodies bathed in the light of the Riviera contrasts with the arch intellectualism of protagonists Adrien (Patrick Bauchau) and Daniel (Daniel Pommereulle) (see figure 2), who only half-heartedly put into practice their professed libertinism in their overtures to Haydée (Haydée Politoff), the voracious 'collectionneuse' of the title. If they lauded Almendros's daringly naturalistic cinematography, critics especially noted the primacy given to language. The danger that speech might degenerate into mere verbiage made Rohmer's enterprise a delicate one, wherein the discursive distance created by Adrien's voiceover narration had to be counterbalanced by sufficient camera distance (Bory 1967). Some critics found that literary ambitions had got the better of Rohmer: 'La parole assassine l'image' (Speech kills the image), contended Pierre Marcabru (Marcabru 1967). Left-wing papers accused the film of promoting reactionary ideology through its portrayal of self-absorbed characters who were blind to society's needs (Martin 1967) or of treating its subjects with the dispassionate gaze of an 'entomologist' (Chapier 1967). Insofar as it provocatively unveiled a cynical, libertine eroticism at odds with prevailing screen conceptions of romantic love (de Baroncelli 1967), *La Collectionneuse* remains a key document of the pre-1968 zeitgeist. It claimed the Silver Bear at the Berlin Film Festival and established Almendros as an innovator in naturalistic cinematography.

In early spring 1968, the French cinema world was rocked by the Langlois affair, in which the founder and director of the Cinémathèque Française, accused of mismanagement, was abruptly relieved of his duties by Minister of Culture André Malraux. Rohmer was among several hundred filmmakers, technicians, actors, and producers to petition for Langlois's reinstatement ('Protestations' 1968: 45), though he was not among those to clash with De Gaulle's riot troops, as did Truffaut and Jean-Pierre Léaud. The director's next outing, shot after the upheavals of May 1968 as if nothing had occurred, was *Ma Nuit chez Maud*. Since it involved name actors Jean-Louis Trintignant (*Un homme et une femme*, 1966) and Françoise Fabian (*Belle de Jour*, 1966), it required levels of financing that Les Films du Losange could not handle alone. Refused an *avance sur recettes* subsidy by the CNC on account of the screenplay's presumed lack of appeal and, one suspects, to its director's poor standing with the cinema workers' union, the film was co-produced with seven other companies for the not extravagant budget of 600,000 new francs. Rohmer and Almendros decided to buck current trends and return to elegant black and white, in part because series coherence demanded it (*Contes moraux* one to three in black and white, four to six in colour), in part because the wintertime setting of Clermont-Ferrand (see figure 3) had a drab look that colour would have made unpleasing to the eye. To ensure tonal contrast in the central sequence that unfolds in Maud's apartment, they adopted an old studio technique: all wardrobe elements and props on the set were chosen in blacks, whites, and greys. Rohmer even eliminated from his screenplay all references to colour (Almendros 1984: 77). Again, in this dialogue-heavy film, the director refused to cover scenes, choosing speaking shot or reaction shot ahead of time and insisting on obtaining a perfect first take – a challenging prospect, because *Ma Nuit chez Maud*, unlike *La Collectionneuse*, used direct sound recording. Rohmer was vindicated in his punctiliousness: the actors' delivery is superb, and editing, done by onetime Godard collaborator Cécile Decugis (*A bout de souffle*, 1959), took just one week to complete.

Selected for the 1969 Cannes Festival, *Ma Nuit chez Maud* narrowly missed a prize for best actress, which Fabian lost to Vanessa Redgrave (*Isadora Duncan*). And while Trintignant took Best Actor for his role as a magistrate in Costa-Gavras's political thriller *Z* (also Best Picture), many thought he equally deserved that distinction for *Maud*'s church-going engineer. Rohmer's popular success mystified industry experts: how could an austere picture that revolves around tableside discussions of probability, fidelity, faith, and Pascal's famous 'wager' have appealed to a quarter-million spectators in Paris, where it ran for thirty-four weeks, and to over a million worldwide? In his pursuit of a literate cinema with intelligent, non-heroic characters, Rohmer struck a chord with adult viewers and enjoyed his warmest critical reception to date, perhaps even of his career. Critics who had dismissed the verbosity of *La Collectionneuse* now underscored the literary qualities of Rohmer's dialogues – the finest in France since Renoir's *La Règle du jeu*, suggested one critic (Garson 1969). The controversy staged between the Catholic moralist narrator and the Marxist professor Vidal (played by theatre director Antoine Vitez) refused facile oppositions, as did Rohmer's portrayal of the seductive free-thinker Maud and her rival Françoise. The often unforgiving satirical weekly *Le Canard enchaîné* roundly approved the picture – the three scenes of Holy Mass excepted – and encouraged Rohmer to pursue his solitary march in the name of a counter-cinema (Duran 1969). Even the editors of the journal *Positif*, who had borne a grudge against Rohmer since the latter's *Cahiers* days, praised the film for instructing through beautifully crafted cinematic 'theorems' (Legrand 1970: 4). As Norman King points out, perhaps the true secret behind *Maud*'s appeal is that the film repressed the collective trauma of May 1968 the better to resurrect a calmer moment when intelligence and bourgeois propriety enjoyed free reign (King 2000: 202–3).

Bolstered by the triumphs of *Ma Nuit chez Maud* and of the European blockbuster *More* (1969), Schroeder's own exploration of drugged-out hippydom, Les Films du Losange reached cruising speed by the turn of the decade. This allowed the company to supply seed money for Rivette's twelve-and-a-half-hour *Out 1: Noli me tangere* (1970), in which Rohmer plays a Honoré de Balzac specialist (he had already cameoed as a linguistics professor in Luc Moullet's *Brigitte et Brigitte* of 1965), and to co-finance with Columbia Pictures the two remaining *Contes moraux*. Both were shot in excellent conditions. *Le Genou de Claire* brought cast and crew in summer 1969 to the shores of the Annecy Lake, at the foot of the French Alps, for five weeks of collective living in borrowed villas. During the shoot, Rohmer would occasionally disappear for hours or a couple days at a time, only to return with the expectation that work recommence at a moment's notice. After these escapes, which were little appreciated by lead actor Jean-Claude Brialy, the director's intensity was such that up to ten minutes of screen time could be put in the can in a single day (Almendros 1984: 91–2). Shot chronologically, and almost entirely in exteriors but without the slick veneer that characterised colour production at the time, *Le Genou de Claire* was released in late 1970 to significant acclaim.

To be sure, it would have been difficult to equal the critical and popular success of *Ma Nuit chez Maud*. Yet once again the press lauded Rohmer's non-judgemental explorations of eroticism. For critic Michel Duran, the 'mythology' that the hero Jérôme creates around a glimpse of Claire's knee (see figure 4) holds more promise than 'toutes les images de femmes nues déferlant sur nos pellicules à la mode' (all the images of nude women that unfurl in today's fashionable pictures) (Duran 1970). Much as in Valéry Larbaud's novellas of the 1920s such as *Beauté, mon beau souci...*, the film's equivocal erotic charge stems from differences in age and mentality between the mature diplomat Jérôme and the two half-sisters, Laura and Claire. As Jérôme (Brialy) recounts his sentimental exploits to the Romanian novelist Aurora (Aurora Cornu), the spectator comes to understand that the most mature characters are perhaps the film's youngest, who are sharp enough to see through Jérôme's idle games. Likened to a Jansenist rereading of *Les Liaisons dangereuses* (Legrand 1971: 54), the film again placed itself at odds with prevailing views of romantic love. If Brialy's almost intuitive grasp of his character's dense text was duly noted, the film's revelation was the wild-haired Béatrice Romand, who plays the mercurial and not-so-innocent Laura. Described by Pauline Kael as an 'exquisitely gawky young beauty who looks like a Pisanello princess' (Kael 1973: 265), Romand comes across as the quintessential *jeune fille en fleurs* or adolescent on the cusp of womanhood, a figure that the filmmaker would revisit across his career to varied effect.

The *Contes moraux* came full circle in 1972 with *L'Amour l'après-midi*, a tale of temptation, rectitude, and reconciliation – a tale more transparently moral than the rest (see figure 5). The return from the Rousseauesque setting of *Le Genou de Claire* to the bustling streets and shops of Paris gave the series' sixth and final chapter a new intensity. Where previous films in the cycle had featured homogenous groups of students, artists, and professionals, *L'Amour l'après-midi* foregrounds the social disparities that separate hero-narrator Frédéric (Bernard Verley), a middle manager who lives a comfortable married life, and Chloé, a self-described 'paumée' (lost soul) down on her luck. Played by Zouzou, who had made her reputation dancing the twist (see Bertrand Blier's *Hitler, connaîs pas!*, 1963) before Philippe Garrel hired her, Chloé disturbs the usually placid atmosphere of Rohmer's universe, using coarser language than is the norm. The narrative turns not on infidelity per se but on the conflicts that arise when two partners enter a relationship on unequal footing and with distinct expectations. If critics on the Left denounced the film as a predictable exercise in bourgeois psychology (Capdenac 1972), others applauded its realism and range of emotion, from Chloé's desperation to the tenderness of Frédéric's wife Hélène (played by lead actor Verley's real-life spouse). The film's lessons on love and commitment attracted over 900,000 spectators throughout France, proving the public's receptiveness to a more conventional screenplay than the admittedly baroque *Le Genou de Claire*. This enthusiastic response spurred many viewers to revisit or to discover for the first time the six-part series, screened in numerous revivals throughout the 1970s. So coherent were the six *Contes moraux* that they seemed to compose a single film, on the musical model of theme and variation or like the chapters of a book (see Chapter 4).

Between cycles: the 1970s

With the *Contes moraux* cycle behind him and his reputation well established at home and in United States, where he was painted as a specialist in 'the eroticism of non-sexual affairs' (Kael 1991: 136), Rohmer took a break from directing. He completed a doctoral thesis on the use of space, movement, and composition in F.W. Murnau's *Faust* at the Sorbonne, where he had been giving classes in *mise en scène* since 1969 and received a lectureship in 1972. The year 1974 saw the publication of *Six contes moraux*, comprising revised versions of the first-person tales Rohmer had adapted for the screen, and the preparation of *Ville nouvelle* with delegated producer Jean-Paul Pigeat. The four-part television programme, broadcast in summer 1975, focuses on the peripheral new towns launched by France's regional planning board as part of decentralisation. On-site interviews with planners, engineers, and the first residents of Cergy-Pontoise, a new town founded north-west of Paris, reflect Rohmer's ethnographic sensibility and concern with the ways in which the built environment fashions everyday life. This fieldwork would directly inform two features of the 1980s, *Les Nuits de la pleine lune* and *L'Ami de mon amie*, set in the postmodern new towns of Marne-la-Vallée and Cergy-Pontoise respectively.

In anticipation of his next project, an adaptation of Heinrich von Kleist's novella *Die Marquise von O....*, Rohmer also took time out to relearn German, which he had studied in high school. A majority West German venture co-produced by Klaus Hellwig of Janus Films and Margaret Menegoz of Les Films du Losange, with additional moneys from German regional television and giants Gaumont and United Artists, *Die Marquise von O...* was a high-culture gamble. The picture was shot in German with seasoned stage actors from Berlin's prestigious Schaubühne and Munich's Kammerspiele, including Edith Clever and the young Bruno Ganz. Legal hurdles notwithstanding, Rohmer smartly retained his usual French-speaking technicians, while deferring to German-speaking collaborators for their expertise in costume and set design. All met up in Franconia at Obertzen Castle, whose sun-drenched corridors, graced with antique textiles designed by Moidele Bickel, lent themselves perfectly to Almendros' soft-edged photography and to experiments in depth staging. Rather than adapt Kleist's text in any conventional sense, Rohmer approached it instead as if it were a shooting script complete with indications of gesture and mood. Unfettered by the task of composition, he was free to focus on actor direction and to indulge his pictorialist sensibilities, through allusions to late eighteenth- and early nineteenth-century European painting (see figure 6). On every level, *Die Marquise von O...* bore the stamp of a master – enough so as to earn a Special Jury Prize at Cannes, where it competed for West Germany.

A difficult subject matter – the Marquise, unaware she has been raped by the Count in her sleep, believes she has conceived immaculately – coupled with the language barrier surely intimidated average

French viewers. Nonetheless, critics praised Rohmer's restrained *mise en scène*, so unlike the overblown costume dramas which disgraced the screens year in year out. Jean de Baroncelli perhaps best summed up the director's inimitable achievement when he called *Die Marquise von O...* 'le premier film du XIXe siècle' (the first nineteenth-century film) (de Baroncelli 1976). It is certainly among Rohmer's deepest pictures, despite its apparently histrionic surface.

In an otherwise impeccable production record, *Perceval le Gallois* (1979) stands out like an indelible stain. Several years in the planning, the film barely got off the ground, and by the time the last scenes were completed at the Epinay studios (see figure 7), it had nearly bankrupted Les Films du Losange. Wisely, Schroeder had pushed Rohmer and his executive producer, Margaret Menegoz, to secure the lion's share of the budget – nearly 8,000,000 francs, a third of which went for decors alone (Thevenon 1978) – from the state television channel FR3 and other stations in Italy, Switzerland, and West Germany. In itself, the decision to adapt Chrétien de Troyes's twelfth-century poem was not uncommercial: there will always be an audience for tales of knights in shining armour and damsels in distress. To insist that actors speak in rhymed octosyllabic couplets, with Chrétien's original Old French ever so slightly modernised by Professor Schérer himself, and steer flesh-and-blood horses through plasticine decors, however, was perhaps misguided. When courting his producers, Rohmer cited the subject's potential appeal for viewers of all ages. But this was not Demy's *Peau d'âne*, and if André Dussolier's handsome Gauvain seduced more than a couple of maidens with his jousting and broad smiles, Fabrice Luchini's comically exalted Perceval, whose trajectory we follow up to the culminating scene of Christ's Passion, left many critics perplexed.

Indeed, Rohmer had perhaps done a kind service to literature professors by respecting Chrétien's poem; he had not, judging from public response, made a very accessible work of cinema. 'Watching the film', wrote Tom Milne, 'is rather like watching the animation of a medieval manuscript, with the text gravely read aloud while the images – cramped and crowded, couloured with jewelled brilliance, delighting the eye with bizarre perspectives – magnificently play the role traditionally assigned to marginal illuminations' (Milne 1981: 194). With only 53,277 tickets sold nationwide in its initial run, and slim prospects for export, the film was an unilluminating flop. Too serious despite its equivocations on the verb *baiser* ('to kiss', but also 'to screw') to be taken as second-degree camp, it was too artificial to convince. This fact much pained Roland Barthes, who suffered at each outburst of laughter from spectators who in place of Rohmer's subtle art of estrangement would clearly have preferred 'un Moyen Age où rien n'est différent d'aujourd'hui, sauf les costumes' (a Middle Ages in which nothing differs from today, save the costumes) (Barthes 1995: 987). If it did not win wide acceptance, at the least *Perceval le Gallois* filled Rohmer's stable with new actors and, especially, actresses: along with Luchini, the affable Dussolier, and the curvy, lark-throated Arielle Dombasle, several ladies-in-waiting who dedicated nearly eighteen months of their teenage years to Rohmer's middle-age project would go on to star in his *Comédies et proverbes*. Fatigued by the shoot, Nestor Almendros lost faith in Rohmer and, his services in high demand in North America as in Europe, would not work with him again until *Pauline à la plage*.

In the meantime, Rohmer corralled together his protégés for a stage production of Kleist's five-act drama *Catherine de Heilbronn*, which ran for one month in the Paris suburb of Nanterre. His translation and staging of Kleist's story of medieval honour, doomed love, and sorcery fell short of the mark. The pacing never recovers from the lumbering first act, in which the Count of Strahl (Pascal Greggory), facing a panel of hooded judges, defends himself against Catherine's father Theobald, who accuses him of sequestering the maiden in his chateau. The eponymous character (played by Pascale Ogier, the daughter of Rivette regular Bulle) spends much of the play prostrate at the Count's feet, imploring his grace in a wisp of a voice. Discrepancies between Rohmer's iconic use of decors and the eclecticism of Kleist's own period, and between the delivery of *Perceval le Gallois* returnees and that of experienced stage actors, further explain *Catherine de Heilbronn*'s tepid reception. One solution that Rohmer might have adopted is the use of projections; indeed, his filmed version of the production skillfully renders the Count of Stahl's visions through silent film conventions, such as circular caches, soft focus, emphatic gestures, and piano accompaniment.

If *Catherine de Heilbronn* is destined to remain a footnote to Rohmer's œuvre, *Perceval le Gallois* has, with time, found critics courageous enough to defend it. Jonathan Rosenbaum ranks Rohmer's 'medieval musical – which actually feels at times like a studio-shot

Western, complete with artificial sky' among fifteen notable works by directors of the New Wave generation (Andrew 2001: 210). All the same, it's not unreasonable to describe the late 1970s as Rohmer's dark ages: eight years after the *Contes moraux*, it seemed that the director had lost (his) touch. To regain public confidence, he had little choice but to return to low-budget filmmaking and to situations of contemporary relevance.

The second series: *Comédies et proverbes*

Completed in 1980 for a pittance, *La Femme de l'aviateur*, the first of the *Comédies et proverbes*, shows the sixty-year-old director rejuvenated and in peak form. Bernard Lutic's 16mm camera explores the hidden underside of Paris, as in the dingy postal sorting centre of the Gare de l'Est, takes to the streets for an audacious shot-sequence that slaloms amidst rows of automobiles, or confines itself to the maid's quarters where the mopey Anne (Marie Rivière), in between visits from her aviator boyfriend, grudgingly receives her insistent suitor, the postal clerk François (Philippe Marlaud). The long central digression in which a pert *lycéenne* (Anne-Laure Meury) joins François in his detective work in the Buttes Chaumont park exudes New Wave spontaneity: delivering her lines with impeccable timing and wily smiles, seventeen-year-old Meury steals the show from Rivière's Anne, who is invariably confined to her bed in her pyjamas, much like the goldfish imprisoned in the fishbowl beside her. Energetic and humorous, *La Femme de l'aviateur* was, in Michel Pérez's estimation, the work of an 'éternel étudiant' [eternal student] who grasped the problems of French young adults without claiming to speak for them (Pérez 1981).

If *Cahiers du cinéma* editors chose the film's release date of 4 March 1981 as one of a 'hundred days' to have marked French cinema across its first century (Magny 1995b), it was not merely because *La Femme de l'aviateur* struck a chord with the public. It was also because Rohmer staged his comeback as a *serial* filmmaker. If the *Contes moraux* had drawn on the novel of psychological analysis, this second cycle of films, which borrows its title from dramatist Alfred de Musset, looks to stage comedy and to popular wisdom (the title sequence of each film concludes with a 'proverb'). Breaking with the waltz-hesitations of the *Contes moraux*'s male protagonists, the films feature dynamic young women in their twenties who assert their dual need for independence and companionship and who most often fail in their designs. Explanations for this move towards female subjects are several. Rohmer, who works as his own casting agent, had been receiving for some years a steady flow of fan mail – in reality, letters from actors eager for work. As one pile of letters ('filles') grew more quickly than the other ('garçons'), it seemed inevitable that the new cycle should shift towards women's experience. Moreover, such a change would avert reproducing the one man/two women schemata of the *Contes moraux*, still in evidence in *La Femme de l'aviateur*. At all events, the prospect of a new series gave the sixty-year-old Rohmer, who already had three or four screenplays in the works, a needed boost: 'J'ai besoin de savoir où je vais' (I need to know where I'm headed) (Montaigne 1980).

Clearly, the filmmaker knew where he was going, for the six *Comédies et proverbes* were released from 1981 to 1987 at the steady rate of one per year, with the sketch film *4 Aventures de Reinette et Mirabelle* thrown in between. More televisual than their predecessors, the features are also, *Le Rayon vert* excepted, more cinematically classical. First-person voiceover disappears, and pictorialism is held in check by taut dramatic construction, with each film clocking in at between 90 and 104 minutes. Variations in cast, locale, and dramatic treatment (there is no assigned series theme) keep audiences guessing from one instalment to the next.

La Femme de l'aviateur was followed by *Le Beau Mariage* (1982), in which Sabine (Béatrice Romand), tired of playing mistress to a painter who won't leave his wife, launches herself in headstrong pursuit of a husband. Taking her dreams for reality, she latches on to the idea that Edmond (André Dussolier), the older barrister cousin of her friend Clarisse (Arielle Dombasle), will give in to her charms and ask for her hand before the year's end. So transparent are Sabine's designs – 'j'vais m'marier' (I'm gonna get married), she repeats time and again – that the spectator may wish to side with the career-driven Edmond. Yet Rohmer's trademark ironic distance makes such secondary identifications tenuous. Until Edmond gives Sabine notice in a painfully courteous monologue delivered from his office desk, it doesn't seem impossible that he might fall for the pesky art-history student after all. Of this tightrope act of narrative distance and sympathy, of tenderness and malice, Michel Mardore wrote that 'on finira par dire, comme pour Lubitsch autrefois, qu'il existe une "Rohmer's touch". Et ce sera vrai' (people will end up saying, as they did of Lubitsch, that there is a 'Rohmer's touch' (*sic*). And they won't be wrong) (Mardore 1982). In its lighthearted theatricality, *Le Beau Mariage* exemplifies French stage comedies of character, wherein a defining trait leads an individual into error. Visually, the 35mm film is a bold manifesto on colour, where wardrobe, available decors (notably the cobblestone streets of old Le Mans), and frame composition create a unified palette of brown, ochre, and pink.

With *Pauline à la plage*, the *Comédies et proverbes* took to the beaches of Normandy for a channel-side romp featuring six stock characters, from the coquettish divorcee Marion and the lascivious seducer Henri to the jealous pretender Pierre. The Pauline of the title, played by a fifteen-year-old whose photograph had made its way into Rohmer's office drawer, Amanda Langlet, is a common-sensical adolescent who finds herself thrown into the restless company of adults on summer vacation. Enamoured of a boy her own age, Sylvain, she falls victim to her elders' games only to emerge very much the moral victor. The film's dialogues, tinged with archaisms, and its scenes of *quid pro quo* recall the French theatrical tradition – 'un peu de Marivaux, un peu de Musset, un peu de Feydeau',[2] as Louis Seguin put it (Seguin 1983). The actors' mien and contemporary dress, from windsurfers' getups and bathing suits to the latest summertime fashions are, by contrast, very twentieth-century (see figure 8). Awarded the Silver Bear at the Berlin Film Festival, *Pauline à la plage* was considered by some as insufferable due to Dombasle's mannered delivery and her come-on smiles (Baignères 1983). But beyond such cosmetic details, critics like Serge Daney, the most influential voice in 1980s French film criticism, saw a system so well-oiled that its efficency was nearly impossible to refute (Daney 1983). The picture had a strong run in the United States, where it was billed as a light-hearted sex comedy with a twist. Apparently Pauline Kael's warning that the director, unlike his more salacious compatriots, 'tells you more than he shows you' did nothing to stop this 'daisy chain woven by a prig' from becoming a hit (Kael 1985: 37; 39). It reached over seventy North American cities, grossing 2.6 million dollars, an impressive figure for a foreign film

2 'a bit of [each dramatist]'; Georges Feydeau is the prolific nineteenth-century author of *boulevard* plays.

without big-name draws of the Isabelle Adjani type or so much as a proper lovemaking scene ([Unsigned] 1984).

The *Comédies et proverbes* proved that working by series was not just an artistic statement, but smart business practice. In consultation with Margaret Menegoz, who headed operations at Les Films du Losange from the mid-1970s onward, Rohmer carefully supervised each film's release. Hoping at first to re-establish his following through word of mouth, he put *La Femme de l'aviateur* on just four screens in Paris, then upped that number to eleven and nine respectively for *Le Beau Mariage* and *Pauline à la plage*. When prints of the fourth series instalment, *Les Nuits de la pleine lune*, were struck in 1984, he could count on a core of series 'subscribers' as well as on viewers familiar with at least one previous film. Aggressive distribution, along with Pascale Ogier's nomination for Best Actress at the Venice Mostra, promised quick returns. At Venice, the film reportedly received a thirty-minute standing ovation (Pantel 1984), and Ogier, who won out over Sabine Azéma and Claudia Cardinale, was hailed as France's rising star. Within just five weeks 175,604 Parisians turned out for the film, which quickly netted 300,000 tickets in the capital and another 100,000 in the provinces; continuous to the year 2000, viewing figures for France are 626,461, which make *Les Nuits de la pleine lune* Rohmer's third biggest domestic success. The film's exemplary run was marred by tragedy when, one month after her triumph at Venice, the twenty-five-year-old Ogier died in her sleep. This was the second actor whom Rohmer had lost in the prime of youth: Philippe Marlaud, the sleep-deprived postal clerk of *La Femme de l'aviateur*, had perished three years earlier in a campground fire at age twenty-one (Beylie 1985: 111).

Les Nuits de la pleine lune is arguably the darkest picture of those that Rohmer has set in contemporary times, and one of few to expose raw emotions. Acting is on a par with *Ma Nuit chez Maud* and *Die Marquise von O....* Tcheky Karyo's athletic frame, atypical in Rohmer's universe where mind and mouth prevail over body, speaks of pent-up frustration, while Ogier's oval-shaped face and svelte figure display at once fragility and 1980s modishness. Even the smooth-talking Fabrice Luchini reveals a sensual side to his screen persona, as Octave, ever clad in his tight, faded jeans and long scarves. Moviegoers were struck by how contemporary and youthful Rohmer's world was: language, dress, decors, and even thumping party music by new wave rockers Elli et Jacno were all very *dernier cri*. Protagonist Louise, an interior decorator, is not just up to date, but well ahead of the curve; her boyfriend Rémy, a town planner working and living in the new town of Marne-la-Vallée is, in his rational way, in lock-step with the times. The breakdown of their couple evinces the conflicts that erupt when individuals, torn between lifestyle choices, are too unsure of their desires to communicate openly. The film's conclusion is caustic, almost cruel: as Louis Seguin remarked, 'Rohmer torture ses personnages pour les faire avouer: il leur fait violence pour arracher leur vérité' (Rohmer tortures his characters to make them confess: he violates them to wring out their truth) (Seguin 1984). Renato Berta's largely frontal compositions provide a cold, hard-edged urgency, reinforced by a colour scheme of gray, white, and red. Detractors who had qualified Rohmer's filmmaking as repetitive were again reminded that the key to appreciating this uncompromising *cinéma de chambre* lay in making connections among elements of the ongoing series. As Serge Daney wrote,

> Il n'y a pas seulement du plaisir à voir un film d'Eric Rohmer, il y a du plaisir à le voir succéder si vite à un autre film d'Eric Rohmer. C'est le plaisir, devenu trop rare, de la *série*.[3] (Daney 1984)

Never one to be drugged by success, Rohmer changed gears for his next project, originally titled *Aoûtiennes* or 'August chronicles'. Abandoning the scripted dialogues that his actors were accustomed to learning to the last syllable, he embarked on an improvisation with a single actress, Marie Rivière. The canvas was inspired by a Miss Lonelyhearts letter from a women's magazine: 'Je suis belle. Je suis de Biarritz. Je devrais plaire et les hommes ne font pas attention à moi, pourquoi?' [I'm pretty. I'm from Biarritz. I should be attractive and yet men pay no attention to me. Why?] (Pantel 1986). The challenge lay in allowing a wholly banal dramatic premise to develop organically: the young secretary Delphine finds herself without plans as dreaded August begins. Shooting in 16mm without a screenplay, contract, or authorizations, Rohmer and his three-woman crew followed Rivière as she criss-crossed France from one vacation spot to another. The foursome were mistaken for amateurs on holiday, vindicating

3 'There is pleasure not just in seeing an Eric Rohmer film, but in seeing one Eric Rohmer film follow so closely another. It's the pleasure, hard to come by nowadays, of the *series*.'

Rohmer's self-description as a *cinéaste du dimanche*. The cast was filled out by Rivière's family and friends as well as a host of strangers who consented to appear on camera, including sailors, Swedish and Spanish vacationers, and the French tourists whom Delphine, when she reaches Biarritz, overhears discussing Jules Verne's adventure novel, *Le Rayon vert*. If the largely improvised work – rebaptised *Le Rayon vert* – at first seemed ill-suited to the *Comédies et proverbes*, closer in spirit to Jean Rouch than to classic Hollywood, its touchingly comic resolution and feminine focus made it a worthy candidate for the cycle, of which it stands as the fifth part.

Le Rayon vert was legally a telefilm, since the pay station Canal Plus had acquired for 850,000 francs rights to premiere it. Telefilm status earned Les Films du Losange a state subsidy of 1.7 million francs, against Rohmer's provisional budget of 2 million, one-fortieth of what Claude Berri's *Jean de Florette/Manon des sources* cost that same year. In the event, the budget nearly doubled due to processing expenses and especially because of the elusive 'green ray' that Delphine glimpses in the final scene. Insistent than no trick photography be used, Rohmer posted a cameraman on the Atlantic coast who, for weeks on end, scoured the horizon each evening at sunset in the hopes of capturing this rare atmospheric phenomenon. Yet nature was more fickle than it had been during production of *Ma Nuit chez Maud*, when snow had fallen on Clermont-Ferrand the very day Rohmer had predicted. 'Le rayon vert', quipped Monique Pantel, 'est aussi difficile à voir que Eric Rohmer ... le cinéaste le plus secret de France' (The green ray is as hard to spot as Rohmer, France's most secretive filmmaker) (Pantel 1986). Though the director's entourage maintained that the ray was filmed off the Canary Islands, it is likely that a lab technician intervened in the end. In any event, the morning after the broadcast premiere, some viewers remained unsure whether Delphine had in fact seen 'son rayon vert', which is said to bestow the ability to read into other people's hearts (Skorecki 1986). A minor conspiracy theory developed suggesting that Rohmer had instructed the lab to create an effect all but imperceptible on video, so that television viewers would head to the theatre for a second opinion!

Just one week after its Canal Plus broadcast took a paltry audience share of 1 per cent, *Le Rayon vert* won top prize at the Venice Mostra, presided by novelist–filmmaker Alain Robbe-Grillet. In its humble way, the picture went on to beat out weightier productions, averaging

4,661 viewers weekly per theatre for its five screens, to the 2,703 of *Jean de Florette*, shown on sixty-five ([Unsigned] 1986). With only 60,000 entries needed to pay back costs, it garnered over 400,000 in France alone and, like *Pauline à la plage*, reached a broad international public, thus confirming Rohmer as the most visible representative of the ageing French New Wave (Truffaut had passed away in 1984). This popular success was surely linked to the frustratingly simple character of its protagonist. Delphine's problems are not so very insoluble, and yet at every juncture she appears ready to break into tears. 'Rivière's Delphine', notes Phillip Lopate, 'cries more than any actress since Maria Falconetti's Joan of Arc, back in 1928' (Lopate 2003: 170). Lopate is perhaps forgetting Ingrid Bergman's Karin in *Stromboli*, but the point is well taken. Again, the press saluted the use of lightweight production to not-so-lightweight results. The film's unassuming surface disguised a keen sense of psychology (Baignères 1986), while its slightly grainy 16mm images stood in stark contrast to the product-advertisements of the decade's *cinéma du look*, exemplified by Luc Besson's *Subway* (1985) and Jean-Jacques Beneix's *37°2 le matin* (1986).

So rewarding was this experiment in improvisation that Rohmer, awaiting completion of buildings in Cergy-Pontoise to be used in his next feature, tried out similar techniques with two twenty-year-old actresses, Joëlle Miquel and Jessica Forde. While the latter had landed a minor role in Jacques Doillon's *La Puritaine* (1986), the former, a department store employee and oil painter steeped in a naive surrealism, had no acting experience (Pantel 1987). On the basis of tape-recorded interviews with his players, Rohmer devised four interrelated sketches opposing city mouse and country mouse. Mirabelle has never seen a garden patch or experienced the silence of the countryside just before daybreak, while Reinette, a wild child who leaves her rustic surroundings for Paris, discovers how little she knows of the capital's insufferable waiters, con artists, and art world. *4 Aventures de Reinette et Mirabelle* was released on four screens in Paris, though Rohmer maintained that, for his purposes, one would have sufficed (Trémois 1987). Critics found that the adolescent charm of these so-called 'adventures' quickly wore thin. If Serge Daney could appreciate Rohmer's coupling of refinement and triviality at a midpoint between television and the cinema (Daney 1987), others confessed their disappointment outright: 'Après vingt ans de fidélité, c'est la rupture:

je n'aime plus ce que fait Rohmer' (My twenty years of fidelity are over: I no longer like what Rohmer is doing) (Pangon 1987). Sophie Maintigneux's underdressed 16mm cinematography prompted some to reconsider their opinions of *Le Rayon vert*: were not critics wasting their time by investing such films with a significance that was in the beholder's eye alone? 'Le roi est nu et il s'est lui-même dévêtu' (the emperor is naked and he's taken off his own clothes), wrote Pierre Ajame of *Le Nouvel Observateur* (Ajame 1987). Co-produced by Les Films du Losange and the newly founded Compagnie Eric Rohmer (CER), *4 Aventures de Reinette et Mirabelle* remains the prototype of the 'film-intermède' in its director's career, a light yet, like Renoir's later work, not inconsequential interlude between two acts of greater importance (Pérez 1987). Lighter still was the droll 'Bois ton café', a video clip of a pop song performed by Rohmer protégée Françoise Quéré (a.k.a. Rosette) in which a woman is reminded by her boyfriend (Pascal Greggory) that if she doesn't rise from her slumbers or her bubble bath, her morning coffee will be cold.

Unlike the *Contes moraux*, whose number was fixed from the start, the *Comédies et proverbes* were an open series. Reasons of symmetry, or simply the desire to move on, may have pushed the filmmaker to end this second cycle with instalment number six, *L'Ami de mon amie* (1987). Like *Les Nuits de la pleine lune*, the picture showcases the postmodern decors of a suburban new town. But whereas Louise did her best to flee Marne-la-Vallée and establish a foothold in the centre of Paris, the young inhabitants of Cergy-Pontoise in *L'Ami de mon amie* are happy to go it alone on the suburban frontier. The ingénue Blanche (Emmanuelle Chaulet), in her search for friendship and romance, first befriends Léa (Sophie Renoir), then steals Léa's boyfriend from behind her back, only to confess and make amends in a jubilant final scene. That uplifting ending, together with vibrant green-and-blue 35mm cinematography by Bernard Lutic, photogenic actors in up-to-date attire, and a failsafe screenplay 'réglé comme un mouvement d'horlogerie' (that runs like clockwork) made *L'Ami de mon amie* a resounding success (Boujut 1987). Unaffected delivery and matter-of-fact dialogue combine with a plot again reminiscent of Hollywood's sophisticated comedies and the eighteenth-century French stage. Jean Roy welcomed Rohmer's return from improvisation to a cinema where nothing is left to chance:

> ce magicien de l'équilibre instable n'est aussi parfait que lorsqu'il contrôle tout lui-même ... Il n'y a que dans la contrainte de l'œuvre que le spectateur peut expérimenter sa propre liberté.[4] (Roy 1987)

Produced for 3,000,000 francs, or one-quarter of the average French feature budget that year (Frodon 1987), the film reached nearly a half a million spectators across France. While many were curious to see what new lifestyles the postmodern *villes nouvelles* had to offer, others cherished the ironic gaze that Rohmer levelled at his characters, trapped in an artificial, purpose-built environment miles away from the only city that mattered.

After seven years of intense activity, Rohmer again took a break from filmmaking to direct Pascal Greggory (*Pauline à la plage*) and Jessica Forde (*4 Aventures de Reinette et Mirabelle*) in his own *Trio en mi bémol* at the Théâtre Renaud-Barrault. The stage play presents the month-to-month meetings of Paul, a classical music aficionado, and his ex-girlfriend Adèle, who has since taken up with a fashionable rock music critic. Consumed with jealousy, Paul resigns himself to playing Adèle's confidant. Plot turns on the fact that Adèle, unbeknownst to Paul, never discovered the recording of Mozart's Trio in E-flat Major (whence the play's title) he had given her as a present. With its two-person cast, the play lapsed into sing-songy repetition, and its pared-down stage design, limited to changes of season as viewed through Paul's apartment window, won few adherents. Far more satisfying is *Jeux de société* (1988), produced for a public television series on the history of private life inspired by historians Georges Duby and Philippe Ariès. Its eight vignettes re-enact the games that the French have played to pass the time, from the medieval game of kings and queens and seventeenth-century blind man's bluff to Restoration-era charades. As Joël Magny points out, Rohmer's focus is on games in which rule-bound social interaction, rather than pure chance, is at stake (Magny 1995a: 222). A model of pedagogy and visual pleasure, the one-hour telefilm explores the workings of dissimulation and wit with a touch so light that even Patrice Leconte's César-winning *Ridicule* (1996) may appear weighty and anachronistic by comparison.

4 'this magician specialised in balancing-acts is never so perfect as when he controls everything himself. ... Only because of the work's constraints can spectators experience their own freedom.'

The third series: *Contes des quatre saisons*

As he neared the end of his seventh decade, Rohmer embarked on his 'homage to meteorology', the *Contes des quatre saisons*. He made no secret that this third cycle responded as much to commercial logic as to artistic imperatives, noting that he preferred to work for 'une assistance réduite mais fidèle, plutôt que pour des spectateurs nombreux et versatiles' (a limited but committed public rather than for many viewers with varied interests) (Riou 1990). The *Contes des quatre saisons* would be looser in nature than the previous two series, having no predetermined theme or subject. As Rohmer noted,

> Il s'agit simplement d'un petit exercice de discipline, d'une soumission modeste à l'air de la saison, sans lui accorder d'autre signification que celle que son climat suggère.[5] (Riou 1990)

Viewers were forewarned that the cycle might take a good while to complete, as side projects were not excluded, and that the seasons might not be treated in proper order. At the least, each feature would be set in, and, in a savvy marketing ploy, released during 'its' season.

Save Hughes Quester, who had his acting debut in Patrice Chéreau's *Le Lys et l'orchidée* (1976), the principals of *Conte de printemps* (1990) were new to the screen, in keeping with Rohmer's policy of giving work to as many young actors and actresses as possible. As the film opens, Jeanne, a high-school philosophy teacher, finds herself between two apartments in sentimental flux, with a week's vacation in store. At a party, she is befriended by Natacha, an outgoing but immature conservatory student who wraps her up in a matchmaking scheme. Like *La Femme de l'aviateur*, the plot employs Hitchcockian suspense (a necklace has inexplicably disappeared), but in the end that dramatic element is secondary to the treatment of female friendship, rivalry, and seduction. Festival-goers at Berlin scoffed at the film's references to Kant, notably in the meal-time discussion opposing the born pedagogue Jeanne and the tempestuous show-off Eve (Levieux 1990). But for *Cahiers* critic Antoine de Baecque, the film was not so much about philosophy as it was a demonstration of philosophical method itself: like Socrates, Jeanne patiently teases out the truth from

5 'It's just a little exercise in discipline, a humble submission to the feel of each season, to which no other meaning is given aside from what its climate suggests.'

her interlocutors (De Baecque 1990). Despite warm press in France and fine appearances by Florence Darel and Anne Teyssèdre, the latest in a long line of *Rohmériennes*, the picture reached only half the attendance figures of *L'Ami de mon amie*. At the start of each new series, Rohmer, who refused to squander Les Films du Losange's money on advertising, could count only on a core of unconditionals. The rest he left to word of mouth.

One of the unsolved mysteries in Rohmer's career is why the second tale of the four seasons met such cool reception in its country of origin. On the surface, *Conte d'hiver* (1992) had much to appeal to a broad public: a middle-class protagonist with ordinary problems and baggage to boot (Félicie, a hairdresser, is a single mother); themes of steadfastness and faith; relatively high-keyed lighting; and a storybook ending. Félicie's sentimental travails are rendered with sympathy as she leaves one man for another, knowing all the while that she remains bound to a third, a Prince Charming named Charles who during a summertime fling unwittingly left her with a 'souvenir' she cannot forget, namely her daughter Elise. As is often the case in Rohmer's universe, failed communication drives the plot. Through a slip of the tongue, Félicie stupidly gave Charles a mistaken postal address and lost touch. Against all odds, she hopes one day for his return, as is evident in the performance of *A Winter's Tale*, which she interprets as a magical sign. Like Hermione who rises from the grave before the eyes of her incredulous family, the father of her own child, thinks Félicie, must one day return from the beyond.

In her screen debut, the unassuming Charlotte Very crafts a new manner of Rohmerian heroine akin to Marie Rivière's Delphine of *Le Rayon vert*, who similarly believed in the irrational and shed tears of joy at picture's end. While stalwarts defended tooth and nail the surprise-filled *Conte d'hiver* (Siclier 1991), they emphasised its high cultural references to Shakespeare, Pascal, and that other winter's tale, *Ma Nuit chez Maud*, perhaps to the detriment of its melodramatic appeal. The film's tactfully seasonal message went untapped, with fewer than 100,000 spectators turning out for its Paris run.

Not until the series' two final instalments would Rohmer harvest the fruits of his mature commercial sensibility. Before concluding his season cycle, however, he attended to two side projects. The first was a test to see how resilient his own 'parallel' cinema had become. In February 1993, word got around Paris that a new Rohmer film on the unlikely subject of electoral politics had opened at a single theatre in Saint-Germain-des-Prés. Caught unawares, the press rushed to confirm the rumour: *L'Arbre, le Maire et la Médiathèque ou Les sept hasards* was indeed a 'political' film, starring Rohmer veterans Fabrice Luchini, Arielle Dombasle, and Pascal Greggory. The title is a programme unto itself. Set in the rural Vendée, the story pits an idealistic schoolteacher, Marc Rossignol (Luchini), against the socialist mayor (*le Maire*) of Saint-Juire, Julien Deschaumes (Greggory), who in his bid for a seat in parliament dreams of building a lavish cultural centre (*la Médiathèque*) in town. Through his friend, the high-society novelist Bérénice Beaurivage (Dombasle), Deschaumes meets a press agent who makes him the focus of a magazine feature on rising stars in the Socialist Party. The reporter sent on assignment to Saint-Juire is seduced by Deschaumes' vision, but sympathises with the inspired Rossignol, who notes that the mayor's pet project requires felling an age-old tree (*l'Arbre*). In a number of *cinéma-vérité* moments, we see the journalist conversing with townspeople who weigh in on the mayor's priorities. In the final edit of her article, made unrecognisable by the press agent's cuts, Deschaumes is cast as a foe of the environment in league with Parisian bureaucrats. He loses his campaign, and the young journalist moves on to other pursuits.

Critics were sharply divided by Rohmer's approach to politics, which amounted to defending no one thesis or party line, but weighing the discourses of each. While some, pointing to the film's irreverent portraits of technocrats and society butterflies, placed Rohmer in a lineage with Sacha Guitry or Jean Renoir (Riou 1993), others felt he had missed the mark: in sequence upon sequence, whether in the fields or in Paris, wrote Jean-Marie Frodon, his protagonists 'débitent avec véhémence une série de platitudes' (passionately reel off platitudes) (Frodon 1993). Second-degree interpretations, Frodon argued, were bound to fail, since Rohmer opts for neither ironic distance nor satire. This was, perhaps, to leave aside another second-degree reading, namely to consider *L'Arbre, le Maire et la Médiathèque* a tongue-in-cheek reflection on the screen personalities of returning actors Greggory, Dombasle, and Luchini.

Produced by the Compagnie Eric Rohmer without the requisite application to the CNC, the 16mm feature was initially denied an exhibition visa. This was patently retaliation against Rohmer, for, as his associates pointed out, it was common in the industry to authorise a shoot after the fact, to employ different technicians or actors from those specified in preproduction files, or to circumvent requirements for permits (PL 1993). The difference was that Rohmer flaunted his disrespect of regulations while moralising his low-budget ways, stating that anyone else would have spent twice the money, using state aid and burdensome bank loans.

> [J]e n'ai pas à avoir honte de mes méthodes: j'enrichis le fonds de soutien, qui permet de produire d'autres films français, et j'enrichis le commerce extérieur, car mes films se vendent plutôt bien à l'étranger! Si tout le monde faisait comme moi, le cinéma français se porterait beaucoup mieux![6] (Pascal 1993)

Statements such as these were disingenuous to a point, since the lead actors of *L'Arbre, le Maire et la Médiathèque* had lent their star power for free, taking a cut of proceeds. As in many of Rohmer's ventures – and this was his cheapest yet –, the film 'cost' merely what it took in (Prédal 2002: 24). This thriftier-than-thou attitude surely infuriated many filmmakers seeking distribution, since the condition for streamlined production à la Rohmer was a notoriety that only an initial breakthrough could bring – a long shot in prevailing market conditions.

As he planned the remaining two *Contes des quatre saisons*, Rohmer capitalised on the flock of actors who had congregated around the CER to shoot *Les Rendez-vous de Paris* (1995). Unlike *4 Aventures de Reinette et Mirabelle*, its three vignettes feature different characters and story lines, linked only by common themes of courtship, chance, and seduction. Wishing to engage his subject in as free a manner as possible, Rohmer again took to the streets without a permit, arguing that his crew's equipment was no more intrusive than the video cameras wielded by the tourists who each day mob central Paris. To play by the rules, he remarked, would destroy whatever magic the city's open public spaces had to offer: 'l'autorisation [de tourner] ne correspond pas à mon idée d'un tournage léger et inscrit dans le réel' (official permits [to shoot] don't fit with my idea of a lightweight shoot embedded in reality) (Kaganski and Blumenfeld 1995). There is something to be said for this: never had Rohmer's camera been so mobile as in the hands of Diane Baratier, who in 'Le Rendez-vous de 7

6 'I needn't be ashamed of my methods: I contribute to the fund that supports French film production, and I enrich foreign trade, since my films sell rather well overseas! If everyone did things the way I do, French cinema would be much better off!'

heures' manoeuvres through densely packed markets and the throngs gathered near the Pompidou Centre. As it explores the four corners of the capital, from the heights of the Belleville Gardens to the Marais district near the Picasso Museum, however, the film takes on a made-for-export character; like so many postcards from Paris, its episodes are framed by shots of a Piaf-like street singer and her accordionist. Rohmer's gambit – in his own words, 'faire quelque chose à partir de rien' (to make something out of nothing) (Kaganski and Blumenfeld 1995) – was to some critics' eyes too precious by half. *Le Figaro* thus lamented the actors' artificial tone, out of phase with the cynical times the French were living through (Baignères 1995). To his credit, noted Frodon, Rohmer had seen fit to produce neatly accessible films entirely on his own terms (Frodon 1995). The forced charm of these vignettes recalls *Le Petit Théâtre de Jean Renoir* (1969), while the use of urban space as a backdrop for conversation, notably in 'Les Bancs de Paris', prefigures Richard Linklater's similarly talkative *Before Sunset* (2004).

The release in summer 1996 of *Conte d'été* prompted *Sight and Sound* critic John Wrathall to write that had Rohmer not discovered film, he might well 'have ended up a travel agent', for 'no other director has chronicled in such minute detail what people do – or, more to the point, don't do – on holiday' (Wrathall 1996: 53). The subject of *Conte d'été* – how to spend a vacation when plans fall apart – was familiar to viewers of *Le Rayon vert*. But this time around, the hapless vacationer was a man, played by New French Cinema fixture Melvil Poupaud. What Poupaud's Gaspard, a maths student and aspiring composer, does during his stay in Brittany as he awaits his would-be girlfriend Lena, is to confide his woes to Margot, an ethnology student, and to win the affection (but not the last favours) of the fiery Solène. What he does not do is to take any of these three women on a promised boat trip to the island of Ouessant (Gaspard leaves his girl troubles behind to pursue his music). Apparently, the prospect of seeing Poupaud bare-chested for much of the film, not to mention the thrill of stumbling upon Amanda Langlet at the beach a dozen years after her debut as Pauline, had significant appeal. Released in June 1996, *Conte d'été* had a strong domestic run, with nearly 60 per cent of the 318,739 tickets sold going to the provinces.

A move away from Paris and its mentality likewise fuelled the wild audience success of *Conte d'automne* (1998), hailed as a minor triumph for a director then nearing his eightieth year. Co-produced, like *Conte d'été*, by Les Films du Losange and television channel La Sept, with help from the Rhône-Alpes regional film board, the final series instalment enjoyed the healthy budget of 13,000,000 francs, or half the average cost for features that year. Early in the project, Rohmer decided to unite two handpicked 'stars' who, after first working with him in the 1970s, had taken leading roles in the *Comédies et proverbes*: Béatrice Romand (*Le Genou de Claire*; *Le Beau Mariage*) and Marie Rivière (*Perceval le Gallois*, *La Femme de l'aviateur*); both appear in *Le Rayon vert*. Magali (Romand) is a widowed winemaker and her best friend, Isabelle (Rivière), a bookstore manager bored with her lot as a provincial *bourgeoise*. Unbeknownst to Magali, Isabelle places a personal ad to find her stay-at-home friend a match. Among the respondents is the Algerian-born Gérald, who rachets up his expectations until Isabelle confesses to her bait-and-switch stratagem. A second plot line complicates this first strand as the young Rosine tries to set up Magali with her philosophy professor and former lover, Etienne. Everything comes to a head at the wedding reception for Isabelle's daughter, a sequence brimming with misunderstandings, disappointments, and surprises (see figure 9) in which the film achieves a happy medium between control and spontaneity, dramatic precision and openness to the unexpected (Lalanne 1998: 44). It is little surprise that the picture took the prize for Best Screenplay at Venice, a festival which, unlike Cannes, had always shown goodwill towards Rohmer.

Thankfully, the rural *Conte d'automne* describes France's viticultural heritage without embellishment or idealisation. There are no close-ups of wine labels or clinking glasses, and little wine talk. When Magali and Isabelle amble through the vineyards under the early autumn sun, a nuclear power plant looms in the distance, recalling the region's fragile environmental balance. In addition to its description of a corner of France that Rohmer had not yet explored, the film showed how a slight departure in casting – namely, shying away from pretty twenty-somethings – could re-energise the director's system. While the Rivière/Romand billing enticed many of the 370,000 French spectators, the real surprise lay in Alain Libolt's Gérald. A stage actor whose last major screen appearance had been in Jean-Pierre Melville's chilling Resistance epic *L'Armée des ombres* (1969), Libolt introduces the un-Rohmerian element that lifts the picture to a new level. His exploration of the states of male vulnerability and confusion make for a performance as convincing as Jean-Louis Trintignant's in *Ma Nuit chez Maud*. One can't help but wonder, on the basis of *Conte d'automne*, how different Rohmer's career might have looked had he written more roles for mature actors.

The director's chair: the studio years

At century's end, Rohmer had been playing the 'cinéaste debout' (standup filmmaker) for over four decades, and while he still prided himself in his pseudo-amateur status, he also needed a change from the demanding pace he had set himself. From 1980 to 1998, aided by his assistant and sometime producer Françoise Etchegaray, he had completed thirteen features from original screenplays, attending to all aspects of production from location scouting to final edit, and had overseen, as president of the CER, a further half-dozen shorts written by his younger associates, from *Les Amis de Ninon* and *Des goûts et des couleurs* (both 1996) to *Heurts divers* (1997), *Le Modèle*, and *Le Cambrure* (both 1998).

For his next project, his largest since *Perceval le Gallois*, he retreated to the studio and recast himself as a 'cinéaste assis', comfortably seated in the director's chair. Set during the French Revolution at the height of Robespierre's Terror, *L'Anglaise et le Duc* adapts the memoirs of Scottish aristocrat Grace Elliott, an intimate friend of the King Louis XVI's regicide cousin, the Duke of Orléans. Ostensibly written in 1801, her *Journal of My Life During the French Revolution* struck Rohmer as rich in atmospheric detail and so precise in its narrative logic that the film's sequences were all but traced out (Elliott 2001: 7). Like Kleist's *Die Marquise von O…*, the text called for direct *mise en scène*; for the screenplay to take shape, the memoirist's indirect discourse needed merely to be transposed into dialogue form. More of a challenge were the numerous exterior scenes set in and outside Paris: how to recapture the eighteenth-century city, whose character was all but obliterated under Napoleon III? Rohmer dismissed two common solutions, either to build costly studio sets or to piece together a simulacrum of Paris from location footage culled at different sites, in France or abroad. His response was instead, as with *Perceval le Gallois*, to abandon photographic realism for artifice: 'Je préférais trouver le vrai par le faux, plutôt que de faire du faux en me servant de bouts de vrai'

(My preference was to find truth through artifice, rather than to make something fake with pieces of truth) (Tranchant 2001). The solution lay in new digital imaging techniques whereby live-action footage could be integrated with still images representing exterior decors. Working from period representations of Paris, Rohmer commissioned thirty-five cityscapes and landscapes painted in three-point perspective, through which his actors, filmed in digital betacam on an empty soundstage, would appear to move about once the images – often five or more layers' worth – were synthesized by computer. The cumulative effect is unorthodox: stylised, yet strangely plausible.

Given the picture's heavy technical requirements, for the first time in his career Rohmer turned to a major production company, the storied Pathé. The film benefited from the presence of Jean-Pierre Jeunet and Marc Caro regular Jean-Claude Dreyfus (*Delicatessen*; *La Cité des enfants perdus*), whose grovelling Duke of Orleans is given to outbursts of rage and acts of tenderness, and of the more obviously Rohmerian Lucy Russel (*Following*), whose melodically accented French is a wonder in itself. Full of intrigue, violence, and suspense, the narrative alternates between conversations in Lady Elliott's private chambers and her journeys by coach or on foot through a city in Revolutionary turmoil. We witness history firsthand, as when a mob parades the head of the Princesse de Lamballe about on a stake, and as it is reported, as when Lady Elliott and her aristocrat peers await the result of the Convention's vote on the fate of Louis XVI. A sense of tragedy looms over the film's second half as the Terror spreads: Rohmer's heroine is arrested as a suspect, then thrown into Robespierre's prisons, only to be released.

Pathé proudly marketed *L'Anglaise et le Duc* as the first all-digital French production, and one which singularly enriched the scope of period recreation. For most French critics, however, the picture was, like Renoir's Popular-Frontist *La Marseillaise* before it, a political film. By giving expression to Elliott's royalist sympathies (this in spite of the fact that she by no means supported absolutism) and by depicting rank-and-file revolutionaries in an unflattering light, the film deviated from historiographical doxa, which continued to toe the Jacobin line. While the film was not blacklisted by the press outright, its middling box-office take (under 250,000 tickets sold in France) can be attributed to the tacit sentiment that a director who had taken pains to represent an aristocrat's point of view could only have been a royalist himself. The fact that noted historians were invited to comment on the 'politics' of *L'Anglaise et le Duc*, whether they had seen it or not, indicates how volatile the place of the Terror in the French Revolutionary narrative remains today. Foreign markets, Italy in particular, were far more receptive to Rohmer's iconoclastic elegance.

The espionage film *Triple agent* (2004) forms a diptych of sorts with *L'Anglaise et le Duc*. Both films address the dilemmas of mature women born outside France who are thrown into the whirlwind of history and who must pay dearly the price of their allegiances. Set in the 1930s as fascist and communist blocs rear their heads against one another, *Triple agent* takes its inspiration from the Skobline Affair, a kidnapping incident of some importance in the annals of European espionage. Newsreel footage of the Popular Front coalition's electoral victory of 1936 opens the picture, setting the stage for an intimist drama that foregrounds the duplicity of language in lieu of the action scenes spectators expect from the spy genre. Under Rohmer's gaze, domestic space itself becomes the theatre of operations in a battle between suspicion and trust (see figure 10). Heroine Arsinoé (Katerina Didaskalou) is the Greek spouse of Fiodor (Serge Renko), a White Russian army general in exile who conducts secret intelligence missions – for which European power, Arsinoé, and the spectator, are unsure. As Fiodor's behaviour turns increasingly erratic and his explanations more jumbled, Arsinoé suspects him of betraying the expatriate group that employs him. Her suspicion is confirmed – and her life put in jeopardy – when Voronine's hierarchical superior is abducted by two 'German' agents, believed to be Soviet operatives in disguise. Tightly framed in enclosed spaces, the actors excel in communicating the tragic sentiment that historical forces beyond their control shape their destiny or, inversely, the conviction that individual actions may make a difference on the world stage. *Triple agent* falters somewhat in its epilogue, which offers, against the background of German Occupation, an explanation of the espionage affair. It remains enticing to the eye throughout: Diane Baratier's cinematography reveals deep reds, browns, and shades of ochre in studied interiors, and costumes and hairstyle, from Renko's luxuriant moustache to Didaskalou's *décoiffé*, are meticulous as ever.

Co-produced for 6 million euros by Rezo Films and the CER with funds from France 2 and from Italy, Spain, Greece, and Russia, *Triple agent* reflected an increasingly international, European motion picture industry. Yet in an era when English-language films made in non-English speaking countries for international distribution were fast becoming the norm, Rohmer remained steadfast in his quest for cultural authenticity. Long stretches of Russian-language dialogue in *Triple agent* certainly detracted from its commercial potential. Presented by critics as a model of refinement that distills 'les puissances du faux' (the powers of falsehood) (Frodon 2004), *Triple agent* was, despite its subtly Hitchcockian verve (Cerisuelo 2004: 22), too recondite for viewers little interested in retellings of obscure events. The picture failed to reach even the 100,000 mark in France, where it ranked 226th for the year 2004. This unimpressive result must be considered in the context of declining theatre attendance and the rise of home viewing – a practice for which Rohmer, whose own excursions to the movie theatre had already become rare by the 1980s, has never hidden his enthusiasm.

The director's last feature at the present writing, *Les Amours d'Astrée et de Céladon* (2007), mines the same literary vein as *Perceval le Gallois*. Based on the central plot thread of Honoré d'Urfé's baroque pastoral novel of 1606, the film explores the working of passions, magic, and disguise in the druidic Gaul of the fifth century, a setting whose patent uncommerciality typifies Rohmer's late literary-historical bent. Whether portraits of star-crossed shepherds and spritely nymphs – filmed in the scenic Sioule River Valley of the Auvergne and along the Loire – can lure a larger swath of the French public than did the knights and damsels of *Perceval le Gallois* remains to be seen.

Conclusion

> Je n'aime pas tellement les jeunes filles, mais je ressens la jeune fille qu'il y a en tout homme.[7] (Guibert 1984)

Feted in spring 2001 with a lifetime achievement award at the Venice Mostra and in 2004 by a forty-film retrospective at the Cinémathèque Française, the very institution that had sparked his filmmaking career, Rohmer is perhaps on the eve of retirement. The parting words of a *Cahiers du cinéma* interview granted in conjunction with that crowning event suggested as much: 'je ne regrette rien et, en fin de

7 'I'm not especially fond of young girls, but I do feel the young girl who dwells in every man.'

compte, je n'ai rien dans mes tiroirs' (I don't regret a thing and, in the end, I've nothing left in my desk drawers) (Burdeau and Frodon 2004: 23). Whether Rohmer will cease making films altogether and turn to other, less demanding pursuits, including two of his personal causes – advocacy for the preservation of historical buildings and of the French language – is anyone's guess. At the least, it is certain that the bulk of his life's work for the screen is behind him.

Three observations regarding production, casting, and reception can be made in conclusion to the present overview. First, few contemporary French directors have exerted budgetary restraint to such consistent results as Rohmer. In an age of 20-million-dollar behemoths like Claude Berri's *Germinal* or Régis Warnier's *Indochine*, he has regularly made do with budgets in the mid-hundreds of thousands, limiting his ambitions and adhering to a production model that all but guarantees a profit. In a national climate where state support is the norm, his pictures – only six of which received any CNC money – pay for themselves at the ticket booth (Carrière 2004). Hence Rohmer can describe himself as both 'un cinéaste purement commercial' (a purely commercial filmmaker) and an enlightened amateur who was wont to turn down dividends from Les Films du Losange, arguing that it was enough that the company continue to produce and distribute his films as he saw fit (Carrière 2004). It remains that the legendarily frugal Rohmer, who long refused to eat in restaurants or to take taxis (Smith 1995: 73), is very much in it for the money. Whatever ups and downs his features have weathered domestically have been offset by robust foreign sales, to North America and Japan as well as to the European market. This has given Rohmer a financial buoyancy enjoyed neither by Rivette, whose films are thought too hermetic or too lengthy to please, nor by the later Godard, whose turn to essayism has limited his exposure to the high end of the art-house circuit. Confidential sources claim that owing to his stake in Les Films du Losange, which ensures him a cut of foreign sales, Rohmer has amassed a *very* sizable personal fortune – a rumour that the ever-discreet filmmaker is surely not about to confirm, nor to dispel for that matter.

The subject of casting would merit a chapter unto itself. What stands out over five decades is a significant gender imbalance – not in the number of men and women hired, which averages out to a very *paritaire* fifty–fifty, but in the status that playing in a Rohmer film holds in the career paths of actors and actresses respectively.

While the director has employed name actors on several occasions, like Jean-Louis Trintignant, Jean-Claude Brialy, or Jean-Claude Dreyfus, only rarely has he looked to well-known actresses. Indeed, where female leads are concerned, his preference lies in discovering talent, often recruited from the stage. And talent has come by the bucketful, for, as Brialy once quipped, the dream of all young girls '[est de] tourner avec Rohmer' ([is] to shoot/spin about with Rohmer) (Brialy 1987). Working with Rohmer has had, all things considered, marginal professional impact for dozens of young women, whose best chance for finding work in the cinema thereafter may well be in another Rohmer film... The same is not true of the actors to whom Rohmer gave exposure early in their career. Roles have come easily to *Comédies et proverbes* veterans André Dussolier, Pascal Greggory, Tcheky Karyo, and especially Fabrice Luchini (Vincent, *La Discrète*; Molinaro, *Beaumarchais l'insolent*; Leconte, *Confidences trop intimes*), now recognised as one of France's leading comic actors and not the uptight 'Rohmer protégé' he was considered to be in the mid-1980s.

Third and finally, Rohmer's career points up the strengths and weaknesses of auteurism in the public eye. Reception history shows that even in a country so politically fraught as France, aesthetic conservatism can generate consensus. One is hard-pressed, especially where Rohmer's three cycles are concerned, to find in the French press any outright pans. Left-leaning papers from *L'Humanité* to *Libération* have defended the director despite his putative right-wing political beliefs, while Catholic journalists of *La Croix* and *Télérama* have reacted positively to the ambiguities that his narratives propose in place of univocal example. Anglophone critics, to their credit, have been less reluctant than their French counterparts to poke fun at characters who spend their youth drowning themselves in words. But those same voices from abroad have also done much to promote the 'Rohmer film' as the quintessence of Frenchness: a sex comedy without the sex or, as the case may be, without the laughs (something that the African-American comedian, director, and actor Chris Rock seems bent on rectifying in his 2007 remake of *L'Amour l'après-midi*, entitled *I Think I Love my Wife*). Certainly there are worse things one can spend one's pocket change on than the 'serio-comic triviality' that is Rohmer's strong suit, if not everyone's cup of tea (Kael 1991: 58). As an Arthur Penn character famously says of *Le Genou de Claire*, watching a Rohmer film can be 'like watching paint dry'.

Needless to say, true popular success has eluded Rohmer. His features have garnered half a dozen major prizes at European festivals, but not one has been nominated for a César, the chief distinction awarded by the French motion picture industry. This comes as no surprise given the barely veiled condescension Rohmer has shown for reigning production models. Loathe to play the sales representative for films that, if they are well-made, should find a public on their own, he has long considered advertising – beyond the requisite press release, trailer, and poster – to be a waste of resources. If the public is small, so be it. If it is larger than the last time around, better yet. If it reaches the benchmark of 1,000,000 tickets sold, as was the case of *Ma Nuit chez Maud*, well, then a miracle has occurred. What matters in the end is that the films get made and reach the screen. The rest is for the public to decide, in an exercise of individual taste that exemplifies Rohmer's conception of the cinema as a space of individual freedom.

References

Almendros, Nestor (1984), *A Man with a Camera*, tr. Rachel Phillips Belash, New York, Farrar, Straus, Giroux.

Andrew, Geoff, ed. (2001), *Film: The Critics' Choice*, New York, Watson-Guptill.

Baignères, Claude (1983), 'L'art du ridicule', *Le Figaro*, 25 March.

Baignères, Claude (1986), 'La caméra invisible', *Le Figaro*, 5 September.

Baignères, Claude (1995), 'Intermittences du cœur', *Le Figaro*, 24 March.

Barthes, Roland (1995), 'Perceval', in *La Chronique*, *Œuvres complètes*, III, 1974–1980, ed. Eric Marty, Paris, Seuil: 987.

Beylie, Claude (1962), 'Les trois cordes de la lyre', *Cahiers du cinéma* 133, July: 53–7.

Beylie, Claude (1985), 'Mourir à vingt ans', *L'Avant-scène cinéma* 336, January: 111.

Bontemps, Jacques (1965), 'Le cinéma parallèle', *Cahiers du cinéma* 165, April: 65.

Bory, Jean-Louis (1967), '"La Collectionneuse" d'Eric Rohmer', *Le Nouvel Observateur*, 1 March.

Boujut, Michel (1987), 'Eric Rohmer', *Evénement du jeudi*, 17 September.

Brialy, Jean-Claude (1987), 'Rohmer ausculte l'âme des petites filles dont il fait des modèles', *Pariscope*, 26 August.

Burdeau, Emmanuel and Jean-Michel Frodon (2004), '"J'ai tout de suite pensé..."', *Cahiers du cinéma* 558, March: 16–23.

Capdenac, Michel (1972), 'L'Amour l'après-midi', *Les Lettres françaises*, 6 September.

Carrière, Christophe (2004), 'Mystère Rohmer', *L'Express*, 15 March.

Cerisuelo, Marc (2004), '*Triple Agent*: A spy in the house of love', *Positif* 518, April: 21–2.
Chapier, Henry (1967), '"La Collectionneuse" d'Eric Rohmer', *Combat*, 1 March.
Crisp, Colin (1993), *The Classic French Cinema: 1930–1960*, Bloomington and Indianapolis, Indiana University Press; London, I.B. Tauris and Co.
Daney, Serge (1983), 'Rohmer à la plage', *Libération*, 23 March.
Daney, Serge (1984), 'Rohmer aime bien et châtie bien', *Libération*, 4 September.
Daney, Serge (1987), 'Rohmer côté court', *Libération*, 4 February.
De Baecque, Antoine (1990), 'Jeanne, ou l'idée d'enseigner', *Cahiers du cinéma* 430, April: 22–3.
De Baroncelli, Jean (1967), 'La Collectionneuse', *Le Monde*, 8 March.
De Baroncelli, Jean (1976), 'Un conte romantique d'Eric Rohmer', *Le Monde*, 19 May.
Douchet, Jean (1996), 'Un esprit "NV": les Films du Losange', in Jacques Aumont, ed., *Pour un cinéma comparé*, Paris, Cinémathèque française: 69–76.
Duran, Michel (1969), '"Ma Nuit chez Maud" (Le Pascal des provinciales)', *Le Canard enchaîné*, 11 June.
Duran, Michel (1970), '"Le Genou de Claire"', *Le Canard enchaîné*, 16 December.
Elliott, Grace (2001), *Journal de ma vie durant la Révolution française*, Paris, Les Editions de Paris/Max Chaleil.
Ferenczi, Aurélien (1990), 'Rohmer: l'ouverture des quatre saisons', *Le Quotidien de Paris*, 4 April.
Frodon, Jean-Marie (1987), 'Rohmer, l'homme tranquille', *Le Point*, 24 August.
Frodon, Jean-Marie (1993), 'L'embardée de Rohmer', *Le Monde*, 13 February.
Frodon, Jean-Marie (1995), 'Trois petites histoires d'Eric Rohmer', *Le Monde*, 23 March.
Frodon, Jean-Marie (2004), 'Rohmer l'intimiste dans l'écheveau de l'histoire', *Le Monde*, 17 March.
Garson, Claude (1969), '"Ma Nuit chez Maud": une intelligence constante', *L'Aurore*, 16 May.
Goudet, Stéphane (2004), '"On-dit" ou l'Histoire hors champ', *Positif* 518, 23–28 April: 23–7.
Guibert, Hervé (1984), 'On pourra toujours parler d'amour', *Le Monde*, 30 August.
Kael, Pauline (1973), 'Eric Rohmer's refinement', *Deeper into Movies*, Boston, Little, Brown & Company: 264–7.
Kael, Pauline (1985), 'Sex and politics', *State of the Art*, New York, E.P. Dutton: 37–9.
Kael, Pauline (1991), *5001 Nights at the Movies*, New York, Henry Holt.
Kaganski, Serge and Samuel Blumenfeld (1995), 'Discours de la méthode', *Les Inrockuptibles*, 22 March.
King, Norman (2000), 'Rohmer's "Ma Nuit chez Maud"', in Susan Hayward

and Ginette Vincendeau, *French Film: Texts and Contexts*, 2nd ed., London and New York, Routledge: 202–12.
Legrand, Gérard (1970), 'Sur une convergence de plusieurs films récents', *Positif* 112, January: 1–7.
Legrand, Gérard (1971), 'Un genou ...et un autre genou', *Positif* 125, March: 54–7.
Levieux, Michèle (1990), 'Les comptes de Rohmer', *Révolution*, 6 April.
Lopate, Phillip (2003), '*Le Rayon vert* (The Green Ray)', in Mary Lea Bandy and Antonio Monda, ed., *The Hidden God: Film and Faith*, New York, Museum of Modern Art: 170–3.
Magny, Joël (1995a), *Eric Rohmer*, 2nd ed., Paris, Payot & Rivages.
Magny, Joël (1995b), 'Rohmer revient', *Cahiers du cinéma*, special issue '100 journées': 121.
Marcabru, Pierre (1967), 'Les dangers de la littérature', *Arts* 75, March: 121.
Mardore, Michel (1982), 'Une jeune femme très comme il faut', *Le Nouvel Observateur*, 22 May.
Martin, Marcel (1967), 'Libertine et point ingénue', *Les Lettres françaises*, 9–15 March.
Milne, Tom (1981), 'Rohmer's Siege Perilous', *Sight and Sound*, summer: 192–5.
Montaigne, Pierre (1980), 'Rohmer: le meilleur cinéma français est en péril', *Le Figaro*, 23 December.
Pangon, Gérard (1987), 'Pas d'accord', *Télérama*, 4 February.
Pantel, Monique (1984), 'Ovation pour les inconnus des "Nuits de la pleine lune"', *France-Soir*, 8 September.
Pantel, Monique (1986), 'La lettre d'une femme belle et seule a déclenché "Le Rayon vert"', *France-Soir*, 4 September.
Pantel, Monique (1987), 'Reinette et Mirabelle, les bavardes d'ER', *France-Soir*, 5 February.
Pascal, Michel (1993), [Interview with ER], *Le Point*, 27 February.
Pérez, Michel (1981), 'Jeunesse et classicisme d'un éternel étudiant', *Le Matin*, 4 March.
Pérez, Michel (1987), 'Un intermède lumineux dans l'hiver', *Le Matin*, 4 February.
PL (1993), 'Un film qui manque d'agrément', *Le Canard enchaîné*, 3 March.
Prédal, René (2002), *Le jeune cinéma français*, Paris, Nathan.
'Protestations' (1968), *Cahiers du cinéma* 199, March: 45–6.
Riou, Alain (1990), 'Ma règle du jeu', *Le Nouvel Observateur*, 5 April.
Riou, Alain (1993), 'Eric Rohmer en campagne', *Le Nouvel Observateur*, 18 February.
Rohmer, Eric (1955), 'Redécouvrir l'Amérique', *Cahiers du cinéma* 54, December: 11–16.
Roy, Jean (1987), 'Les signes de la balance', *L'Humanité*, 26 August.
Seguin, Louis (1983), '"Pauline à la plage"', *La Quinzaine littéraire*, 1 May.
Seguin, Louis (1984), '"Les nuits de la pleine lune"', *La Quinzaine littéraire*, 1 October.
Siclier, Jacques (1991), 'La coiffeuse errante', *Le Monde*, 31 January.

Skorecki, Louis (1986), 'La disparition du rayon vert', *Libération*, 3 September.
Smith, Gavin (1995), 'The Joyous Pessimism of Barbet Schroeder', *Film Comment*, March-April: 64–7.
Thevenon, Patrick (1978), 'Le nouveau Rohmer: le Roman de Perceval', *L'Express*, 20–6 March.
Thomas, François (2005), 'Rohmer 1952: *Les Petites Filles modèles*', *Cinéma 09*, spring: 33–47.
Tranchant, Marie-Noëlle (2001), 'Entretien avec Eric Rohmer', *Le Figaro*, 7 September.
Trémois, Claude-Marie (1987), 'Un air de liberté', *Télérama*, 4 February.
Truffaut, François (1975), *Les Films de ma vie*, Paris, Flammarion.
Truffaut, François (1978), *The Films of My Life*, tr. Leonard Mayhew, New York, Simon and Schuster.
[Unsigned] (1984), 'French Side Story', *L'Express*, 12 October.
[Unsigned] (1986), 'Un rayon d'or', *Libération*, 11 September.
Williams, Alan (1992), *Republic of Images: A History of French Filmmaking*, London and Cambridge, MA, Harvard University Press.
Wrathall, John (1996), 'A Summer's Tale/Conte d'été', *Sight and Sound*, October: 53–4.

1 Salvation comes in extremis for Pierre Wesserlin (Jess Hahn) in *Le Signe du Lion* (1962)

2 Homosocial pacts: modern-age dandies Adrien (Patrick Bauchau) and Daniel (Daniel Pommereulle) in *La Collectionneuse* (1967)

3 A winter's tale: the churchgoer Françoise (Marie-Christine Barrault) confesses her sins to the narrator (Jean-Louis Trintignant) in *Ma Nuit chez Maud* (1969)

4 False heroism and narrative complicity: Jérôme (Jean-Claude Brialy) corners Claire (Laurence de Monaghan) in *Le Genou de Claire* (1970)

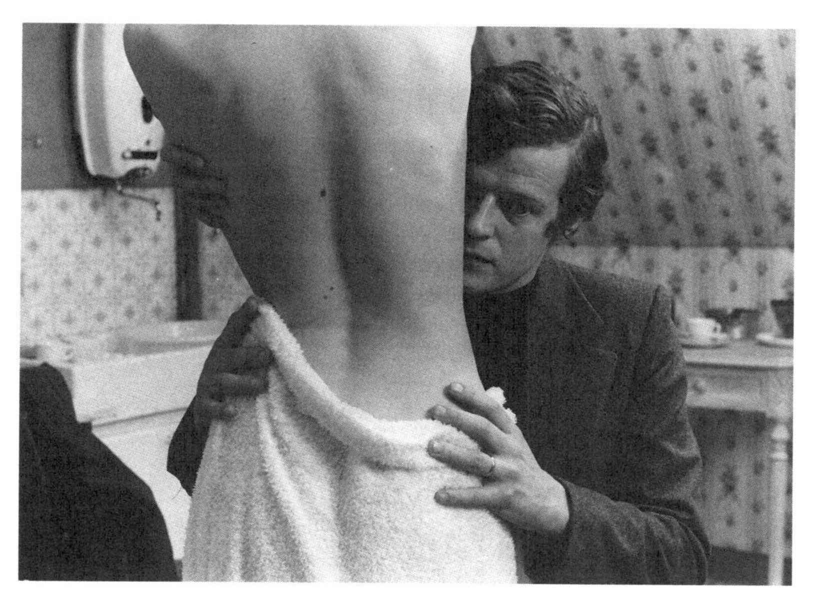

5 Temptations of the flesh: Frédéric (Bernard Verley) and Chloé (Zouzou) in *L'Amour l'après-midi* (1972)

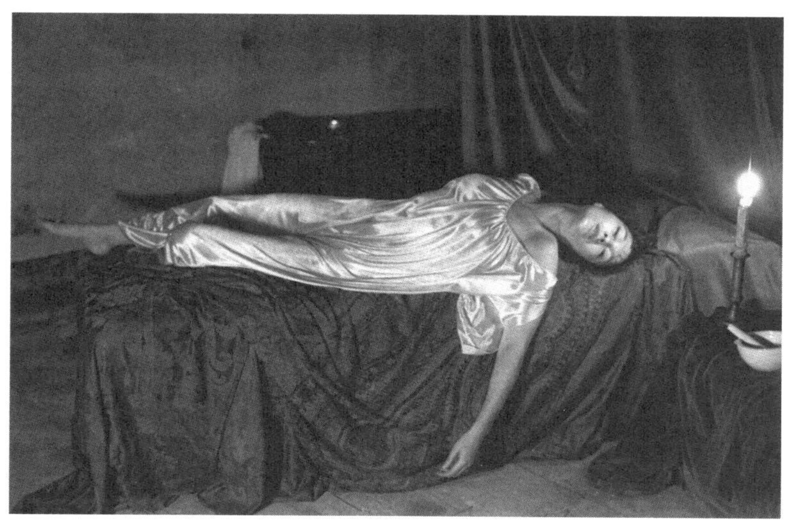

6 Pictorial quotation: the sedated Marquise (Edith Clever) as viewed by the Count in *Die Marquise von O...* (1976)

7 Rohmer's middle ages: the director on the set of *Perceval le Gallois* (1979)

8 The light of the world: actors Amanda Langlet, Pascal Greggory, and Arielle Dombasle in a contre-jour shot from *Pauline à la plage* (1983)

9 Maturity and companionship: Magali (Béatrice Romand) and Isabelle (Marie Rivière) make up in *Conte d' automne* (1998)

10 As suspicion mounts, the marriage of the Voronines (Serge Renko and Katerina Didaskalou) unravels in the domestic spy drama *Triple agent* (2004)

2

Theory and criticism

When France's leading postwar film critic, the wildly prolific André Bazin, fell ill with leukaemia in the late 1950s, he left in Eric Rohmer's hands the editorship of *Cahiers du cinéma*, the internationally renowned journal he had founded in 1951 with Jacques Doniol-Valcroze and Jean-Marie Lo Duca. Two years Bazin's junior, Rohmer was seen as his natural successor: an early contributor to the magazine, he had astutely defended in its pages the precepts that Bazin held essential to the seventh art, namely that film enjoys an objective relation to reality; that it is impure by nature among the arts; and that it evolves towards an ever more precise reproduction of the world, which itself reflects the order of creation. These notions not only grounded the idealist aesthetic theory that Rohmer developed as a critic from the late 1940s until 1963, when he was ousted from *Cahiers* by the journal's pro-modern wing of contributors, but also proved crucial to his understanding of filmmaking, pointing to a transparent visual style and a conception of *mise en scène* rigorously bound to the real.

With Bazin's untimely death in 1958 at age forty, the sense of obligation at *Cahiers* to continue a rich but as yet under-appreciated legacy was great. Perhaps greater still was the impression that Bazin, the author of over 1,300 articles, had set the bar too high. Reviewing the major pieces his friend had assembled for publication under the title *Qu'est-ce que le cinéma?* (*What Is Cinema?*), Rohmer confessed mixed feelings of exaltation and discouragement: 'Tout a été dit, par lui, et l'on vient trop tard' (Everything has been said by [Bazin], and we've come too late) (Rohmer 1984: 164/1989: 105 [tr. mod.]). These words should be taken less as the admission of a debilitating 'anxiety of influence' than as a homage to the quality and scope of Bazin's teachings, which almost single-handedly set the critical agenda for film comment in France after the war up through the early 1960s. Rohmer was and would remain indebted to the axiom he identified as his mentor's 'first principle': '*Le cinéma apparaît comme l'achèvement dans le temps de l'objectivité photographique*' (*Cinema appears as the completion in time of photographic objectivity*) (Rohmer 1984: 153/1989: 97). This thesis of film's mechanical, objective character, which Bazin first proposed in a landmark essay of 1945 on the 'ontology' of the photographic image, heralded in Rohmer's view a Copernican revolution, for it set cinema firmly apart from the other arts under whose shadow it had long remained. By subscribing to Bazin's axiom that the cinema's essence lay not in its potential for subjective expression, but in its objectivity as a pure emanation of the filmed motif, Rohmer placed himself in a lineage that sang the virtues of the real over those of the image, the prosaicism of the Lumière brothers over the trickery of Méliès, Murnau's world-bound poetry over Eisenstein's dialectics of montage.

If Rohmer's abundant writings on film aesthetics relied upon Bazin's 'ontological realist' assumptions, in other key respects they owed less to the co-founder of *Cahiers* than to the Young Turks who imposed a pro-Hollywood line on the magazine, over Bazin's reservations. Antoine de Baecque has retraced the battles waged between *Cahiers*' yellow covers that led to the editorial take-over at mid-decade by the 'hitchcocko-hawksiens', a group comprised of Truffaut, Rivette, Godard, Chabrol and presumably led by Rohmer himself – whence Pierre Kast's disobliging epithet 'l'école Schérer' (the Schérer school), which was meant to underscore those critics' dogmatism. Very much the elder statesman and *éminence grise* of the group (De Baecque 1991: I, 75), Schérer/Rohmer[1] expounded a theory of the cinema's classicism at mid-century, praised the technical achievements of Hollywood in the age of sound and colour, and elaborated, in contrast to Truffaut's sharp polemics and ad hominem attacks, a theory of film authorship based on literary criticism and art-historical connoisseurship. This is not the place to retell *Cahiers*' conflicted internal history, in which Rohmer played a key role as both actor and victim. Suffice it to say that the critic should be categorised not as the strict Bazinian some assumed him to be, but as a figure who mediates between the

1 Hereafter, 'Rohmer'; articles signed Maurice Schérer will be identified 'MS' in parentheses.

venerable tradition of idealist aesthetics one the one hand, and, on the other, the director-based, pro-American 'politique des auteurs' or auteur theory that came overtly to challenge it in the mid-1950s – only to implode with the rise of structuralism, the dismantling of the Hollywood studio system, and the emergence of world cinema on the heels of the French New Wave.

This chapter aims to present and contextualise Rohmer's primary theoretical and critical insights. The task is not an easy one, for save the accessible *Hitchcock* (1957) co-written with Claude Chabrol, Rohmer's critical writings, partly anthologised in *Le Goût de la beauté* (*The Taste for Beauty*), are notoriously difficult and at times uninviting. They couple a refined style of argument with a complex grasp of French syntax that lends itself poorly to English translation. References are invariably high cultural, drawn as often from literature (Aristophanes, Molière, Goethe), painting (Titian, Goya, Cézanne) and philosophy (Parmenides, Plato, Hegel) as from the history of film, and a Catholic subtext, coloured by Jansenism, is often present (Crisp 1988: 3). Rohmer's self-description as an *honnête homme* possessed of an innate taste for classicism and unconcerned with things ephemeral (political and social change first among them) recalls a bygone era in which disinterested critical judgement was prized above the 'commitment' (*engagement*) called for by Sartre. Yet Rohmer's writings warrant attention not simply as a pillar of high criticism within the local history of postwar French film comment. They reflect too a formative moment in an individual's apprenticeship to the medium and in the evolving understanding of film's responsibility with respect to the visible world. The act of critical judgement becomes a manner of filmmaking in its own right, a way of discerning an ideal state of cinema to which the practising director can aspire.

His own declarations notwithstanding, criticism was not for Rohmer – as it was for Chabrol and initially for Godard – a mere stepping-stone to professional directing, a stopgap solution at a time when funding was scarce and the industry closed off to newcomers unwilling to climb the ranks. Rohmer's critical temperament was far too assertive, and his dedication to the daily running of *Cahiers* too deep. As De Baecque points out, to ask whether criticism was either a means or an end for future New Wave directors is a false question to begin with (De Baecque 1991: I, 291). Rather than to seek causal relationships between criticism and creative work, then, it is best to imagine Rohmer's early writings as a reflection upon a vast intertext of images, forms, and concepts that his own films, through their attendant stylistic choices, will reflect on in turn (see Chapter 3). We will see that despite the enthusiasm for Hollywood he shared with the Young Turks, Rohmer remains at base a Bazinian, for whom the cinema is inseparable from the belief in the camera's capacity for revealing the world in a manner unique among the arts.

Ontological realism and technical change

Efforts toward the postwar reconstruction of France went beyond removing rubble from bombed-out city districts, relocating displaced families, and rebuilding infrastructure. Out of the widespread optimism of the 1944 Liberation sprung new cultural organisations which sought to re-establish national unity and to lessen the burdens of everyday living in a time of continued shortages. For André Bazin, whose sympathies lay with the Left but whose liberal Catholic beliefs allied him with the 'personalism' of Emmanuel Mounier's journal *L'Esprit*, the cinema, thanks to its wide appeal, ease of distribution, and visual immediacy, was the best tool for re-educating French society and rekindling its war-weary spirit. The viewing and group discussion of films ranging from Chaplin's comedies and Carné's poetic realist works of the 1930s, to Italian neo-realist pictures like *Rome, Open City* (1945) and *The Bicycle Thief* (1948) encouraged individuals both to appreciate the seventh art as such and to identify political and moral priorities through reflexive analysis (Andrew 1978: 64). It was this pedagogic value of cinema, at the crossroads of phenomenology, ethics, and politics, that brought Bazin to cultural activism, leading him to deliver countless lectures in factories and meeting-halls, to coordinate *Objectif 49*, a prominent *ciné-club* which rallied left-leaning intellectuals of all stripes, and to write for publications as diverse as the Communist *L'Ecran français*, Sartre's *Les Temps modernes*, and the populist daily *Le Parisien libéré* (De Baecque 2003: 45–7). Bazin may have exhausted himself in the process, yet he achieved his goal of 'set[ting] Paris aflame with cinema' (Andrew 1978: 83).

The staple of postwar cinephilia, and the breeding ground for the generation of aspiring filmmaker-critics who would gain notoriety at the end of the 1950s as the French New Wave, were the weekly meetings of the *ciné-clubs*. Such groups had existed in France as early as the 1920s, when in the heyday of the art cinema they had promoted the international avant-garde. Those few that remained by 1940 were forced to operate clandestinely under German Occupation. While many clubs founded after the Liberation, like Bazin's *Objectif 49*, had individual betterment and community-building in mind, others followed the museographical approach of the voracious Henri Langlois, the director of the Cinémathèque Française, whose seemingly countless archival treasures drew packed houses, however 'minor' the programme.

Among the more prominent Parisian organisations to call for a renewed cinema culture divorced from escapist entertainment was Maurice Schérer's Ciné-Club du Quartier Latin. When a former student, F.C. Froeschel, approached him with funds to organise screenings, Schérer consented immediately (De Baecque 1991: I, 222). By the close of the 1940s, the club's Thursday afternoon meetings attracted a core of followers that included Jacques Rivette (b. 1928) and Jean-Luc Godard (b. 1930), enticed as they were by the unorthodox choice of films, many of which were little-known American genre pictures (Rohmer 1984: 17). The club's modest *Bulletin*, edited by Schérer and later renamed *La Gazette du cinéma*, allowed fledgling critics like Truffaut, then André Bazin's personal secretary, to cut their teeth, while leaving enough space for pieces by Alexandre Astruc and for Sartre's major essay on film, 'Le cinéma n'est pas une mauvaise école'. Schérer owed his prestige in student circles to his age and professorial demeanour – he was reputedly a hard-nosed discussion leader – and to the quality of three articles of the late 1940s which appeared in Jean George Auriol's *Revue du cinéma* and in *Les Temps modernes*. Directly inspired by Bazin's theses on the 'realism' of the photographic image, these early pieces defend an evolutionary theory that relates the history of film style and technical change to the medium's ontology.

In 'Le cinéma, art de l'espace' ('Cinema, the Art of Space', MS 1948), Rohmer opposes the consensual view that narrative cinema, following Lessing's distinction, is a temporal art. Logically and historically, he contends, it is space that provides cinema with its essential form of sensibility, inasmuch as the medium relies on visual perception (Rohmer 1984: 42). Film's spatial aspect is not to be confused with pictorialism or composition. It extends rather to the 'totality' of filmed space, by which Rohmer understands the dialectical relationship between the finite projection screen and the unbounded setting in which the filmed action is imagined to take place (Rohmer 1984: 42). Films are of cinematic value not if they aspire to formal esthetic autonomy, as the beaux-arts tradition had perhaps assumed, but because they use means specific to the medium – framing, depth of field, rhythmic editing – to convey a total sense of space that reflects the world's own complexity. Individual directors are sensitive to cinema's spatial qualities to varying degrees. The comic genius of Buster Keaton, for instance, would lie less in the psychology of the sight gags than in the way gesture inhabits the screen itself, as if to inquire into 'le "pourquoi" des trois dimensions' (the 'workings' of the three dimensions), whereas the humour of Charlie Chaplin, socialised and humanistic, is little attuned to the medium's spatial constraints (Rohmer 1984: 47/1989: 23). Period and group styles similarly diverge in their treatment of space. The same cinemagoers who in the 1920s could naively enjoy the deformed angles of *The Cabinet of Dr Caligari* and the meaning-laden poses of Murnau's actors in an experience of 'pure vision', are driven in the 1940s to rationalise each image, interpreting it such that they no longer show any interest in 'la *réalité même* de son aspect' (the *reality* of what they see) (Rohmer 1984: 52/1989: 28). Incessant shuttling between sign and signification blinds the viewer to photography's fundamental objectivity, which alone justifies in Rohmer's view the 'fascination' of cinema. The movie screen confronts us directly with the phenomenological experience of seeing.

Rohmer closes 'Le cinéma, art de l'espace' with the argument that great filmmakers are those who are best able to reconstitute a full spatial universe. This goal Soviet montage and German expressionism had all but achieved in their celebration of shapes and movement. But it is for Rohmer contemporary Italian neo-realism that elevates spatial coherence to its highest level yet, with its reportage-like techniques and authentic locales. Praising Rossellini's *Paisà* (1946), which charts the Liberation of Italy by Allied forces and the linguistic and cultural encounters that ensue, Rohmer affirms that realism can best be achieved when a director does not rely on editing to transmit an idea: 'le mérite de Rossellini dans *Païsa* est d'avoir misé le moins possible sur des effets de montage et évité un trop grand morcellement en plans' (Rohmer 1984: 53) (Rossellini's success in *Paisan* is to have relied as little as possible on the editing and to have avoided breaking up his work into too many shots' [Rohmer 1989: 28]).

We may think here of the River Pô episode, where long takes and slow pans capture the movement of Italian partisans who scurry about in their boats as German forces close in from all sides. Rohmer thus upholds Bazin's view that the inviolate nature of the real can best be apprehended when editing is least obtrusive (Bazin 1975: 280). Morally speaking, a long take is superior to a sequence of alternating shots that unduly focuses attention and imposes a hierarchy on the visual field. Rossellini's example proves that simplicity of means no more impoverishes our sense of space than the converse search for baroque stylisation guarantees spatial richness, as evidenced by Hitchcock's more heavily edited films.

The term 'realism' emerges from Rohmer's early work as both evaluative and prescriptive. Like Bazin, the critic acknowledges that the cinema is realist by nature. Tied to the laws of conventional photography, the film image wrests a moment out of time and, in Bazin's metaphoric reading, 'embalms' it for posterity, satisfying a deep anthropological urge to stave off death (Bazin 1975: 9). At the same time, certain works of cinema are more 'realist' than others in that they better unveil the ambiguity of the world, encouraging the viewer to participate in its unfolding and to make independent discoveries. Realism is consequently as much an ethical principle as an ontological one.

Philosopher Noël Carroll has pointed to the contradictions attendant to Bazin's position, one which tends to conflate the mechanical process of photographic representation with the aims of one contingent film style – the deep-focus 'spatial realism' of Welles and Renoir (Carroll 1988: 128). While Rohmer's writings contain a similar kind of semantic slippage when they promote cinematic spatial realism as the only legitimate realist art, their logical inconsistencies are less damning than Carroll lets on (Carroll 1988: 142). For a generation as steeped in Hegelian notions of history as was Rohmer's, the evolution of film language is a rational historical fact. Figures like De Sica, Zavattini, and Rossellini are central to cinema's development because their grasp of the medium corresponds to 'une certaine marche vers l'objectivité' (a certain progression toward objectivity) that mirrors history's own movement (Rohmer 1984: 157/1989: 100). The search for representational exactitude thus reveals the objective vocation of film itself, its 'essence' or 'Idea'. But this Hegelian understanding of film's ontology is underwritten by the belief that the world-bound truth exposed by motion-picture photography is itself the truth of divine creation. Even as Bazin refers to the 'scientific' nature of the medium and the 'automatic' nature of its processes, then, the horizon against which he reads film is metaphysical. What Rohmer terms an 'axiom' shoring up his mentor's critical edifice is every bit a credo which he himself, having distanced himself from Sartrean conceptions of liberty and action, adopted from the late 1940s onward.

Rohmer's disquisition on space was followed by the compact manifesto, 'Pour un cinéma parlant' ('For a Talking Cinema' MS). The piece opens with the provocative claim that despite the introduction of sound, the cinema has yet to learn how to talk: 'Il n'y a eu en somme jusqu'ici ... que du cinéma *sonore*' (until now there has only been *sound* cinema) (MS/Rohmer 1984: 57/1989: 29). In response to a technical advance that should have prompted thorough reappraisal of the medium, film theorists and avant-garde directors reaffirmed the primacy of images, dismissing sound as 'parasitic' and leaving its signifying potential untapped. So strong was the equation of the cinema with the visual that twenty years after *The Jazz Singer*, the best films are judged to be those which could do without speech altogether (Rohmer 1984: 56). To overcome this resistance to the sound film, filmmakers must recognise that spoken language is in no way inferior to the 'language of images' championed by the avant-garde. They must not reduce speech to literary dialogues that lie halfway between theatre and the novel (Rohmer 1984: 58). In a novel, notes Rohmer, dialogues conjure up a world that is present only in the reader's imagination; transposed in the sound film, those same dialogues become redundant, since their referent is visible onscreen. Ideally, speech should intersect with, rather than duplicate the filmed world. 'L'art du réalisateur n'est pas fait pour faire oublier ce que dit le personnage, mais, tout au contraire, pour nous permettre de ne perdre aucune de ses paroles (Rohmer 1984: 59) (The director's art is not to make us forget what characters say but, rather, to help us not to miss a word [Rohmer 1989 : 31]).

The sound film is hence defined not as one in which actors reel off memorable lines, but one where words are integral to structure, as in the case of deceitful narration or offscreen commentary conceived as counterpoint (Rohmer 1984: 60). These positions clearly anticipate Rohmer's own mode of filmmaking, which will place speech and image on equal footing, or even favour the former by juxtaposing offscreen narration and dialogue.

The introduction of colour marked a second key step in the cinema's evolution. Only two colour features were made in France before World War Two, with the Francita-Realita process, and it was not until 1953 that the country's colour boom began in earnest (Crisp 1993: 135–6). Few French producers could afford Technicolor, the tricolour dye process that was the jewel in the American industry's crown, and unipack European alternatives were as yet unimpressive. 'Est-ce vraiment couleur, celle qu'on nous offre depuis cinq ans?' (is what we have seen in the past five years really colour?), Rohmer asked his readers in 1949, only to respond that 'l'image en couleurs est laide' (The colour picture is ugly) (MS/Rohmer 1984: 71/1989: 39). The overly contrasted or washed-out hues of available stocks paled in comparison to pristine black and white, which, even in 16mm, presents 'l'exacte copie d'une réalité qui reste seule soumise au jugement esthétique' (an exact copy of reality, which alone is subjected to aesthetic appraisal) (Rohmer 1984: 72/1989: 40). If and when colour does meet the human eye's standard for precision and nuance, affirms Rohmer, rather than become an end in itself it must remain a means by which to access a world-bound beauty:

> Le cinéma malaxe la pâte même du réel, et le plus fort de son ambition est précisément de ne rien refuser de ce qu'il peut devoir à la richesse et à la précision des mécaniques dont il dispose.[2] (Rohmer 1984: 72–3)

Technical progress is only to be embraced to the extent that it affords a more comprehensive and objective grasp of reality.

Many of Rohmer's reviews of the 1950s point to the heightened artistic sensitivity that colour production required of directors and their crews. Speaking of Jean Renoir's *The River* (1950), shot on location in India, the critic notes the audacity of cinematographer Claude Renoir who, rather than seek an even palette, highlighted instead the aggressive 'acidity' of certain tones as if to authenticate the truth of the fictional tale (Schérer 1952b). Howard Hawks' *Gentlemen Prefer Blondes* taunts the spectator with colours so garish that they have a

2 'Cinema kneads the dough of reality; its greatest ambition is to accept as much as possible given the richness and precision of available technology.' (Rohmer 1989: 40)

humour unto themselves (Schérer 1954c: 45), while Hitchcock's *The Trouble With Harry* uses the bright autumn foliage of New England to attenuate the farcical aspects of the film's plot (Rohmer 1956a: 38). By 1956, the year colour production in France reached its peak for the decade (Crisp 1993: 139), processing quality and artistic mastery were such that the once hesitant Rohmer could speak as a convert to colour, which now lent itself to all genres, the thriller as much as the western. Distinctive styles begin to emerge, with some directors aiming for chromatic harmony throughout a picture and others underscoring individual colours to stir up emotions, as in the case of Harriett's blue dress in *The River* or Miss Lonelyheart's green one in *Rear Window* (Rohmer 1984: 109).

For the critic, there is no debating that colour technology marks a new phase in cinema's realist vocation. Deprived of colour, filmed objects now enjoy but partial existence; they *are* fully themselves only through and in colour. 'C'est par [la couleur] seule que l'expression cinématographique atteint un réalisme absolu' (It is only in [colour] that cinematic expression attains absolute realism) (Rohmer 1984: 110/1989: 68). This affirmation does not advocate a painterly approach to the medium, for the film director need only respect what belongs to the real:

> Méfions-nous des filtres, des traitements chimiques de la pellicule, et de tous autres faux-fuyants. Il y a une sorte d'intensité propre à l'image brute que l'on doit humblement respecter.[3] (Rohmer 1984: 112)

This attitude informs the naturalistic approach that Rohmer and his chief cinematographer, Nestor Almendros, would perfect from the mid-1960s onward.

Much like sound before it, colour confirmed the teleology of Bazinian photographic realism. Whether widescreen formats similarly enhanced viewers' grasp of the real was more open to debate. With the Paris premiere of the biblical epic *The Robe* in December 1953, Cinemascope was introduced or, rather, reintroduced to France, since the anamorphic lens was the invention of Henri Chrétien, a Frenchman who had patented his 'Hypergonar' in 1928, to the general indifference of the domestic industry (Crisp 1993: 128). In his reaction piece 'Vertus cardinales du Cinémascope' ('Cinemascope's Cardinal

3 'Beware of filters, of chemical toning, and of all other tricks. There is a kind of intensity belonging to the raw image that we must respect.' (Rohmer 1989: 70)

Virtues'), one of several assembled for the January 1954 issue of *Cahiers*, Rohmer questions the idea that widescreen brings with it a quantitative change – something 'more' to look at; indeed, viewing conditions themselves are transformed (Schérer 1954a: 36). As directors had long crammed the frame to its outer edges, widescreen allows for properly 'aired-out' *mise en scène*, providing cinema – in Rohmer's lofty turn of phrase – with 'le seul élément sensible qui lui échappât: l'air, l'éther divin des poètes' (the one perceptible element that had escaped its grasp: air, the poets' divine ether) (Schérer 1954a: 37). Some pictures shot in standard 1.33:1 aspect ratio, like Renoir's deep-focus *La Règle du jeu*, Welles's *The Magnificent Ambersons*, or Hitchcock's *Rope*, had already given expression to this 'divine' element (Schérer 1954a: 37–8). What remained was to make intelligent use of the outsized format, something *The Robe* did only too rarely. Close-ups should be used sparingly, since long focal lengths distort the image's lateral edges, and interior scenes are less suited to it than natural exteriors. When put in the right hands, Cinemascope promises in Rohmer's view a communion between spectator and image where all that is technical melts into air: perhaps some day, the critic speculates, 'ne parlera-t-on plus de *cadrages* mais de paysages ou de sites, non d'*éclairages* mais de lumière' (one will no longer speak of *framing* but of landscapes or sites, no longer of *lighting* but of light) (Schérer 1954a: 39). Interestingly, fifty years after praising the wide screen, Rohmer would revisit this article in the pages of *Cahiers*, arguing that what he saw as the format's virtues were perhaps vices in disguise, leading to a poverty of the image.

Wary as always of costly capital improvements, French studios and exhibitors equipped for widescreen with reluctance. By 1956, one-third of films produced in France boasted a widescreen format. This figure declined steadily over the decade, to reach a mere 7 per cent in 1959, the year of Truffaut's *Les 400 coups*, shot in the Cinemascope knockoff Dialyscope (Crisp 1993: 131). Colour, of course, had a more lasting impact on the domestic product. Nonetheless, high costs and processing delays dissuaded many French producers from using colour throughout the 1950s, long after it had become the norm in America. Rohmer's pro-Americanism can hence be traced to the unparalleled technical achievements of Hollywood, which was a step or two up on Europe in bringing the world to life onscreen.

Classicism and the seventh art

The question of cinema's autonomy or uniqueness among the arts has long fuelled theoretical debate. In the 1920s and early 1930s, critic Rudolph Arnheim emphasised the medium's 'unreality' and the manner in which it enhanced aesthetic sensibility by limiting natural perception, while Bela Balázs attempted to describe, through comparison to other arts, the unique 'language-form' into which film transforms its raw materials (Andrew 1976). If many avant-garde practitioners thought it possible to forge an abstract cinema wholly uncontaminated by the sister arts, conversion to sound in the 1930s all but guaranteed the dominance of the narrative fiction film. Filmmakers looked to their literary forebears for guidance, much in the way that photographers had deferred to painters in the mid-nineteenth century.

By 1950, the situation was such that André Bazin wondered whether an autonomous art of film could even be said to exist:

> Le cinéma, ou ce qu'il en reste, est-il aujourd'hui incapable de survivre sans les béquilles de la littérature et du théâtre? Est-il en passe de devenir un art subordonné et dépendant en numéro *bis* de quelque art traditionnel?[4] (Bazin 1975: 83)

Even if it were the case that film had been stripped of all autonomy, thought Bazin, it would be no cause for alarm. Far from a shameful aberration in cinema's life course, the turn to literary sources is part of a process of mutual enrichment through which each art explores its possibilities. Rejecting the avant-gardist discourse on purity, Bazin preferred to track general trends of what remained a popular medium. The critic's duty in his view was to point out the inadequacies of current literary adaptations and to identify those works that respect and, ultimately, transcend their source material, such as Robert Bresson's 1950 rendering of Georges Bernanos' *Journal d'un curé de campagne*.

In his own efforts to define cinema's aesthetic, Rohmer echoes the defeatism characteristic of a time when middle-of-the-road adaptations led French production. His second *Temps modernes* piece, 'Nous n'aimons plus le cinéma' ('The Romance is Gone', MS 1949),

4 'Is the cinema or what remains of it incapable of surviving without the twin crutches of literature and theater? Is it in process of becoming an art derived from and dependent on one of the traditional arts?' (Bazin 1967: 54)

condemns generations of filmmakers who, as if suffering from an inferiority complex, adopt rules of composition from the other arts. This imitative behaviour, though intended to prove film's superiority as a synthetic means of expression, effectively deprived the cinema of its ability to recast whatever borrowings it might make (Rohmer 1984: 69). So compromised is film by the 'foreign criteria' of literature that novelists and playwrights who try their hand at screenwriting have little difficulty tailoring their ideas to the medium – evidence enough of film's impurity. Rohmer's point is neither to blame individual directors nor to decry a system of production which relied heavily on adapted screenplays, as it would be later for Truffaut in his diatribes against the Tradition of Quality. At issue is rather the status of cinema as a culminating point in the history of representation in the West. A filmmaker's creations – whatever their origins – may rank among the greatest artworks in history:

> Les adaptations ne sont justifiées que dans la mesure où elles viennent nous confirmer, non plus que *Hamlet* ou *Les Frères Karamazov* étaient du cinéma avant la lettre, mais que le cinéma *peut être* Shakespeare ou Dostoïevski. C'est-à-dire cesser d'être lui-même.[5] (Rohmer 1984: 68)

The cinema aspires to eternal beauty through a dialectical process based on exteriorisation and negation that the critic must to bring to light.

For Rohmer, whose most thorough statement of intent was the five-part 'Le Celluloïd et le marbre', serialised in *Cahiers* in 1955 (Rohmer 1955a–e), a theory of cinema must be grounded in aesthetics (the science of the Beautiful), notably in the Platonic and Kantian traditions which promote the correspondence of object to universal Idea and the coincidence of beauty and truth. In this idealist framework, art's autonomy with respect to historical circumstance and social organisation is taken as a given. The relative weight of each of the arts nevertheless changes with time, moving through stages that mirror human development, from infancy to maturity and old age (Rohmer 1955b: 14). Inverting the traditional hierarchy according to which the noblest arts are those with the longest history, Rohmer contends that,

5 'Adaptations are justified only to the extent that they confirm, not that *Hamlet* or *The Brothers Karamazov* were in fact cinematic works, but that the cinema *can be* Shakespeare or Dostoyevski. That is, it can cease being itself.' (Rohmer 1989: 37)

as the last art to appear on the world stage, the cinema is the only one with its finest years ahead. At mid-century, it finds itself on the cusp of a 'classical age' in which the need for legitimation is no longer felt. Long held to the standards of painting, poetry, music, and literature, cinema now had the right to judge the other arts in turn from its newly consolidated position of artistic maturity.

As early as 1949, in 'L'âge classique du cinéma' ('The Classical Age of Film', MS 1949), published in Albert Camus' journal *Combat*, Rohmer had made the case for film as the consummate art of its epoch, one that literature itself attempted to copy. Having exhausted psychological explanation, modern novelists abandon interiority for the 'spectacle absurde et chaotique des apparences' (the absurd and chaotic spectacle of appearances) (Rohmer 1984: 75/1989: 41). Yet this play of appearances which so interests the school of literary behaviourism, argues Rohmer, is cinema's alone to reproduce. And if film looks to the visible world, it is the better to access an interior world in turn. To the extent that they place their faith in the suggestive power of showing over telling, then, filmmakers are well positioned to revive humanistic categories that novelists had considered outmoded, such as the passions, character, and mood.

Rohmer's first *Cahiers* piece, 'Vanité que la peinture' ('Such Vanity Is Painting', MS 1951), unfolds the hypothesis that cinema's coming of age has revived the ideal of an impermanent beauty to which art gives access. The title quotes Pascal's observation that painting vainly seduces us by offering up mere appearances, while it is the things themselves that alone merit our admiration. If the painter's craft is one of vanity, the filmmaker's is one of humility, for the movie camera accomplishes the essential task of all art insofar as it ushers us back to things: 'La tâche de l'art n'est pas de nous enfermer dans un monde clos. Né des choses, il nous ramène aux choses' (Art's task is not to enclose us in a sealed world. Born of the world, it brings us back to it) (Rohmer 1984: 78/1989: 44). By placing at the forefront of contemporary aesthetics an art whose 'realism' describes its very essence, Rohmer removes film from the formalist teleology of a Clement Greenberg, for whom each art turns inward, moving towards a heightened self-awareness. Indeed, at the very moment at which modernity's imperatives have led the other arts to break with Nature and given free reign to iconoclasm and to the vilification of humankind, cinema, as Rohmer sees it, continues faithfully to copy the world. It has dispelled its initial doubts as to its specificity and as such enters with confidence into its 'classical' phase.

What constitutes 'classicism' for the critic? In the West, where the aesthetic sense is tightly correlated to Nature through the concept of mimesis (imitation), mature or 'classical' periods can be defined as those in which 'beauté selon l'art et beauté selon la nature semblaient ne faire qu'un' (art and beauty in nature seemed to be one and the same) (Rohmer 1984: 80/1989: 45). The author's case in point is Renaissance monocular perspective, which renders objects on the canvas much as the eye perceives them in real life. Since it abandoned perspective in favour of the play of colours (impressionism) or the fracturing of the picture plane (cubism), painting has estranged itself from an ordinary vision of objects, which now are distorted beyond recognition. Yet the greater the exaggerations of the painter's hand, affirms Rohmer, the more sensitive we become to the filmmaker's power to reproduce the unadorned beauty of things:

> une irrésistible envie nous prend de regarder le monde avec nos yeux de tous les jours, de conserver pour nous cet arbre, cette eau courante, ce visage altéré par le rire ou l'angoisse, tels qu'ils sont, en dépit de nous.[6] (Rohmer 1984: 80)

Amidst impatient calls for revolution and revolt, cinema promises a classical simplicity stripped of expressionistic excess. This celebration of photographic objectivity bestows a nobility upon filmmaker and viewer, who each must acknowledge that beauty is everywhere and always *of the world*. Art's attempts to embellish the real or to invest it with symbol and signification pale in the face of creation's inherent beauty.

The radical nature of cinema as a mechanical art, then, is its ability to present the viewer with a totality formed solely of concrete appearances, untainted by metaphor or the mystique of the beyond. From these prosaic appearances the viewer may extract a range of meanings without the risk of exhausting their diversity. All that appears onscreen – a face or the movement of a hand in close-up, a lone human figure set off against a decor – reveals the harmony of nature's distinct realms. But in the world of film, the relationship of

6 'We are tempted to look at the world with our everyday eyes, to hold and keep for ourselves this tree, this running water, this face distorted with happiness or anguish, just as they are, in spite of us.' (Rohmer 1989: 45, tr. mod.)

being to appearance is inverted such that 'l'apparence est l'être, et tire à elle la substance d'un monde intérieur dont elle est l'incarnation, non le signe' (appearance is being, and pulls toward it the substance of an interior world, a world of which it is the incarnation, not the sign) (Rohmer 1984: 77/1989: 43).

This Bazinian poetics of incarnation, which opposes flesh and spirit the better to join them, undergirds much of Rohmer's criticism beginning with his review of *Stromboli* (MS 1950), the film that the critic would credit, some thirty years later, for his conversion from existentialism to a spiritual world view (Rohmer 1984: 22). Published in the fifth and final issue of *La Gazette du cinéma*, the brief article casts Rossellini's film as the story of a 'pécheresse touchée par la grâce' (a sinner who receives God's grace) (Rohmer 1984: 201/1989: 124). While Karin (Ingrid Bergman), a war refugee who is forced to marry a poor fisherman to escape deportation from Italy, grapples with the unforgiving surroundings of the volcanic island and with a culture she has no desire to comprehend, Rossellini's camera withholds sympathetic identification. Confined to the village, the heroine is left to suffer much like the tuna that are netted and put to death at sea in the film's central scene. Karin's endless tears and outbursts reveal the hollowness of her being, or what Rohmer calls her deep 'abjection' (Rohmer 1984: 202). This dispassionate portrayal of human subjectivity sets up the moment of paroxysm where Karin, fleeing the village in ruins, ascends the volcano only to encounter the wrath of creation and, in Rohmer's reading, to receive in extremis the gift of God's infinite grace. Like Karin herself, the spectator is shaken from a state of insensitivity and reminded of divine goodness.

Not all viewers of *Stromboli* would subscribe to Rohmer's Catholic reading, which claims a higher vocation for the seventh art than is often allowed. For those individuals who have tired of art's provocations and who feel alienated from the world, however, the cinema reawakens faith in the existence of eternal beauty, the unification of form and Idea (Rohmer 1984: 88–9). The medium's fundamental realism provides the common ground where the prerogatives of idealism and materialism, luminous incarnation and objectivity intersect (Schérer 1954b: 57). Far from the second-class entertainment many intellectuals made it out to be, the cinema was thus an art capable of fulfilling the highest spiritual and aesthetic goals while reaching an audience more inclusive than that of painting, sculpture, and even literature. The popular art par excellence, it was *the* classical art of the twentieth century and the only one to pursue universalist goals. And curiously enough, it was not France, with its universalist ideology born of Revolution, but Hollywood that owing to its efficiency and elegance came closest to achieving them.

Rohmer's most sustained defence of the American cinema appeared in the December 1955 issue of *Cahiers* alongside surveys on the western, the detective film, and the musical by Bazin, Chabrol, and Jean Domarchi respectively. 'Redécouvrir l'Amérique' ('Rediscover America') opens on a rare autobiographical aside. The critic states that not until he saw Marcel Carné's brooding *Quai des brumes* in 1938 did he consider cinema to be a legitimate art. But cinema's truest face, he notes, came from abroad:

> un beau jour, sous les espèces de Claudette Colbert, de Clark Gable, le cinéma me présentait, sous l'éclairage le plus favorable, un visage sans fard, brut, mais non pas fruste: il me parlait un langage franc, mais sans l'ombre d'une intonation vulgaire.[7] (Rohmer 1955f: 11)

It Happened One Night: the title of Frank Capra's improbable 1934 love story of an out-of-work journalist (Gable) and a high-society girl impatient with her milieu (Colbert) would seem to describe Rohmer's own discovery of a light but sophisticated world where form and content stand in perfect equilibrium. The serio-comic vein in which Rohmer would illustrate himself as a director looks back to such fine-mannered pictures as Capra's, with their signature mix of seduction and talk.

The title 'Redécouvrir l'Amérique' is indicative of the neglect suffered by the American cinema at the hands of the European critical establishment. It is all too quickly forgotten that French critics and directors of the late 1940s and the 1950s persisted in seeing the work of the devil in the American motion picture industry, which they accused of propagating bad taste and right-wing ideas and of acting on the basis of profit alone. For Rohmer and his younger associates at *Cahiers*, however, the films of Capra, Sturges, Lubitsch, and more recently Hitchcock, Hawks, Cukor, and Ray were more than enough proof that the California coast was not the hell some claimed it to be.

7 'Out of nowhere, in the shape of Claudette Colbert and Clark Gable, the cinema displayed, in its finest hour, its unadorned face, raw but not unpolished; it spoke to me honestly, without a hint of vulgarity.'

Hollywood was for Rohmer nothing less than 'cette terre d'élection, cette patrie que fut Florence au quattrocento pour les peintres, ou Vienne au XIXe pour les musiciens' (this chosen land, this homeland which fourteenth-century Florence had been for painters, or nineteenth-century Vienna for musicians) (Rohmer 1955f: 12).

Hyperbolic as it may be, the comparison is meant in earnest. Rohmer credits Hollywood's ascendancy to the importance of subject over treatment, to hardworking, well-trained screen actors, and to a choice of universal themes drawn from a conflicted national past of conquest, voyage, and toil. Working from commonplace oppositions between power and the law, desire and destiny, and individual liberty and common interest, American directors choose situations of significant moral complexity, where action and meaning are one. While French producers and hired scriptwriters continued to rehash bedroom farce, offering the public – as Truffaut had shown in his broadside of 1954, 'Une certaine tendance du cinéma français' (Truffaut 1987) – little more than 'l'éternel rabâchage d'un amour contrarié par un conformisme religieux ou social' (the constant rehashing of loves thwarted by religious or social conformity) (Rohmer 1955f: 16), their American competitors looked modernity squarely in the face, taking into account changing gender roles in the workplace and new constraints of modern life, from speed and the power of machines to the anxieties of middle-class comfort. Studying Hollywood's styles and conventions could help French filmmakers to reclaim the leading role in Europe that since the war they had lost to Italy. Modernity and classicism in this account are not mutually exclusive; to the contrary, classicism stands at the very forefront of modernity. As Rohmer affirmed with a typical taste for paradox: 'Notre époque est ainsi faite que l'originalité, la modernité la plus profonde se cachent sous le masque du classicisme, de la discrétion' (Our time is such that the most profound instances of originality and modernity are hidden behind the mask of classicism and discretion) (Schérer 1954d: 10).

The polemical charge of Rohmer's invitation to 'rediscover' America as the promised land of classicism was surely not lost on his readers, much less on *Cahiers*'s rivals at the left-leaning, para-surrealist *Positif*, with whom Rohmer traded blows in 1956–57 (De Baecque 1991: I, 142–3). To vaunt contemporary American products as the summum of world cinema was to condone capitalist organisation and, albeit indirectly, the witch-hunting institutions that had used blacklisting in response to the Red Scare. If Rohmer points to the congruence of technical, ideological, and creative factors that make America propitious to individual artistic vision, he does not endorse American values per se; the national cinemas of the West are, in the end, to be praised only insofar as they fulfil cinema's universalist potential.

That notion of universalism was, to be sure, no less fraught than the idea of an invariant Nature (or creation) deployed elsewhere in Rohmer's aesthetic theory. The often underhanded references to non-Western cultures that one finds scattered in the critic's reviews of the 1950s merit scrutiny in this regard. If some are mere cause for embarrassment, others may provoke outrage, so entwined are they with Europe's colonialist ideology and division of the world's peoples according to race and milieu. In his review of F.W. Murnau and Robert Flaherty's *Tabu: A Story of the South Seas* (1931), which he effusively qualifies as 'le plus grand film du plus grand auteur de films' (the greatest film by the greatest of film authors) (Schérer 1953: 46), Rohmer all but enlists the cinema in a civilising mission. Whereas Gauguin, during his sojourn in Tahiti, had heaped anathema on Western art and its canons in the name of personal revolt, Murnau brought to those same lands the Occidental values embodied by such works as the *Iliad* and the *Niebelungslied*: 'c'est en conquérant et messager de notre culture que [Murnau] prétendit planter sa caméra' (it is as a conqueror and message-bearer of our culture that [Murnau] set up his camera) (Schérer 1953: 47). Such formula were dated even in their time, and it is particularly odd to see Rohmer pursue his crusade in reference to a film whose actors were primarily islander non-professionals, and where the would-be superiority of Western civilisation is nowhere apparent. Eurocentric assumptions feature similarly in his review of a 1956 survey on Japanese cinema, an industry then known for its love of remakes and traditional genres. While he admits his lack of expertise, Rohmer sees Japanese filmmakers as being at an aesthetic disadvantage. Their culture lacks the Occident's history of pictorial representation, which led from monocular perspective to photography, and its stylised gestures inherited from Kabuki theatre transfer poorly to the screen. The only true path for Japanese cinema, should it wish to progress, is to look westward:

> Qui joue le jeu du cinéma doit se soumettre à la règle qui est la même, qu'on veuille ou non, sous tous climats. ... Le cinéma japonais a, il me

semble, plus à apprendre de nous, que nous, à retenir de lui.[8] (Rohmer 1956b: 54)

A review of Mizoguchi's *Crucified Lovers* from the following year likewise lacks in nuance. It dwells first on the constitutive weakness of the standardised Japanese product, then compares the film at hand to works by Rossellini, Dreyer, Bresson, and Renoir (!). In the end, the critic acknowledges the 'universality' of Mizoguchi's genius. Yet the Japanese director excels not thanks to a cultural particularism that would enrich film's possibilities, but because, like the finest directors from the West, he understands that an actor's gestures are 'truest' onscreen when they are recreated in their arbitrariness (Rohmer 1957: 47).

There can be no doubt that Rohmer's defence of classicism went beyond a qualification of the pleasures of Hollywood gems like *It Happened One Night*. More problematically, by tying the medium's purchase over the contemporary world to the West's aesthetic and industrial hegemony, Rohmer excluded from consideration entire swaths of cinema history – a history that was still very much in the making. Such assumptions were not unique to Rohmer, to be sure; they are symptomatic of the pro-American wing of the *Cahiers*, first led by the 'hitchcocko-hawksiens' and, later, by the overtly right-wing 'Mac-Mahoniens' who, rallying around the screening room of a single Right Bank cinema, the Mac-Mahon, defended Hollywood mavericks like Raoul Walsh with legendary zeal (De Baecque 2003: 212–14). As Rohmer moved away from the evolutionist, Bazinian positions he had espoused in the 1940s, it nevertheless became clear that cinema was for him less a matter of nations and cultures than of individual creators who strove to transcend circumstance and left on their works an indelible stamp. This conviction was expressed in the platform known as the 'politique des auteurs'.

Theories of authorship

The collective nature of film production posed a dilemma to early film critics, who could not rely on the model of individual authorship

8 'Whoever plays the game of cinema must obey a rule which, like it or not, is the same under all climates. Japanese cinema, it seems to me, has more to learn from us than we from it.'

applied to novels, musical compositions, and, to a lesser extent, painting and sculpture. As late as the 1950s, directors, screenwriters, and even producers were singled out as potential candidates for authorship. This confusion attests to the relative discredit of film directing, seen by many scriptwriters as a matter of applied technique rather than of creation. Of Jean Aurenche and Pierre Bost, who signed a flurry of adaptations at mid-century, Truffaut wrote 'le metteur en scène, à leurs yeux, est le monsieur qui met des cadrages là-dessus' (for them, the director is the gentleman who decides what's in the frame) (Truffaut 1987: 224).

For the *Cahiers* critics who so venerated old masters like Dreyer, Griffith, Renoir, and Chaplin, and who strove to liberate cinema from its literary antecedents, there could be no doubt as to the true locus of film authorship: the director alone was responsible for a work's content. Not all directors, however, could aspire to the status of *auteur*. This distinction was merited only by those who recognised the primacy of *mise en scène* and who used the medium to convey a unique world view. Ideally, to maximise control over the creative process, the film author would shoot his or her own original screenplay and employ the 'language' of cinema with a liberty and a precision equal to those achieved by the essayist or novelist: 'l'auteur écrit avec sa caméra, comme un écrivain écrit avec un stylo' (the [film] author writes with his camera just like the writer with his pen), wrote to this effect Alexandre Astruc (Marie 1997: 31).

By the turn of the 1950s, French directors were widely recognised by press and public alike as responsible for the artistic content of their works. The case of Hollywood was quite different. Studio executives required that decisions, however minute, be submitted to producers for approval, such that directorial freedom in choice of subject, casting, staging, and editing was limited. At first glance, Hollywood seemed inhospitable to the expression of personal vision. How, then, to explain the artistic success of its reputedly 'commercial' products? Informally developed in the early 1950s by Truffaut, Rivette, and Rohmer, the 'politique des auteurs' responded to this question by reviving the romantic notion of artistic genius in a domain largely defined by economic and institutional pressures. However constraining the circumstances, they affirmed, an *auteur* manages to convey themes and obsessions which compose an inviolable signature. For the informed spectator, the challenge lay in separating the wheat (directors with a coherent world view and a corresponding mastery of *mise en scène*) from the chaff (the studio hacks and those directors who never rose above strict competence in their craft). Once these initial choices were made, the critic could shed light on those figures and themes that define, in a group of films, an author's personal stamp.

It is significant that in the hands of the pro-American *Cahiers* critics, the 'politique des auteurs' often took as a test case directors like Fritz Lang and Alfred Hitchcock, who left Europe mid-career for Hollywood. Though such filmmakers received preferential treatment on arrival, they did have to adapt their methods to unfamiliar structures and institutional habits. In many cases, the results were considered inferior to earlier works in the director's European œuvre. The case of Renoir merits special note, for it was on his little-appreciated American period (1940–1950) that Rohmer penned an important early position piece for *Cahiers*. A consummate illustration of the 'politique des auteurs', 'Renoir américain' (Schérer 1952a), the pendant of André Bazin's own 'Renoir français' published in the same 1952 issue, is Rohmer's attempt to reverse critical bias through the exercise of disinterested judgement. If French reviewers were in principle well-disposed to Renoir's Hollywood pictures, notably the agricultural family drama *The Southerner* (1945), notes Rohmer, they invariably held those films to standards set by the political works of the 1930s, from the immigrant struggles of *Toni* (1934) and the Popular Frontist *Le Crime de Monsieur Lange* (1936) to the pessimistic, post-Munich *La Règle du jeu* (1939). At best, the American pictures were considered modestly successful reiterations of Renoir's French work; at worst, they proved that his creative energies had been crushed 'dans les rouages de l'imposante machinerie yankee' (by the cogs of the overwhelming Yankee machine) (Rohmer 1984: 279/1989: 174). Rohmer discards both arguments, showing that when making *Swamp Water* and *The Southerner* Renoir enjoyed significant freedom to improvise with actors and to vary camera placement. Of viewers who would see in Renoir's later works signs of artistic decadence, the critic asks that they show the respect due any creative genius:

> [L]'histoire de l'art ne nous offre, à ma connaissance, point d'exemple qu'un génie authentique ait connu, à la fin de sa carrière, une période de vrai déclin: elle nous inciterait plutôt, sous la maladresse ou pauvreté apparentes des films [américains de Renoir], à retrouver la trace de cette volonté de dépouillement qui caractérise les 'dernières

manières' d'un Titien, d'un Rembrandt, d'un Beethoven ou, plus près de nous, d'un Bonnard, d'un Matisse ou d'un Stravinsky.[9] (Rohmer 1984: 280)

Artistic genius does not decline over time, but moves towards greater purity, to the effect that the enlightened critic who looks beyond a work's apparent faults will discover the jewel that lies underneath. To judge present efforts on the basis of past achievements is to forget that every masterwork provides 'une nouvelle définition du Beau' (a new definition of beauty) (Rohmer 1984: 280/1989: 175). Here again, we encounter Rohmer's timeless conception of aesthetic modernity, one which can be confused neither with the neo-classical revival of old canons nor with the cult of originality.

If the 'politique des auteurs' helped to re-evaluate neglected works of established directors, it served also to promote filmmakers who had yet to enjoy critical favour. Hitchcock provides a prime example. An accomplished technician with prolific talent, the 'Master of Suspense' was no more an artist for it; Bazin himself was reticent to admit Hitchcock under the respectable yellow covers of the *Cahiers*. Only after a hard-fought campaign waged by Rohmer, Truffaut, and Rivette through interviews, multiple reviews, and politicking in the *ciné-clubs*, did the director of *Shadow of a Doubt* and *Strangers on A Train* earn his place in the magazine's pantheon. The campaign, which culminated in a 1955 special issue of *Cahiers* on Hitchcock, paved the way for Rohmer and Chabrol's 1957 monograph, the first comprehensive study of the director's work in any language.

Today, *Hitchcock* seems conservative. It is a film-by-film analysis that charts Hitchcock's thematic and formal evolution from his days as stand-in silent director in London to his fecund Hollywood years with David O. Selznick and the majors. Despite its unassuming aspect, the book stands out among studies of its time in that it eschews journalistic anecdote as well as the filmmaker's express designs. Treating Hitchcock's films as model narratives and as interlocking parts of a career that endlessly looks back upon itself, the authors uncover

9 'as far as I know, the history of art offers us no example of an authentic genius who, at the end of his long career, had a period of real decline. Rather, beneath the seemingly unrefined or meager appearance of [Renoir's American films], we are prompted to seek evidence of the desire for simplicity that characterizes the final works of a Titian, a Rembrandt, a Beethoven or, closer to us, a Bonnard, a Matisse, or a Stravinsky.' (Rohmer 1989: 174)

the invariant structures or 'formal postulates' that make Hitchcock's universe unique. At the heart of this investigation lies the idea of exchange, which appears under four guises: moral (the transference of culpability from a guilty party to an innocent one); psychological (suspicion, or generalised doubt about each character's motives); dramatic (blackmail); and material (a to-and-fro motion in *mise en scène*) (Rohmer and Chabrol 1957: 7). Chabrol covers Hitchcock's British period in workaday prose, while Rohmer, with typical literary flourish, treats the Hollywood years beginning with *Rebecca* (1939), in which Hitchcock reached artistic maturity (Rohmer and Chabrol 1957: 63). In his commentaries, Rohmer establishes the film's source material, provides a synopsis, and delves into questions of dramatic structure, genre, acting, camera work, and morality. Rather than cast aside commercial and critical failures, he brings the same scrupulous attitude to each film, culling from pictures like *Lifeboat* or *Under Capricorn* lessons that can be drawn only if spectators open their eyes to inner correspondences that Hitchcock deploys with geometric precision. Conceived as a sort of initiatory journey, Chabrol and Rohmer's study proposes an ever-deeper comprehension of the leitmotifs that lend the director's work its unity. There are no missteps or failures in this vast career, maintains Rohmer, only fresh perspectives on the traps of egotism, diabolical urges, and guilt. 'Si [Hitchcock] se trompe, le cinéma tout entier se trompe avec lui' (If [Hitchcock] has got it wrong, so has the whole of cinema) (Rohmer and Chabrol 1957: 100).

With its overarching Anglo-Catholic thesis on guilt, *Hitchcock* was definitive proof that film comment, newly modelled after literary study, had left behind a policy of 'selections' for the more noble one of 'complete works' (Rohmer 1956c: 55). If a director was indeed an author, it followed that every bit of relevant evidence – every foot of film edited – needed to be taken into account. In this respect, the battle to impose Hitchcock, whose œuvre was consistent in tone and subject, was easier to win than Rivette's parallel campaign behind genre chameleon Howard Hawks. In Rohmer's view, the author of *Monkey Business*, *Red River*, and *The Big Sky* was perhaps not on a par with masters like Renoir, Erich Stroheim, or Jean Vigo. Yet Hawks was no less worthy of praise for all that:

> peut-on reprocher à un cinéaste de n'être que cinéaste, de ne point chercher à faire éclater les frontières de son art, de se garder au

contraire toujours en deçà et porter à une classique perfection le genre populaire du western, du policier, de la comédie musicale?'[10] (Rohmer 1984: 210)

Working under generic constraints was a fine test of directorial vision, and there was no reason to equate artistic integrity with opposition to the industry: a great filmmaker, wrote Rohmer with Hawks again in mind, 'sait battre ses confrères dans la branche réputée pour la plus commerciale' (knows how to beat out his colleagues in what is reputed to be the most commercial branch of filmmaking) (Schérer 1954c: 44). It is wrong, then, to assume that Rohmer, as a priest of 'high' criticism, excludes from his purview the more popular genres. Though the majority of authors he championed were indeed European masters, his admiration for slapstick, farce, screwball comedy, and the occasional western suggests that no one genre should enjoy exclusive critical privilege.

By the time *Hitchcock* appeared, Rohmer and his associates, known since their days at *La Gazette du cinéma* as 'les hitchcocko-hawksiens', had firmly established their foothold at *Cahiers*, rallying around Hollywood newcomers (Cukor, Ray, Mankiewicz) while keeping tabs on the usual suspects (Renoir, Rossellini, Hitchcock). No doubt this auteurist trend went against Bazin's best wishes. Having himself set a precedent of sorts for auteurism with *Orson Welles*, his style study of 1950, Bazin feared the effects of any auteur theory that neglected context. A defensible position in principle, the 'politique des auteurs' risked becoming in practice an exclusionary policy wherein the arbitrariness of taste interfered with informed historical judgements. It was preferable, thought Bazin, to chart cinema's evolution in its full breadth, and in this respect the study of genres, national schools, or individual works of sociological interest was more urgent than scouting out the latest unrecognised 'genius', of which California seemed to contain a disproportionate number around 1955. Were authorship solely a matter of finding a critic willing (and rhetorically able enough) to impose a filmmaker's work as a 'must', what was to stop the whole of Hollywood from becoming a community of authors?

Given *Cahiers*' reputation as the world's premiere film magazine,

10 'can we blame a filmmaker for being merely a filmmaker, for not seeking to transgress his art's boundaries, for remaining, on the contrary, always within them, and for bringing the popular genres of the western, or the adventure story, or the musical comedy, to a classical perfection?' (Rohmer 1989: 131)

read by lay and professionals alike, auteurism looked suspiciously like a self-fulfilling prophecy: it was enough that a director be treated in its columns as an author for him to become one. Some *Cahiers* contributors took auteurism as a licence to praise lesser-knowns: Truffaut went out on a limb on more than one occasion, vaunting under an assumed name (Robert Lachenay) or his own signature the latest B-movie or lost treasure. More circumspect in his judgements than Truffaut, Rohmer chose to comment on works by directors whose mastery of the medium was beyond debate. The list of titles he reviewed in 1956 is telling: save the Soviet filmmaker Frederick Ermler's *Unfinished Novel* and Anthony Mann's *The Last Frontier*, all are by well-known European or American directors: *Ordet* (Dreyer), *The Trouble with Harry* (Hitchcock), *Rebel Without A Cause* (Ray), *La Voix humaine* (Rossellini), *Lifeboat* (Hitchcock), *Confidential Report* (Welles), *The Court Martial of Billy Mitchell* (Preminger), *Elena et les hommes* (Renoir), *Picnic* (Joshua Logan), and *Un condamné à mort s'est échappé* (Bresson). What some have called the critic's conservatism might also be called his solidity of judgement.

By the mid-1950s the auteurist line had replaced the productive dissension that had marked *Cahiers*' early years, when left-leaning critics like Pierre Kast counterbalanced the unabashed pro-Americanism of 'l'école Schérer' (De Baecque 1991: I, 215–16). With Bazin's departure, auteurism became an official editorial line, which Rohmer attempted to recast as an untranslatable 'critique des beautés' perhaps more elusive than auteurism itself. Under his leadership, the journal became more coherent and more pro-American than ever, taking a clear stand against the modern European eclecticism of its rival *Positif*. Commitment to an intransigent auteurism blinded *Cahiers* to contemporary developments both on the world stage and at home. Ironically, the very institution that had allowed the Young Turks to live and breathe cinema without committing to years of industry apprenticeship, paid only moderate attention to the New Wave itself. During the pivotal years from 1958 to 1960, and especially after Truffaut's May 1959 triumph at Cannes, instead of defending the French New Wave, *Cahiers* showed guarded enthusiasm. This was intended, in part, to avoid accusations of self-promotion and to protect the journal's hard-won reputation of objectivity (De Baecque 1991: II, 13). More crucially, it may have been a function of the theoretical weaknesses of Rohmer's own version of auteurism, too dedicated to 'eternal' values to comprehend a mode of filmmaking that was very much of the moment and that brought Astruc's ideas of personal expression to fruition.

When Rohmer did address the New Wave in *Cahiers*, it was neither as a witness to nor as a participant in the movement, though he, like Godard, had begun shooting a feature in summer 1959 (*Le Signe du Lion*). Rather, he spoke as the exacting critic of 'beautés' he had long styled himself to be. While he was ready to acknowledge that the New Wave would go down in history, he was reluctant to say which films by contemporary French directors would rise above the fray, with the exception of *Hiroshima mon amour*, discussed in a *Cahiers* roundtable shortly after its release (Domarchi *et al.* 1959). If Rohmer allotted many three-star and even four-star ratings to New Wave films in the *Cahiers*' monthly 'Conseils des dix', among his articles as chief editor of the magazine, only 'Le Goût de la beauté' of 1961 ('The Taste for Beauty') highlights films by New Wave friends and fellow travellers, namely Chabrol's *Les Godelureaux*, a box-office disaster and critical disappointment, and Jean Rouch's ethno-fiction shot in Ivory Coast, *La Pyramide humaine*, one of the most pointed explorations of colonial race relations of its time. These works he championed not on account of their social relevance but again from the point of view of a cinema 'en soi' (in itself) (Rohmer 1984: 114/1989: 71). His gloss of *La Pyramide humaine* brackets the film's political charge in the name of idealism:

> [Le cinéma] possède, en quelque sorte, la vérité d'emblée, et se propose la beauté comme fin suprême. ... La difficulté pour lui n'est pas, comme on le croit, de forger un monde à lui avec ces purs miroirs que sont les outils dont il dispose, mais de pouvoir *copier* tout bonnement cette beauté naturelle.[11] (Rohmer 1984: 121)

If this passage eloquently redefines *cinéma vérité* along ontological realist lines, it leaves aside the transformational nature of Rouch's project, which goes beyond the logic of mimesis or the copying of reality to touch on the very workings of society.

In many ways 'Le goût de la beauté', which reprises arguments voiced in earlier essays, is the last hurrah of a critic who laboured to change focus under pressure yet who never abandoned Bazin's first

11 '[Cinema], in a sense, possesses the truth right from the beginning and aims to make beauty its supreme end. ... The difficulty is not, as we think, in creating a world of its own with mirrors – the tools at its disposal – but in managing simply to *copy* this natural beauty.' (Rohmer 1989: 77)

principle of photographic objectivity. The final two years of Rohmer's tenure at the monthly were, as De Baecque recounts, fraught with difficulties as 'pro-modern' contributors voiced the need to throw *Cahiers*' clout behind the French New Wave, which was faltering after 1961, and the emergent cinemas of Brazil and eastern Europe (De Baecque 1991: II, 21–6). Directors as important as Fellini and Antonioni had until then met with cautious praise, as if any deviation from a strict pro-Hollywood line would throw the *Cahiers* off course. From the outside, the journal seemed out of phase with a changing world, where insurgents in Europe's colonies pressed for political independence and new paradigms of thought, structural linguistics and anthropology in particular, toppled humanist idols one by one.

In the summer of 1963 tensions at *Cahiers* came to a head, and, after a siege led by Rivette and supported by the publication's board of directors and a remorseful Truffaut, Rohmer found himself on the way out. He had, to the fullest possible extent, embraced classical values of harmony and elegance under the aegis of the Beautiful. In an about-face that was a sign of things to come, the new *Cahiers* lent its support to a cinema that was both modernist and international. By the end of the decade, it would enter its political phase of opposition and protest, moving away from narrative cinema altogether and, in the wake of May 1968, embracing Rohmer's twin *bêtes noires* – Marxism and psychoanalysis – in the name of ideology critique.

Conclusion

After his split with *Cahiers* in 1963, Rohmer turned to full-time direction, working on his *Contes moraux* cycle and preparing documentaries for French television. While he was not to return to regular film criticism thereafter – the 1972 thesis on the uses of space and movement in Murnau's *Faust* is an isolated outing –, he remained on collegial terms with *Cahiers*' editorship. Over the years, as *Cahiers* moved back into the mainstream of film comment, that relationship would flourish. Himself a former *Cahiers* interviewer who had presented the likes of Rossellini, Cukor, Astruc, Preminger, Langlois, and Rouch to the Francophone public, Rohmer now ranks among the most interviewed directors in the magazine's history.

Rohmer's criticism might well have been forgotten were it not for the efforts of Jean Narboni, who approached the author in the early 1980s with the idea of assembling a volume of his major articles. Then hard at work on his *Comédies et proverbes*, Rohmer was less than enthusiastic. He recognised that much of his thinking of the 1940s and 1950s was prisoner to its time, burdened by historicist assumptions that were part of any film critic's baggage. If he did not oppose republication of his articles, except the serial essay 'Le Celluloïd et le marbre' whose reprinting he tabled *sine die*, he expressed no desire to revisit them either (Rohmer 1984: 10–12). 'Le Temps de la critique' ('The Critical Years'), the 1983 interview with Narboni that prefaces *Le Goût de la beauté*, shows the extent to which the director had distanced himself from aesthetics and film history. Yet his fundamental conviction inherited from André Bazin remained unshaken: cinema is not an art that says differently the same thing as the other arts, but one that says something wholly distinct because of its privileged relationship to the real. In the cinema, '[l]'essentiel n'est pas de l'ordre du langage mais de l'ordre de l'ontologique' ([t]he essential part is not in the realm of language but in the realm of ontology) (Rohmer 1984: 25/1989: 11). Rohmerian 'realism' thus presupposes a Platonic equivalence of the Beautiful, the Good, and the True, such that artistic creation cannot but be a search for beauty. As Marion Vidal has written,

> loin d'être une simple alternative à l'exaltation du laid ou du grotesque, la recherche de la beauté est la meilleure approche possible de la réalité, donc le seul véritable réalisme.[12] (Vidal 1977: 22)

This idea informs all of Rohmer's work as a director, which, as we will see, humbly brings the viewer into contact with reality even as it celebrates the creative freedoms of fiction.

References

Andrew, J. Dudley (1976), *The Major Film Theories*, Oxford, Oxford University Press.

Andrew, J. Dudley (1978), *André Bazin*, Oxford, Oxford University Press.

Bazin, André (1967 and 1971), *What is Cinéma?*, vols. 1 and 2, tr. Hugh Gray, Berkeley, University of California Press.

12 'The search for beauty, far from being a simple alternative to the exaltation of ugliness, is the best possible way of approaching reality, and hence the one true realism.'

Bazin, André (1975), *Qu'est-ce que le cinéma?*, Paris, Le Cerf.
Carroll, Noël (1988), *Philosophical Problems of Classical Film Theory*, Princeton, NJ, Princeton University Press.
Crisp, C.G. (1988), *Eric Rohmer: Realist and Moralist*, Bloomington and Indianapolis, Indiana University Press.
Crisp, Colin (1993), *The Classic French Cinema: 1930–1960*, Bloomington and Indianapolis, Indiana University Press.
De Baecque, Antoine (1991), *Cahiers du cinéma, histoire d'une revue, t. I, À l'assaut du cinéma; t. II, Cinéma, tours, détours*, Paris, Cahiers du cinéma.
De Baecque, Antoine (2003), *La Cinéphilie: invention d'un regard, histoire d'une culture 1944–1968*, Paris, Fayard.
Domarchi, Jean *et al.* (1959), 'Hiroshima, notre amour', *Cahiers du cinéma* 97, July: 1–18.
Marie, Michel (1997), *La Nouvelle Vague: une école artistique*, Paris, Nathan.
Rohmer, Eric (1955a), 'Le Celluloïd et le marbre: le bandit philosophe', *Cahiers du cinéma* 44, February: 32–7.
Rohmer, Eric (1955b), 'Le Celluloïd et le marbre: le siècle des peintres', *Cahiers du cinéma* 49, July: 10–15.
Rohmer, Eric (1955c), 'Le Celluloïd et le marbre: de la Métaphore', *Cahiers du cinéma* 51, October: 2–9.
Rohmer, Eric (1955d), 'Le Celluloïd et le marbre: beau comme la musique', *Cahiers du cinéma* 52, November: 4–12.
Rohmer, Eric (1955e), 'Le Celluloïd et le marbre: architecture d'apocalypse', *Cahiers du cinéma* 53, December: 22–30.
Rohmer, Eric (1955f), 'Redécouvrir l'Amérique', *Cahiers du cinéma* 54, December: 11–16.
Rohmer, Eric (1956a), 'Castigat Ridendo', *Cahiers du cinéma* 38, April: 36–8.
Rohmer, Eric (1956b), 'Shinobu et Marcel Ginglaris: *Le Cinéma japonais*', *Cahiers du cinéma* 60, June: 53–4.
Rohmer, Eric (1956c), 'Les lecteurs des "Cahiers" et la politique des auteurs', *Cahiers du cinéma* 63, October: 54–8.
Rohmer, Eric (1984), *Le Goût de la beauté*, ed. Jean Narboni, Paris, Cahiers du cinéma (reprinted 2004).
Rohmer, Eric (1989), *The Taste for Beauty*, tr. Carol Volk, Cambridge, Cambridge University Press.
Rohmer, Eric, and Claude Chabrol (1957), *Hitchcock*, Paris, Editions Universitaires.
Schérer, Maurice (1952a), 'Renoir américain', *Cahiers du cinéma* 8, January: 33–40.
Schérer, Maurice (1952b), 'La Robe bleue d'Harriet', *Cahiers du cinéma* 8, January: 62–4.
Schérer, Maurice (1953), 'La Revanche de l'Occident', *Cahiers du cinéma* 21, March: 46–8.
Schérer, Maurice (1954a), 'Vertus cardinales du Cinémascope', *Cahiers du cinéma* 31, January: 36–40.
Schérer, Maurice (1954b), '"L'Amour du Cinéma" de Claude Mauriac', *Cahiers du cinéma* 37, July: 56–8.

Schérer, Maurice (1954c), 'Le Meilleur des mondes', *Cahiers du cinéma* 38, August–September: 41–5.
Schérer, Maurice (1954d), 'A qui la faute?', *Cahiers du cinéma* 39, October: 6–10.
Truffaut, François (1987), 'Une certaine tendance du cinéma français' [1954], in *Le Plaisir des yeux*, Paris, Champs Flammarion: 211–29.
Vidal, Marion (1977), *Les* Contes moraux *d'Eric Rohmer*, Paris, Pierre Lherminier.

3

Style and technique

> What has happened to stasis as a parameter of filmic imagery? Is there no one among the younger generation of directors capable of producing visuals of a genuinely passive, contemplative quality, a quality which would allow the spectator to reach out towards the screen rather than recoiling from it – that quality, in short, which characterises the work of Godard, Rohmer, Oliveira, Iosseliani and Straub, the true masters of the modern art movie? (Adair 1997: 103)

In the narrative cinema, style is often assumed to lie on the side of visible excess. It is the domain of the provocateur, the virtuoso, the formalist, the mannerist. What then of the understated *mise en scène* espoused by Rohmer, whose work displays few hallmarks of 'great' filmmaking – no apparent risk-taking in getting the shot, no undermining of narrative codes, no 'laying bare of the device'? On first viewing, his films may leave the impression that they give us a good bit more to listen to than to look at. Yet we need not conclude from this apparent lack of a strong visual programme that they are uncinematic in any way. The ballet-like camera movements of an Ophuls or a Truffaut, the discontinuous editing of an early Godard, the obsessive tracking shots and montage sequences of a Resnais are not the only means to assert the medium's potential as art. Ever one to contest avant-garde doxa in the name of a measured classicism, the director, interviewed by *Cahiers du cinéma* in 1965, affirmed to this effect that '[u]n cinéma où la caméra est invisible peut être un cinéma moderne' (a cinema where the camera is invisible can be a modern cinema) (Biette *et al.* 1965: 34).

In its respect of linear temporality, human-centred action, and clarity of image and speech, Rohmer's film language aspires to the status of 'prose', a vehicle for transmitting a story and revealing a world, in contrast to an autonomous poetic construct that would take form as an end in itself (Biette *et al.* 1965: 33). Subordinating the expressive qualities of film to communicative ends, the director paints himself a worthy successor to figures like Howard Hawks, Frank Capra, and Otto Preminger, who each considered *mise en scène* and acting best served by cinematographic restraint. Critics have qualified Rohmer's classical style as 'transparent', an adjective easily misconstrued to mean facile or naïve. Its transparency corresponds, quite to the contrary, to a state of lucid self-awareness. As *Positif* critic Gérard Legrand has written,

> chez d'autres la mise en scène n'est invisible que parce qu'elle n'existe pas, alors que chez Rohmer ... elle n'est invisible que parce qu'elle existe complètement – et donc soulève un coin de voile.[1] (Legrand 1971: 56)

Far from a default position dictated by industrial organisation and corporatist habit, as is the case of Hollywood continuity editing, 'invisible' *mise en scène* expresses the ontological realist's desire humbly to access phenomenal reality even as it patiently serves narrative designs.

Despite his deep knowledge of film history, Rohmer has crafted a style that is anything but self-reflexive. His work eschews the *mise-en-abîme* (film-within-a-film) and emphatic formal devices common to modernist works of the 1960s from Resnais' *Hiroshima mon amour* and Varda's *Cléo de cinq à sept* to Godard's *Vivre sa vie* and *Le Mépris*, as well as the cinephilic allusions and quotations that have become staples of postmodern filmmaking. But the most telling sign of Rohmer's refusal of meta-cinema is, like Poe's 'Purloined Letter', so obvious as to escape notice. If one can spot here and there the odd television set – always turned off, as it happens –, the cinema itself is altogether absent from Rohmer's fictional universe. Characters do not attend movies, speak about them, imitate characters from them, or tack film memorabilia on their bedroom walls. Paradoxically, the world they inhabit is utopic precisely because it is a *world without cinema*. Conspicuous as it may be coming from a fellow traveller of

1 'For others *mise en scène* is invisible only because it is nonexistent, whereas for Rohmer it is invisible because it exists completely – and thus lifts up a corner of the veil.'

Truffaut and Godard, who wore their love of cinema on their sleeve, this discretion with respect to the seventh art should not be used as licence to consider Rohmer merely as a literary moralist or a quizzical entomologist of modern French society. Quite the opposite: the fact that his fictions do not take film as their object makes it all the more essential that we investigate, in cinematic terms, what lies behind their supposedly 'transparent' rendering of reality – as well as the ideological stakes this stance implies.

One could argue that the filmmaker's ethic of transparency, itself an extension of his aesthetic theory, is complicit with the dominant cinema's attempt to conceal its status as representation the better to 'naturalise' its depicted contents. In this reading, under cover of the camera's invisibility Rohmer's narratives would disavow the class character of their predominant theme, namely the role of individual choice in matters of the heart. While it is undeniable that Rohmer's fictions employ classical form in the service of a universalising bourgeois humanism, they do not do so uncritically and hence belie any tendency toward 'mythologisation', in Roland Barthes's sense of the term (Barthes 1957). By lifting up ever so slightly the veil of representation, to recall Legrand's phrase, they help us to see that art never deploys its mimetic powers so fully as when it recognises that its realism cannot be taken as a given. Photography may well possess, following Bazin's theory, an indexical relationship to the filmed object, but that first-level representational realism is subject to an array of artistic decisions from which arise distinct styles, only some of which will be perceived as 'realist'.

It should come as no surprise that a cinema of prose like Rohmer's should shy away from the meta-cinematic. But for all his commitment to shooting in natural locations with direct synchronous sound, Rohmer is not a naturalistic filmmaker either. The portrayal of life as it is lived, whether in its everydayness or in its dramatic upheavals, does not interest him as it does contemporaries Maurice Pialat (*A nos amours, Police*) and Jean-Pierre and Luc Dardenne (*La Promesse, Rosetta*) among others. In place of social observation, Rohmer's films develop schematic representations of human psychology by grafting theatrical simulacra onto a world that spectators recognise as coextensive to their own. This approach recalls that of Jean Renoir, whose views on realism Rohmer quotes in his article of 1952, 'Renoir américain'. Filmmakers wishing to achieve a truly modern form of expression must not, thought Renoir, confuse realism with a random sampling of reality:

> Vouloir 'faire vrai' est une erreur colossale; l'art doit être artificiel et constamment recréé. C'est cette facilité de recréation qui était la raison d'être du cinéma et, en l'oubliant, il se perd lui-même. La base du péché mortel du cinéma est d'oublier qu'il doit rester une fiction.[2] (Rohmer 1984: 284)

By rejecting the assumption that a directly observed reality would carry greater weight than an artificially recreated one, the director of *La Règle du jeu* (1939) and *Le Carrosse d'or* (1954) recalls the primacy of *mise en scène* in eliciting the suspension of spectatorial belief. This lesson is fundamental to Rohmer, who aims to create self-aware fictions that derive their power, in one case (that of films set in the contemporary era), from the cognitive dissonance between staged events and authentic locations, and, in the other (that of the costume films), from the acceptance of artifice as the sole means of making past epochs present.

Since *Ma Nuit chez Maud*, his first feature to use direct sound, Rohmer has espoused the same principles of economy and intelligibility regardless of personnel, technical advancements, period fads, and budget. Across his fifty-year career, style is so consistent as to call for synchronic treatment; even those projects which seem to promise rupture, like the medieval epic *Perceval le Gallois* or the Revolutionary costume drama *L'Anglaise et le Duc*, which was shot in digital video, betray their identity as Rohmer films quickly enough (for a detailed appraisal of these pictures' stylistic difference, however, see Chapter 5). A common understanding of human communication, a consistent manner of attending to dramatic development, and an aesthetic economy coupled with moral and financial restraint undergird Rohmer's work in its entirety.

In addressing cinematography, *mise en scène*, sound design, and music in synoptic fashion, this chapter aims to show why Rohmer's deceptively prosaic mode of presentation is ultimately so effective in sustaining and critiquing cinematic illusion at one and the same time. Less unassuming than it looks, the filmmaker's practice runs

2 'To want things to "seem real" is a colossal mistake. Art must be artificial and constantly recreated. This facility to recreate was cinema's reason for existence, and if this is forgotten, cinema will lose its way. The root of cinema's deadly sin is in forgetting that it must remain fictional.' (Rohmer 1989: 178; tr. mod.)

slightly against the grain of what Noël Burch calls the institutional mode of representation (IMR), prompting viewers to listen and look closely at the texture of a film and to question assumptions about how film language works in its classical and modernist guises.

The ordinary face of cinema

Film style is notoriously difficult to pin down. David Bordwell defines it as, 'minimally, the texture of [a] film's images and sounds, the result of choices made by the filmmaker(s) in particular historical circumstances' (Bordwell 1997: 4). As such, style is everywhere and nowhere all at once. Lighting, actor blocking, framing, depth of field, film stocks, camera movement, shot duration, punctuation, sound – all these elements decisively contribute to a film's texture. As the basic unit of film editing, the shot is a common point of departure for analysis: rich in information, it organises the represented motif, establishing centres of interest and demarcating dead zones the spectator need not explore, and calls forth a horizon of expectation as a function of photographic conventions. The shot's analytical relevance has however been questioned by many film theorists who instead emphasise syntax in the construction of meaning, or how the 'signifying chain' of linked images produces effects.

Other approaches to style are attuned less to the building blocks of editing than to the imaginary processes whereby film language configures a story world and invites the spectator to suspend disbelief. In this latter vein, Jacques Aumont's study of the face in cinema is particularly useful. Aumont argues that before sound was introduced in the narrative cinema, the face 'spoke' primarily through gesture. This 'primitive' face of cinema was a 'use value', a site of expressiveness that directors often endowed with the auratic quality known as *photogénie*. The 'ordinary face of cinema' which emerged in the 1930s is, by contrast, a pure 'exchange value' whose primary function is to solder together disparate elements of the fictional world. Both the actor's gaze and the spoken word govern the flow of meaning, within the frame and in relation to offscreen space. For filmic representation to function smoothly in this cinema of exchange, writes Aumont, the face must be accessible to characters and spectator alike: 'un visage transitif, phatique, il doit tout faire pour être vu et entendu par son destinataire' (transitive and phatic, the face must do everything necessary to make itself seen and heard by its interlocutor) (Aumont 1992: 46). This means that compositions are most often centred; that *mise en scène* is frontal, with dialogue filmed in shot–countershot to avoid awkward two-shot profile; and that the soundtrack is weighted toward speech. All the more persuasive for the fact that it usually goes unnoticed, the 'ordinary face of cinema' produces an impression of 'togetherness' that makes the spectator forget the fragmentary nature of individual shots (Aumont 1992: 46). But if classic Hollywood directors found in the human face a model of narrative efficiency, they also tended to exploit it in mechanistic fashion, leading to the dominance of continuity editing. Whence, remarks Aumont, the modernist obsession with an intransitive, distorted, or opaque face – one that inhabits the films of Bergman or Antonioni, where players turned in opposing directions dramatise their failure to communicate, or, much later, the films of Leos Carax (*Boy Meets Girl*, *Mauvais Sang*), in which the face becomes a landscape all its own.

Rohmer can be classified as an anti-modernist in that he upholds a functional cinema of exchange. This is made clear by his reluctance to autonomise the human face. Since the face is both the fantasmatic point of origin of language and its point of impact, in Rohmer's language-bound universe it must lay exposed to the viewer's gaze. At the same time, it cannot be endowed with dimensions it rarely possesses in everyday life, lest its excessive presence arrest the flow of meaning. Consequently, close-ups are uncommon and extreme close-ups non-existent, as if the *gros plan*, like the French *gros mot* or swear word, were itself unpolished or indecorous. The glamour that accrues to facial close-ups in mainstream cinema as a conjunction of flattering cinematography, make-up, and perceived star persona, is replaced in Rohmer's films by a matter-of-factness. If a face projects beauty, that beauty is of the world, not of the image. When the camera does dwell on faces at close range, it may connote a hard-earned intimacy (see Maud as she tries to lure the reluctant narrator into her bed in *Ma Nuit chez Maud*, or Félicie, enraptured by a performance of Shakespeare's *A Winter's Tale* in *Conte d'hiver*). Yet the close-up may equally well signify entrapment and fragility, so accustomed are we to seeing Rohmer's characters evolve at their leisure in an aired-out frame (see Chloé in *L'Amour l'après-midi*, subjected to Frédéric's indecisive game-playing, or Arsinoé in the psychological showdown with her husband Fiodor in *Triple agent*). It is revealing that decorative objects like teapots, vases, lamps, and plates command nearly as many close-ups as do actors' faces in Rohmer's films. Mute objects such as these hold no promise of returning a gaze, and thus do not threaten to disrupt communication.

More propitious to the director's designs is the medium shot and in particular the *plan américain* (see figures 3, 8, and 9), in which the frame cuts off actors between the knees and the waist. Bazin once described the *plan américain* – so-called thanks to its heavy use in American comedies – as the framing to which spectators are spontaneously drawn, 'le point d'équilibre naturel de [leur] accommodation mentale' (the natural point of balance of [their] mental adjustment) (Bazin 1975: 72/1967: 32). Medium camera-to-subject distance leaves the actors room for manœuvre, making gestures of the hands, shoulders, and hips fully legible while limiting the need to reframe on action with each new movement. It facilitates communicative exchange inside the frame and towards offscreen space yet requires fewer edits than do tighter framings to preserve spatial coherence. The medium close-up, taken from the shoulders up and often as part of a shot–countershot exchange, is a virtual stop-point in Rohmer's scalar vocabulary: relatively intimate, it is not invasive (see figure 2). Establishing shots are preferably taken from a middle range, such that the human body, never lost in its environment, remains the measure of all things.

Photography

This anthropocentric sense of scale extends to the means of photography themselves, which have a decisive effect on how human actions are rendered. Even as theatrical aspect ratios have widened, Rohmer has stood by the standard 1.33:1 image and has used the 1.66:1 aspect ratio only when exhibitors have required it (*Pauline à la plage* was shot to accommodate both projection formats). He has avoided scope altogether, though the aspect ratio of the Pathé production *L'Anglaise et le Duc* is a generous 1.85:1. This preference for the classically proportioned image reflects not only the idea that the human figure should not be lost in the frame, but also the demands of television and video. Second, the director associates human vision and the camera by restricting focal lengths to those which approximate the capacities of the unaided eye. These range from 25mm to 75mm, with a preference for 50mm. The telephoto lenses wielded in the first and third prologues of *La Collectionneuse*, in the hilltop winter scene in *Ma Nuit chez Maud* (see figure 3), or in the sidewalk scenes of *L'Amour l'après-midi*, all but disappear in work after the *Contes moraux*, like an item of clothing gone out of fashion or a newfangled toy that restricts the imagination instead of stimulating it. The director's point in privileging the 50mm lens is not to efface the traces of the camera – a task that the frame and the splice make impossible – but to instate a comfortable distance from which the spectator is free to judge events in keeping with 'normal' ocular perspective and in sufficient depth of field. Third, camera height, at or near eye level with the actors, suggests that we are not fundamentally different from the characters they play. The camera neither rises up to diminish their stature nor dips below them to exaggerate their traits. In *Perceval le Gallois*, when the knights trot about on horseback against the open sky or through the forest, the camera stays at eye level with the rider, not the mount (compare with Bresson's *Au hasard Balthazar*, shot level with the lumbering beast of burden that is the film's protagonist). The elimination of expressive angles prohibits caricature and sarcasm, even if some characters' behaviour would seem to invite such a treatment (see figure 5). Subtle ironic distance is better suited to Rohmer's humanist concerns and his wish to preserve ambiguity.

Camera placement further feeds Rohmer's realist agenda in that it obeys the physical constraints of locale. There are no false partitions, trick doors, or 'impossible' shots, of which Jean-Pierre Jeunet and Marc Caro, like studio magicians Jean Cocteau and Max Ophuls before them, are so fond. The filmmaker's aversion for trickery and sleight-of-hand is such that when shooting a single scene from various angles, the crew may not be permitted to rearrange furniture lying outside the frame, as is habitually done for comfort's sake (Almendros 1984: 159). Studio sets used for the dinner and sleepover scenes in *Ma Nuit chez Maud*, the workplace and maid's chambers scenes in *L'Amour l'après-midi*, or the drawing-room interiors of *L'Anglaise et le Duc* incorporate a fourth wall and, in the first two cases, even a ceiling, thus reinstating, against common practice, 'real' decors in an artificial environment. As a result, our position as spectators who experience primary identification with the camera is one of measured implication in the scene, never of encroachment. What hints of voyeurism there are should be attributed not to the camera (and even less so to the filmmaker!) but to individual characters whose point of view the narration temporarily adopts. If we consider Jérôme's ogling of Claire's knee in the fifth of the *Contes moraux* to be an invitation to fantasise along with him (see figure 4), we are clearly missing the point. The value of such point-of-view shots, of which a given film may contain but a handful, is relativised by countless 'objective' ones that point up the paltry nature of what Jérôme calls his romantic heroism.

As a general rule, point-of-view shots tend to be informational rather than psychological. Take the inserts of the snowbound hills of Ceyrat viewed from the Michelin engineer's chalet in the opening scene of *Ma Nuit chez Maud*, or of the vast, horseshoe-shaped courtyard of Ricardo Bofill's postmodern housing development admired by Léa from Blanche's apartment window in *L'Ami de mon amie*. Even those 'subjective' shots which incorporate movement tend to de-accentuate psychology. When the schoolteacher Jeanne enters her boyfriend's apartment at the beginning of *Conte de printemps*, the camera describes the room's contents by panning from right to left. Yet we do not return to Jeanne's reaction as classical grammar would require. Consequently, the shot becomes detached from her point of view and the objectivity of its content is reaffirmed. For Rohmer, the only true psychological cinema is a cinema of restraint:

> la description et des comportements et des propos doit se faire sans que le cinéaste essaie de les expliquer. Il faut que le cinéaste respecte la liberté de ses personnages, c'est-à-dire qu'il doit les laisser s'expliquer eux-mêmes.[3] (Séailles 1985: 9)

Composition and focus

The impression of narratorial objectivity given by aspect ratio, choice of focal lengths, and camera placement is singularly reinforced through control over photographic depth of field. In the 1940s and 1950s, Bazin had heralded deep focus as an antidote to analytic editing, which cut needlessly into the fabric of the real. The greater the depth of field, he

3 'both behaviours and intentions should be described without the filmmaker trying to explain them. The filmmaker must respect his characters' freedom, that is, he should let them explain themselves.'

reasoned, the greater the spectator's interpretive freedom. Rohmer is on this count Bazinian up to a point. In a majority of compositions, front and middle planes are crisply defined, with slight to appreciable blurring in the rear plane depending on available light. Focus in the colour *Contes moraux* is shallower than in the second two cycles, a discrepancy that is explained in part by the quality of colour stocks at the turn of the 1970s – 100 ASA for colour compared to 400 ASA for black and white (Revault d'Allones 1991: 21). Even when 'pushed down', colour stocks of the period demanded amounts of light Rohmer and Almendros were unwilling to supply, intent as they were on retaining the natural ambience of each location. To Almendros' mind, nothing was more 'monstrous' than Gregg Toland's deep compositions in *Citizen Kane* and *A Touch of Evil*, focused from three inches all the way out to infinity (Russell 1981: 60). The eye has limits that the camera itself should respect in the interest of verisimilitude.

While Rohmer favours generous depth of field on realist principle, he does not take up in earnest Bazin's related call for depth staging, whereby elements of dramatic interest simultaneously occupy distinct image planes from foreground to rear (Bazin 1975: 73). Staging in depth occurs primarily in scenes where architectural layout requires it, for example in the offices of Frédéric's firm in *L'Amour l'après-midi*, the linked chambers and hallways in *Die Marquise von O...*, or Natacha's father's spacious apartment in *Conte de printemps*. In such interiors, doorways and thresholds provide secondary frames within the frame. As the players distance themselves from the camera, the director is left to decide whether to cut to the next room through a match on movement or to let them play on in deep space. In either case, choice of lens and camera height provide an image free of perspectival distortion (for example foreshortening or parallax).

The prevalence of deep compositions makes shallow or selectively focused ones stand out, signalling a distinct narrative register and quality of attention. The prologue of *L'Amour l'après-midi*, for instance, contains telephoto shots of fashionable women on the sidewalks of Paris, their bodies defined against a general blur. Voiceover commentary tags these images to the dreamy narrator Frédéric. Later in the prologue, in full focus, we see crowds of suburbanites in the same Right Bank neighbourhood heading to and from the train station. Here, the extended depth of field has a levelling effect, suggesting the indifference to Frédéric's reveries of individuals who go about their everyday business. The deep focus used to show the protagonist's spouse, Hélène, back in the couple's suburban apartment, similarly contrasts with the shallow focus of the dream sequence in which Frédéric wields a magnetic charm against the heroines of the previous *Contes moraux*. But scenes such as these are rare, and selective focus appears retrospectively to have been a period trait, shared in the 1970s with Claude Lelouch and Truffaut among others, instead of a feature distinctive to Rohmer. Generally, writes Joël Magny, simplicity and openness win the day:

> chaque plan semble avoir pour seul but de nous montrer le plus clairement et le plus simplement possible ce que le cinéaste a choisi d'offrir à notre regard et à notre jugement.[4] (Magny 1995: 19)

Why this insistence on proportion and clarity in the image? In Rohmer's fictional world, it seems that characters must everywhere appear on equal footing as participants in a game who attempt to prevail less through physical means than verbally, through reasoning and persuasion. The communicative pact to which they subscribe would make staggered or recessional formations impossible. Even those who practise deceit must comply with an unwritten rule of transparency and offer up face and body for exchange. Action consequently centres on a comfortable middle ground, often on a line off the perpendicular to the camera's axis so as to avoid a 'clothesline' effect. This sets off actors against the background – an effect difficult to achieve in colour cinematography, where the human figure appears less sculpted than in back-lit black and white – without effacing the socio-cultural cues supplied by their surroundings. Foregrounds are free of incident so as to afford an unobstructed view of the players and decor. On a fantasmatic level, this empty foreground might well be described as the space of language itself, the zone across which speech is left to travel unimpeded from speaker to listener.

Camera work

As one might expect from a *cinéma de chambre* featuring little conventional action, camera movements are limited in range and number.

4 'each shot seems to have as its sole aim to show as clearly and simply as possible whatever the filmmaker has chosen to submit to our eyes and to our judgement.'

Few accommodations are made to dramatise *mise en scène*, the inherent rhythmic qualities of which the camera need only transcribe. That said, Rohmer's camera work is far from unflinching. If it eschews lyricism, spontaneity, or humour, it shares none of the rigidity of much art cinema, from the long (rather than leisurely) takes of Marguerite Duras' *India Song* to Chantal Akerman's high formalist masterwork *Jeanne Dielmann, 23 Quai du Commerce, 1080 Bruxelles*, composed in its near entirety of fixed horizontal shots taken at right angles to the furniture and walls of the title character's apartment. For Rohmer, it is again the speaking, gesticulating human body that presides over all other elements. The principle is simple: when a character who gets to talking has trouble staying put, the camera must respond accordingly.

In the director's first two cycles, preference goes to fixed shots taken from a tripod. Lateral and vertical reframings (pans and tilts) are justified by character movement, such that we tend to 'forget' the camera's presence. However, the camera's capacity for independent movement may be asserted to support *mise en scène*, especially in later 16mm projects. The hand-held shot-sequence of *La Femme de l'aviateur*, where François and Anne argue all the way up the sidewalk and spill out into the street, points towards both Sophie Maintigneux's highly mobile camera in *Le Rayon vert* and Diane Baratier's work of the mid-1990s. In the sketch film *Les Rendez-vous de Paris*, Baratier's camera plunges into the crowd of an open-air market or of the Beaubourg plaza ('Le Rendez-vous de sept heures') and tags alongside two lovers as they walk alongside the banks of the Seine ('Les Bancs de Paris'). Hand-held camera work is not meant to simulate emotion or authenticity, as is the case with much contemporary cinematography with its video-clip aesthetic; it is rather the logical expression of a lightweight production model which reaffirms the French New Wave's core values of economy and freedom.

Though not inimical to camera movement as an accompaniment to action, Rohmer is curiously adamant in his opposition to the tracking shot, whatever its application. If, as Jean-Luc Godard – inverting an expression forged by Luc Moullet – famously remarked, 'les travellings sont [une] affaire de morale' (tracking shots are [a] moral affair), then it's not unreasonable to say that Eric Rohmer is one of France's most immoral directors. The cinema workers' unions would probably agree, albeit for different reasons: rarely since *Le Signe du Lion* has Rohmer hired labourers to lay down track. To be sure, tracking shots of a sort do find their way into his films, most often variants of the fixed shot taken from moving vehicles, from the slow-moving motorboats of *Le Genou de Claire* and *Conte d'été* to the automobiles of *La Collectionneuse*, *L'Ami de mon amie*, and *Conte d'hiver*. But rarely are these high-speed affairs. The night-time motorcycle ride in *Les Nuits de la pleine lune*, where Pascale Ogier's character cruises the Paris streets with the lanky musician played by Christian Vadim, is an exception to the values of stasis and gentle accompaniment ordinarily upheld by Rohmer's camera. The zoom, or 'travelling optique' as it is also known in France, has nonetheless found favour with the director, especially in the *Contes des quatre saisons*. Zooms in those pictures are measured, sometimes imperceptibly slow; never do they brusquely shift attention from one object to another through rack focus. The resulting visual rhetoric is one of stability and subtlety where each movement, however slight, can generate unexpected surges in intensity and psychological depth.

Lighting

Since his first collaborations with Nestor Almendros in the mid-1960s, Rohmer has made a point of intervening as little as possible in the transcription of available light. He has rejected the cumbersome industrial battery of spots and fills, as well as the technicians and grips who operate them, in favour of simple reflectors, mirrors, and household-current minibrutes. If there are fewer, and less powerful, lamps to illuminate actors and decors in his films, it is not solely for economy's sake. For the ontological realist, natural light has a inviolate beauty that is best left untouched, with reinforcements only as film stock and the legibility of action require.

Particularly useful for understanding Rohmer's approach to lighting is Fabrice Revault d'Allones' *La Lumière au cinéma*. The author's premise is that if light, as it is encountered in the world, is devoid of purpose and signification, in the cinema it necessarily partakes in the construction of meaning along two possible paths (Revault d'Allones 1991: 7). The first, 'classical' lighting, deliberately arranges zones of shadow and luminosity to create specific connotations. Whether it is created in the studio *ex nihilo* or on location, it is (1) *dramatic* in that it serves narrative ends; (2) *hierarchical* in that it privileges some objects (actors) over others (decors); and (3) *legible* in that it offers up clear contrasts as a function of genre and style (Revault d'Allones 1991: 31–2). Modern lighting, by contrast, aims to render the light of the world in its givenness. Abandoning photographic polish for the techniques shared by reportage and documentary filmmaking, directors from Renoir and the Italian neo-realists to the French New Wave have given legitimacy to this unstructured, denotative light which is both 'insignificant' and laden with truth (Revault d'Allones 1991: 8).

Aside from studio pictures like the shadowless *Perceval le Gallois*, lit with powerful arc lights in order to approximate the look of medieval miniatures (Schaefer and Salvato 1984: 21), or *L'Anglaise et le Duc*, with its fishbowl-like blue-green hues, lighting in Rohmer's films is unequivocally modern, in the sense that it surrenders to the moment rather than serves symbolic or narrative designs. In accordance with this modern conception of lighting, meaning arises freely through 'une rencontre fortuite et saisissante [qui] a tout d'un instant de grâce' (a striking chance encounter [that] wholly resembles a moment of grace) (Revault d'Allones 1991: 126). It is no accident that so many scenes in Rohmer's work take place out of doors or in apartments with broad windows and light-coloured walls, for it is in natural light's variations in intensity and direction that we register the concrete presence of the real – in a word, the world's 'grace'. Nonetheless, the concern for legibility remains such that never does Rohmer push the limits of what the eye will tolerate. Though some early pictures sport dangerously low light levels (see the *contre-jour* shots taken from inside the villa in *La Collectionneuse*), there are no burned-out or severely underexposed zones or sharp contrasts between neighbouring shots, which characterise the work of Philippe Garrel (*Naissance de l'amour*). To insist on an even illumination without hard shadows, careful light matching from shot to shot, and a unified palette as does Rohmer is consistent with practice in comic genres. Yet there is little risk that we confuse his realism with the high-key lighting of Hollywood comedy. Following Almendros' basic principle, any and all light sources must be justified diegetically, either shown within the image or pointed to offscreen (Russell 1981: 77). The ethereal qualities of *Die Marquise von O...* come precisely from this documentary appreciation for light in its daily fluctuations; Almendros quipped that it was not he himself 'but an eighteenth-century architect' – namely the designer of Obertzen

Castle – who created the lighting for the 1976 film (Almendros 1984: 155). *Pauline à la plage*, for which Almendros used little more than styrofoam panels to reinforce natural light, is similarly a documentary study on the changing hues of the beachside resort near Granville (see figure 8). The spatial realism practised by Rohmer suggests a state of grace in which, to recall a line from his 'Vertus cardinales du cinémascope', one speaks 'non de *cadrages* mais de paysages ou de sites, non d'*éclairages* mais de lumière' (not of *framing* but of landscapes or sites, not of *lighting* but of light), bringing us into imaginary contact with the thing itself (Schérer 1954a: 39).

Editing

In an important essay of the mid-1950s on the evolution of film language, André Bazin has the following to say about the 'invisible montage' of classic Hollywood:

> Le morcellement des plans n'y a pas d'autre but que d'analyser l'événement selon la logique matérielle ou dramatique de la scène. C'est sa logique qui rend cette analyse insensible, l'esprit du spectateur épouse naturellement les points de vue que lui propose le metteur en scène parce qu'ils sont justifiés par la géographie de l'action ou le déplacement de l'intérêt dramatique.[5] (Bazin 1975: 64)

Rohmer's editing style largely conforms to the 'invisible montage' described here: monstrative rather than demonstrative, it excludes arbitrary changes in scale and camera angle that would steer attention and control pacing independently of the scene's dramatic content. Meaning is assumed to pre-exist its capture, and cuts should reflect a dynamic inherent to the action. These principles, which exclude the parallel montage, accelerated montage, or montage by attraction pioneered by Griffith, Gance, and Eisenstein respectively, are in line with critic Dominique Vilain's contention that 'la force d'un montage n'est pas de se faire voir, mais de faire voir' (editing's power lies not in making itself seen, but in making seen) (Vilain 1991: 52).

5 'Scenes would be broken down just for one purpose, namely, to analyse an episode according to the material or dramatic logic of the scene. It is this logic which conceals the fact of the analysis, the mind of the spectator quite naturally accepting the viewpoints of the director which are justified by the geography of the action or the shifting emphasis of dramatic interest.' (Bazin 1967: 24)

What Rohmer wishes to 'make seen' is predominantly the act of speech – the most immediate and far-reaching activity in which his characters engage. The plot turns on a verbal exchange between lovers, friends, and acquaintances; in groups of two, three, four or more; indoors, out, or in-between; sitting or standing; immobile or agitated. This promotion of dialogue as dramatic motor has a significant incidence on editing. First, narrative segmentation of individual films may recall more the acts and scenes of a stage play than a standard film script, where we expect part of the narrative interest to be carried by non-verbal events, and plot to flow out of an inaugural complicating action to which the hero(s) must respond by making choices. Such arborescent decision-making structures, which give rise in mainstream pictures to cross-cutting between two or more strands of plot, are foreign to Rohmer's screenplays, where what matters most is an individual's verbal posturing in relation to a stated ideal or moral principle. Second, the preponderance of dialogue is such that the director must devise ways to break down a conversation (during the shoot) and piece it back together again (at the editing table) without suppressing the spectator's critical faculties.

Few filmmakers have given so much thought as Rohmer to the different techniques for filming dialogue; perhaps fewer still have understood that the interest generated by dialogue is not proportional to the sheer number of shots or to the briskness of cuts. Two-person exchanges are a case in point. Traditional practice for 'covering' such dialogues would be to film a master shot with actors at opposite edges of the frame, then to re-shoot the scene twice, capturing each actor separately from an oblique angle at equivalent distances (the shoulders or head of the actor opposite may appear in 'cutaway'). When edited together, these two shots, each of which is the countershot of the other, give the impression of two intersecting gazes; they can be fleshed out with portions of the master take or with additional takes from other distances and angles, provided all are photographed on the same side of the 180 degree line.

It is well known that the counter-cinema of the 1960s did its best to dispense with shot–countershot configurations, which embodied mechanistic habit and the ideological illusion of 'suture', wherein the gaze binds spectators into a film's imaginary network and deactivates their critical judgement. Thus, in the opening sequence of *Vivre sa vie* (1962), Godard films his players backs to the camera, the faces of Nana (Anna Karina) and her estranged husband Paul (André S. Labarthe) visible only as blurred reflections in the mirror behind the bar at which they are seated. In a later café scene where Nana and her pimp Raoul (Sady Rebbot) face each other across a table, the camera swings back and forth behind, and then between, the two characters along the arc of a half-circle. The incongruity of these reframings pushes the spectator to reflect on the means of the cinema in keeping with the film's Brechtian programme.

On first appraisal, it would seem that Rohmer, who returns time and again to streamlined shot–countershot editing, supports an aesthetic conservatism that his peers had largely rejected. Yet careful viewing shows that he throws a grain of sand – in place of a Godardian monkey-wrench – into the well-oiled machinery of classical editing. Short supplies of film stock during the shooting of *La Collectionneuse* forced Rohmer to break down mentally each exchange so that only those shots intended for use in the final edit would be filmed (Almendros 1984: 56–7). Mental *découpage* became habit, such that even as material constraints ebbed, Rohmer continued to decide whether the shot on speaker or the reaction shot would be more appropriate to a scene's dramatic shape. In some cases, the edited reaction shot anticipates the shift in dialogue from one character to the other, in other cases it follows it; both solutions avert the 'ping-pong' effect endemic to much conventional editing, whereby image slavishly accompanies speech.

The well-known dinner table conversation of *Ma Nuit chez Maud* exemplifies Rohmer's oblique manner of attending to speech. The film's unnamed protagonist, inspired by the Chanturgue wine that has accompanied the meal, explains his views on Pascal's Catholicism to his bemused friend Vidal and to their hostess Maud. The scene opens with a medium two-shot of the protagonist, to the left, and Maud, to the right. She pours him a glass of wine, and as he continues to speak, the camera pans right, resolving on a second two-shot, this time of Maud and Vidal. The frame's composition, coupled with Vidal's body language, reminds us that the two adults were once lovers. We cut to a medium shot of the narrator alone, who continues his Pascalian meditations. The camera dwells on him even as Maud and Vidal, in offscreen space, interrupt (Vidal: 'Pascal n'a pas été condamné par l'Eglise' [Pascal wasn't condemned by the Church]) or encourage him to continue (Maud: 'Très bien répondu' [Good answer]; 'Alors vous disiez' [You were saying]). Before conversation ends, perspective shifts three more times, each time through a simple cut. The sequence has an average shot length of forty-five seconds, and yet the actors' pacing gives the scene a brisk feel. Narrative interest is heightened by the pairings worked out by the camera: while the scene first suggests that the freethinking Maud and the narrator could form a couple, it repeatedly underscores thereafter both the narrator's diffidence – he is interested only in a 'serious' relationship, namely marriage – and Vidal's regret that he himself will likely not be the one spending the night at Maud's.

Scenes such as this one, or the outdoor discussion of vegetarianism in *Le Rayon vert* or the lunchtime showdown on the nature of *a priori* judgements in *Conte de printemps*, tend to erode the divide between shot on speaker and reaction shot, so entwined are the activities of listening and speaking. As our awareness of the editing process subsides, dialogue itself becomes an object of fascination, provided that we are minimally receptive to its content. But receptive we must be, for when Rohmer's characters believe they have something to say (and when is this not the case?), they may take a good while to say it.

A second component shared by Rohmer's films provides structural contrast to ubiquitous conversation. Like connective tissue, intermediary sequences chart characters' movements from one place to another, on the way to the beach or on the way to work, on foot or by bus, train, metro, or car. Whereas dialogue scenes may create the illusion that screen time and diegetic time are equivalent, the spatial descriptions that connect them are elliptical, with average shot lengths from four to eight seconds. Their function is to recall the situated nature of everyday human endeavours. Take, for instance, in *Conte d'hiver*, Félicie's morning commute from her boyfriend Loïc's suburban flat to the hair salon in Belleville run by her employer and lover Maxence. The sequence begins with an establishing shot of a modern apartment dwelling in the blue morning twilight. We cut to a bedroom, in golden hues, where Loïc and Félicie discuss their plans for the day as the camera slowly zooms in. The forty-five-second shot ends when Félicie looks at her wristwatch. We cut to a residential street, where the heroine trudges down the sidewalk (screen movement is from left to right). Seven images then summarise her daily encounters with public transport: (1) the arrival of a suburban commuter train viewed from the platform, moving towards the frame's lower left edge;

(2) Félicie in medium close-up against the yellow interior of the train as it hurtles towards Paris (right to left); (3) a point-of-view shot of the industrial landscape as seen through the fogged-over train window; (4) commuters on a people-mover in the underground transit station (movement towards the camera, slightly off the vertical axis); (5) a hand-held shot of Félicie making her way through the corridors of the Paris underground and down to a platform; (6) a medium close-up of Félicie inside the subway car; and (7) a ground-level shot of the entrance to the Belleville métro station, where Félicie finally comes up for air. The average shot length for the sequence, starting with Félicie's departure from Loïc's house, is six seconds.

In this transitional scene as in others, shot order precisely conforms to use patterns, meaning that the director does not 'cheat' with geography or character trajectories. If we are familiar with the city of Paris, we know, for example, that Félicie's daily grind includes the dreaded underground changeover at the Châtelet-Les Halles station from the RER to métro line number 9. Importantly, the shots employed are not compilation images of the type often used to evoke place (for example, Paris monuments, cultural clichés), nor are they 'subjective' shots, since narrative focalisation remains external to the character. Their effect is to open up the texture of the spaces traversed and to situate the character with precision. In the case of Félicie, we understand that her problems in love are perhaps related to the complexity of working in a north-east district of Paris and splitting time between two different suburbs; indeed, her trip to her mother's that same evening is summarised with a comparable amount of detail.

In the classic Hollywood cinema, editing is often a matter of punctuation, of finding expressive links between shots and sequences. In nearly every instance, Rohmer prefers simple cuts – the equivalent of the full stop – to other transitional marks such as the fade, lap dissolve, or iris. When punctuation marks do appear, it is often to signal key omissions. Such is the case of the fade to black on the Count as he looks offscreen at the supine Marquise von O... (see figure 6); we will later understand that the black of the ellipsis corresponds to the rape scene. The same goes for the iris around which the Hitchcockian *Triple agent* revolves: Fiodor's alibi rests on the moment of absence that corresponds to the closing and opening of the camera 'eye' in the dressmaker's shop. The only significant exception to this lack of expressive punctuation are title cards. These may underline the passing of time, ticking off the days in any number of summer vacation films (*Le Genou de Claire, Le Rayon vert, Conte d'été*); set off prologues and epilogues from the body of the film (*La Collectionneuse, L'Amour l'après-midi, Triple agent*); preface the action and divide it into a series of chapters (*L'Arbre, le Maire et la Médiathèque ou Les sept hasards*); or authenticate the picture by quoting the language of a source text (*Die Marquise von O..., L'Anglaise et le Duc*).

Sound

In its dominant form, the sound cinema is, in Michel Chion's words, a 'vococentric' medium, one that privileges voice over all other auditory elements (Chion 1994: 6). Even in the presence of acoustical events like offscreen gunshots, the noise of a bustling street, or recorded music, the viewer is instinctively drawn to the human voice. This can be attributed to the semantic burden placed in film on spoken language. If we cannot follow the dialogues or commentary, we risk missing out on characterisation and plot development. Added to this is the aesthetic appeal of the human vocal imprint, whose unique timbre allows us to distinguish one actor from another with greater certainty than do his or her outward physical traits. In its approach to sound, the dominant cinema has consistently privileged intelligibility over fidelity, the functional over the expressive (Chion 1994: 6). What fault lines there are have been drawn primarily between those directors who prefer the flexibility and layered effects of studio postproduction and those who vaunt the purity of synchronous recording.

As in cinematography, Rohmer's views on sound reflect the need to respect the phenomenal world in its givenness. Verbal exchanges open up our senses most fully when they take place in a precise auditory environment. Each sound possesses qualities of attack and decay, reverberation, and modulation that are inseparable from its place of production. In Rohmer's view, the acoustical image must conform to what can be seen onscreen or intuited in contiguous offscreen space; since the world we inhabit is one, the filmed world must it too appear as a unified sensory totality. The dislocation and recomposition that characterise expressivist filmmakers such as Jacques Tati or Robert Bresson, who treat the soundtrack as if it were a musical score, have no place here, no more than does the manipulation of light or the use of lenses that exceed the capacities of the human eye. The ontological realist position excludes on principle disjunctive or contrapuntal uses of sound as well as the use of extradiegetic or 'pit' music, the melody and rhythm of which cannot but interfere with the spectator's interpretive liberty by creating residual emotions. As we will see, only rare allowances are made in Rohmer's films for music whose source cannot be localised in the diegesis.

Since the turn of the 1970s, Rohmer has stood at the forefront of the direct sound movement in France, along with Jean Rouch, Jacques Rivette, and the tandem of Jean-Marc Straub and Danièle Huillet. It should be recalled, *pace* Michel Marie, that direct sound was not a hallmark of the New Wave in its initial phase (Marie 1997: 63). Though synchronous location recording had been employed to naturalistic effect since the early 1930s, it became technically and financially viable only after 1960, the year the first high-quality 'portable' magnetic tape recorder, the Nagra, came out on the market. Godard, for example, postsynchronised all his films up to *Vivre sa vie* of 1962, and those directors who did try their hand at location sound, like Jacques Rozier for his *Adieu Philippine*, struggled to obtain usable takes (Marie 1997: 85). Ironically, turning to the city streets or, in Rozier's case, to the beaches of Corsica in the interest of documenting reality, obliged many filmmakers to return to the recording booth, where actors or their voice doubles could dub their lines in peace and quiet.

Rohmer's early works up through and including *La Collectionneuse* (1967) were postsynchronised. As such, they offer instructive lessons in period sound design. In keeping with the tight dubbing preferred by French audiences, as opposed to the looser Italian style of Cinecittà, they closely coordinate speech and lip movements. Ambient and incidental noises stand out as purposeful, such that the hearer–viewer is immediately drawn to the corresponding visual cause. Such sounds create what Chion calls 'added value', calling up impressions that the image alone – an abstraction to begin with – does not contain. In *La Boulangère de Monceau*, the tinkling of a bell emphatically marks the protagonist's entrances and exits from the pastry shop; a crinkling noise invites us to focus on the hands of the shop assistant who wraps with care the hero's purchases; the shuffling of feet signals the shopkeeper's imminent return from the back room. These sounds should not be considered as redundant. To use Chion's distinction, they *bring about* rather than *duplicate* meanings.

Produced with a higher budget than the first two *Contes moraux*, *La Collectionneuse* mixes dialogue and ambient sounds subtly enough so as to pass at times for authentic location recording. But this result is achieved less through fidelity to nature than by the search for a precise audiovisual equilibrium. In scenes shot in and around the villa, the chirping of crickets is a convenient signifier for the calm French Riviera setting, consonant with the soft afternoon and early morning light that bathes characters and decors alike. The protagonists' listlessness is reflected by the lack of incident on the soundtrack early in the film, over which the narrator's commentary ebbs and flows. As the narrative progresses, however, disputes over the young 'collectionneuse' Haydée come to disturb this calm summer retreat, pointing up the inability of Adrien and Daniel to escape the modern world through meditation and fuelling the sexual rivalry between them (see figure 2). The crash of a Chinese vase in the scene with the antique dealer confirms the spectator's impression that the film's serene acoustic façade, like the vase itself, existed only to be broken, as if to expose the derisory nature of Haydée's self-absorbed male companions.

Voiceover narration in the first three *Contes moraux* erodes the impression of a world-given immediacy in favour of a literary anti-illusionism. *Ma Nuit chez Maud*, which limits voiceover to two key passages, arguably achieves greater acoustic authenticity through its use of direct sound, notably in the three cathedral scenes and in the Suffren café discussion between Vidal and the protagonist. But only with *Le Genou de Claire*, which includes no offscreen commentary, does Rohmer's purist approach to location recording come into full force. The cries of 'Aurora' heard over the din of his motorboat as Jérôme passes under the bridge in the film's opening shot; the echo of a sparsely furnished, high-ceilinged room adorned with frescoes of Don Quixote where Jérôme explains his predicament to his novelist friend; the rustling of the Alpine meadows where he steals a kiss from Laura; or the rain that beats down upon the lakeside shelter as he caresses Claire's exposed knee (see figure 4) – these are all so many examples of the acoustic intimacy that location sound alone can project. Slight alterations in voice colour and depth with the change in direction of the wind or actor movement serve to authenticate the fiction of an unmediated acoustical reality.

With thirty-five years of direct sound recording behind him,

Rohmer has attained mythic status among French partisans of 'le son direct'. He was among the first in France to use buttonhole remote microphones (in 1980) and portable DAT recorders (in 1992). Yet careful listening reveals his films to be so doggedly vococentric that they come insidiously to question the acoustic naturalism to which they aspire. *Conte d'été* of 1996 sheds light on the ambiguities of synchronous recording and mixing. Its action is set in a coastal town in Brittany where the mathematics student and aspiring composer Gaspard awaits his girlfriend Léna. Not one to seek out company, he is befriended by Margot, with whom he takes daily walks around the port, along the town's ramparts, or on the outlying sand dunes. As they roam about in the open air, the two carry on about their amorous expectations and moral conundrums. Whatever the atmospheric conditions or camera distance, their voices are audible down to the last syllable. This is true even of actor Melvil Poupaud (Gaspard), whose delivery is more muddled than Rohmer, a stickler for elocution, usually allows. The effect is at once theatrical and eminently ordinary. Voices are contextualised by sounds we associate instinctively with seaside settings, like the crash of surf, the shouts of children playing, or the cries of seagulls, but never are they washed out. The Breton coast becomes a soundstage where not a word of dialogue gets lost in the wind.

At issue in these scenes is not fidelity but rather, in Michel Chion's words, the 'rendering' of a sonic environment as a function of mental representations and cinematic codes: 'The film spectator recognises sounds to be truthful, effective, and fitting not so much if they reproduce what would be heard in the same situation in reality, but if they render (convey, express) the feelings associated with the situation' (Chion 1994: 109). The use of lavaliere and directional microphones lends Margot and Gaspard's conversations a presence difficult to achieve in less controlled settings. What we assume, based on Rohmer's preference for direct sound, to be an 'objective' auditory point of view, then, is in reality a matter of convention. It is enough to compare Gaspard's arrival at Dinard in the film's opening sequence, which contains no dialogue, with the focalised auditory point of view employed during his outdoor conversations with Margot, to see how oriented for consumption a supposedly 'direct' soundscape can be.

The boat outing at *Conte d'été*'s midpoint hints at the artifice implied in 'rendering' acoustic events. The episode marks Gaspard's momentary triumph as a composer and as the would-be lover of Solène, the long-haired woman whom he first glimpsed in a discotheque. As Solène starts in on the first verse of 'Fille de corsaire', the mariner's song that Gaspard has dedicated to her, her husky alto and the pulsating accordion that accompanies her rise above the churning motor. The effect in this shot-sequence is both realistic – Solène must push her voice make herself heard – and at the limit of what is acoustically plausible, as those who have attempted to converse or, for that matter, play the accordion on a motorboat should know. Enthralled by the performance and by the celebratory mood (all the passengers join in on the chorus), we as spectators gladly accept the convention, which creates an auditory point of view marginally at odds with the camera's own. This is part of the 'white lie' committed by all sound filmmakers, who must exaggerate contrast the better to channel our sensations (Chion 1994: 115).

Such scenes remind us never to autonomise a film's soundtrack: sound has value only in relation to the image (the converse is also true). Indeed, depending on the film, acoustical definition at all frequencies may not be desirable. In *Le Rayon vert*, for example, snatches of conversation are lost and the pitch of characters' voices is modulated with head movements. This unpolished sound harmonises with the slight grain of 16mm and the picture's impromptu *mise en scène*. The rough-and-ready charm of a quintessential French vacation film like Jacques Rozier's *Du côté d'Orouët* (1970) likewise derives from a balance of sound and image: just as the wind and surf drown out the characters' voices and shouts, so too do sun and shadow inscribe on the filmstrip's visible grain burned-out and underexposed zones. Sound must be considered from a total point of view, as one part of the sensory field.

There are limits, of course, to what can be effectively captured on location. As Cécile Decugis, Rohmer's editor for nine projects for between 1969 and 1984, has revealed, the director has on more than one occasion added overdubs to the original location recordings (Vilain 1991: 76). It may be tempting to use such information to demystify 'direct' sound as a reconstructed artefact no less functional than postsynchronised sound. Michel Chion does as much in his commentary on the Buttes-Chaumont park sequence of *La Femme de l'aviateur* (Chion 1994: 105). In that scene, François (Philippe Marlaud), seated on a low stone wall overlooking a reflecting pool, distractedly converses with the high-school student Lucie (Anne-Laure Meury) while surveying from afar the aeroplane pilot and the mysterious woman who accompanies him. Throughout this exchange, Chion remarks, the city park remains uncannily quiet: 'All events that usually intrude on sound recording in a city or in the country have been completely eliminated, but the life that can come with them has also been eliminated in the process' (Chion 1994: 105). It is perhaps true that the scene lacks anecdotal noise. Yet this cleansing effect, Chion neglects to mention, is obtained not through postproduction trickery but by careful scouting for a place and time of day when conditions closest to ideal will prevail. It is not because the scene was shot during off-hours, when park traffic lulls, that spectators will cease to suspend disbelief – no more so than if a sequence set in the morning were shot at dusk with the appropriate filter. The soundtrack, in a word, is 'cleaned up' before the tape begins to roll; what we hear is a direct acoustical imprint of auditory events contemporaneous to the take we see. Why this would constitute a breach of contract for the partisan of direct sound, as Chion contends, is not entirely clear (Chion 1994: 106). A well-selected auditory environment is surely not the same as an artificially constructed one, even if we admit that postproduction mixing always reintroduces some measure of artifice.

The search for hygienic sonic environments outside the confines of the studio has influenced Rohmer's *mise en scène* itself. Sound technicians Jean-Pierre Ruh and Pascal Ribier have noted the extreme lengths to which the director goes to ensure perfectly audible takes: shots are more likely to be discarded because the sound is unacceptable than for reasons related to the image or acting. Nearly all of Rohmer's films – whatever the season – feature exterior locations that are set off from crowds, streets, or other sources of noise. Gaspard and Solène of *Conte d'été*, for example, discuss their trip to Ouessant at a lookout point whose half-circle architecture gives their conversation a theatrical feel, each character being free to move about and declaim at ease. In *Conte d'hiver*, Félicie and Maxence discuss their past and future loves at a similar lookout point above the Loire river, on the outskirts of Nevers. In protected auditory environments such as these, long takes with multiple reframings are viable. In less-secluded spots, however, long takes may become impossible. When Rohmer shot *L'Ami de mon amie* in the new town of Cergy-Pontoise, he had to reckon with the fact that his exteriors lay under the flight paths for the heavily trafficked Roissy-Charles de Gaulle airport. Entire scenes between water sports enthusiasts Fabien and Blanche on the Etangs de Neuville had to be broken down into short takes that could be squeezed in between flyovers (Hertay 1998: 116). Here, the cult of direct sound prompts modifications in staging and in editing.

In the end, Rohmer's experiments with direct sound betray the contradictions of ontological realism. Sound recording and mixing tear us away from the phenomenal real with the same violence as does standard cinematography, however 'objective' the means employed. The fact that Rohmer records all source materials live in the field – including the silence proper to each locale, should overdubs be necessary – suffices nonetheless to distinguish his approach as naturalistic. In today's ear-pounding Dolby Stereo and Surround-Sound media culture, a non-emphatic, effectless treatment of sound like Rohmer's may come as welcome relief. Much can be said for intensive listening to these films which attune us to what Chion calls 'territorial' noise – the variegated sonic landscapes of France, from its ports to its city streets – and especially to vocal timbre and the inflexions and accents of the French language. It's not for nothing that a French language instruction programme was based on *4 Aventures de Reinette et Mirabelle*, nor that the director has often chosen to cast non-native French speakers. In the end, the ontological realist's respect of the world is subsumed to the respect of the word, and it is this privilege granted to speech that makes Rohmer's cinema one of the most musical in its class – paradoxically so, as we shall see.

Music

Vocal or instrumental, period or contemporary, up-front or in the background, continuous or intermittent, music is largely taken for granted in the narrative cinema. As Claudia Gorbman has shown in *Unheard Melodies*, uses of 'extradiegetic' or 'pit' music have varied little since the 1930s (Gorbman 1987: 73–91). While music is invisible by definition, film music, Gorbman argues, is 'invisible' in a more radical sense: whereas spectators may mentally visualise the camera as the site of production of a film's images, they must not imagine the musicians who execute the score or the devices used to record it. An accompaniment to the diegesis, film music must go 'unheard'

– not actively listened to – even as the spectator registers its presence. Furthermore, it can signal emotional intensity in contrast to scenes which do not include it; distinguish among levels of narration; demarcate beginnings and endings; or underscore changes in point of view. More generally, its rhythmic continuity attenuates the spatio-temporal fragmentation implied by shot editing.

Extradiegetic music is a tool most directors could scarcely do without, so effective is it in stirring the emotions, controlling narrative flow, and unifying a work around an acoustic signature. For Rohmer, however, these functions are reason enough to dispense with pit music altogether:

> Je suis hostile à la caméra subjective et également au cinéma sentimental pris dans un sens très large et qui établit entre un personnage et le spectateur une complicité émotionnelle. Pourquoi? Parce que l'émotion ne sera jamais obtenue que par des 'trucs'. Au nombre de ces 'trucs', je place toute la musique, quelle qu'elle soit.[6] (Baby 1967)

Emphatic and manipulative, non-diegetic music can only compromise the prized ironic distance that Rohmer strives to achieve. To add music to a scene which itself contains none is to suggest that actors, dialogue, and *mise en scène* are unable to convey sentiment on their own terms. A proscription against music thus inhibits psychological identification, helping to preserve the spectator's freedom.

More often than not, music will impress itself on Rohmer's viewer negatively, as a lack. The case of *Die Marquise von O...* (1976), set in Napoleonic Europe, is revealing. Most producers would have thought it indispensable to include period compositions from the classical repertoire to establish mood and to reinforce the high-culture connotations of Kleist's text. Yet the emotions delivered by the actors as well as the impression of historical reality are strengthened by the absence of musical reinforcement. Each silence is pregnant with meaning and recalls the atmosphere of studious calm that filled bourgeois households of the time. Where the industry tells us, 'this is where the strings come in', Rohmer gives us a film with no strings attached.

When non-diegetic music does appear in Rohmer's œuvre, its role is far from innocent. It figures prominently in the debut feature *Le*

6 'I'm against subjective camera and sentimental filmmaking in the broad sense, which creates emotional complicity between character and spectator. Why? Because emotion will only ever be arrived at through effects. Among these effects, I include all music of all types.'

Signe du Lion, the story of a professional musician out of work and too proud of his bohemian ways to find any. Much like the partygoer (played by Jean-Luc Godard) who repeatedly cues up a few bars of a Beethoven chamber piece on a record player, Pierre Wesserlin (Jess Hahn) is in a rut. He is struggling to finish his long-awaited symphony, whose melody he claims to have heard in a dream. When his family inheritance falls through, Wesserlin finds himself on the street, and as he walks about Paris under the unforgiving sun, a brooding theme for solo violin brings out his disarray and isolation. Comfortably located outside the diegesis, this skeletal melodic line returns like a leitmotiv to illustrate the hero's grim prospects and deteriorating mental state. When all hope seems lost, a comical bum encountered on the banks of the Seine ropes Wesserlin into presenting a condensed pseudo-Wagnerian opera (in pidgin German) to Saint-Germain café-sitters. Disgusted to see how low he has fallen in his search for pocket change, Wesserlin moves away from his winesoaked partner, who continues his aria in outlandish falsetto. A third-rate street violinist approaches the café terrace. When his screeching ceases, Pierre borrows his instrument and produces a strangely familiar air – the very melody we have been hearing on the soundtrack all along. It is as if the film's vocation were to fold the leitmotiv, initially perceived as illustrative 'pit' music, back into the story world and to expose Pierre's decline as the internal creative struggle it always was. In the event, much like the phonograph blaring from a record shop in the final scenes of Vigo's *L'Atalante* (1934), this sudden retrieval of the lost melody is providential. For just as music helped Père Jules (Michel Simon) track down the newlywed Juliette (Dita Parlo) lost in the big city, so too in *Le Signe du Lion* does it lead two of Wesserlin's acquaintances to identify their now all but unrecognisable friend (see figure 1). The good tidings they bring – the inheritance is Pierre's after all – are almost an afterthought, so ingenious is the soundtrack's formal conceit.

Le Signe du Lion is uniquely complex in Rohmer's œuvre when it comes to the use of music, and it seems plausible that Agnès Varda had it in mind when editing her 1985 masterwork on solitude and suffering, *Sans toit ni loi* (*Vagabond*). *Le Rayon vert*, which dates to that same period, implicitly rewrites *Le Signe du Lion* in a lighter, feminine key. Ill at ease with others and with her self-image, the protagonist Delphine moves about from one lent apartment to another with no clear destination in mind. At various points a seven-note staccato line for solo violin underscores her movements, connoting both the monotony of her predicament and the lingering possibility that fate will come to her aid (Delphine is a soul mate of Pierre Wesserlin, who, born under the sign of Leo, proudly refers to astrology as 'la science la plus exacte de toutes' [the most exact science of them all]). Far from mere narrative accompaniment, the insistent melody becomes an assertive signature for the film as a whole.

Conte d'hiver similarly capitalises on the music lessons of *Le Signe du Lion*. In a crucial scene at the film's narrative midpoint, Félicie, who has just moved to the provincial city of Nevers to join the hairdresser Maxence, visits the cathedral with her young daughter. When she seats herself in front of the altar, we cut to a point-of-view shot showing the stained-glass windows of the apse, justified by a view in medium close-up of Félicie, her eyes upraised. At this point, seven pizzicato quarter notes plucked on a string instrument can be heard. After a pause, the same progression, now louder, is repeated lower on the scale; a third iteration of the statement resolves on the dominant. This 'subjective' musical theme suggests that Félicie has thought something over, or perhaps asked for a bit of divine intercession in finding her long-lost love, Charles. Our suspicions are confirmed, for she and her daughter leave Maxence that very afternoon for Paris. Later that week, a sign that her prayers may soon be answered appears when she attends a performance of *A Winter's Tale*. In Act V, scene III, Leontes, invited to the house of Paulina, shows his daughter the statue of her disappeared mother, a work of art so lifelike that it seems that it could speak. When Paulina calls for music to bring Hermione's effigy to life, the notes played on a wooden flute are the same as those that Félicie 'heard' earlier in the chapel (both, in fact, are reductions of the piano arrangement the spectator may recall from the film's credit sequence). As in *Le Signe du Lion*, the melody subtly steps across the boundary that separates subjective from objective reality, bringing the two realms together and foretelling the fairy-tale ending of Félicie's story. The heroine's auditory hallucination turns into a concrete sign of the force of belief and of the upward turn of fortune's wheel.

Equally worthy of note in its treatment of music is *Perceval le Gallois*. Against the doctrine of 'invisibility' described by Gorbman, the film displays the 'instance of musical production' from the start (Gorbman 1987: 75). Shots of musicians and a chorus, all dressed in brightly coloured tunics, precede the enactment of Perceval's journey to King Arthur's court. Texts adapted from Chrétien's poem and set to twelfth- and thirteenth-century airs comment on the action, prefacing episodes or summarising them, and punctuating Perceval's and Gauvain's travels with chants of 'Et tant et tant il chevaucha' (And he rode and he rode). Since the singers and musicians occupy the same physical space as do the characters, the distinction between diegetic and non-diegetic music collapses, inaugurating a third space of representation – that of theatrical performance itself. As Jean Douchet shows in his 'making-of' *En répétant Perceval*, Rohmer conceived of the film as one continuous performance and insisted that musical accompaniments be played live.

The spare instrumental illustration of *Le Signe du Lion*, *Le Rayon vert*, and *Conte d'hiver* as well as the integrated performances of *Perceval le Gallois* share little with the mainstream cinema. Ostensibly, other *Contes des quatre saisons* are the work of a director more amenable to common practice. The opening sequence of *Conte de printemps*, for instance, pairs a Beethoven piano sonata with a tracking shot taken from heroine Jeanne's car, while the closing credits of *Conte d'été* feature a 'sailor's rock' tune of the kind that protagonist Gaspard might be expected to pen and record a few years down the road. These are, however, rare occurrences in the work of a filmmaker for whom music and cinema simply do not mix. If this is so, it is because all music worthy of the name requires the listener's complete and undivided attention – an attitude perhaps best illustrated by the concert sequence in *Ma Nuit chez Maud*, where a tightly framed extended take forces the spectator to concentrate on Léonide Kogan's performance of a Mozart violin sonata, rather than on audience members. Music is shown to be the 'other' of cinema: either one talks, or one listens.

Curiously enough, coming from the author of a book on the notion of 'depth' in the classical repertoire, *De Mozart en Beethoven*, the one musical genre to appear with any frequency in the world of Rohmer's characters is pop. Men, little interested in dancing apparently, are dragged by their female counterparts to discothèques (Pierre in *Pauline à la plage*, Gaspard in *Conte d'été*), Parisian *soirées* (Rémi in *Les Nuits de la pleine lune*), teenage birthday parties (Edmond in *Le Beau Mariage*), and wedding receptions (Etienne and Gérald in *Conte d'automne*). Most of these episodes, rather than capture contemporary musical sensibility (for example, by featuring a top-selling single), underscore the blandness of popular music. Typically, Chion points out, the selection will be 'aussi incolore que possible, écrite, orchestrée et enregistrée pour ne rien graver dans l'attention et la mémoire' (as colourless as possible, written, arranged, and recorded so as not to capture the attention or to be remembered) (Chion 1995: 380). The tune to which Reinette and Mirabelle dance in the farmhouse the evening before they rise to see 'L'heure bleue' is one such example. The fact that Rohmer should seek such anonymity through canned music is, reasons Chion, proof *a contrario* that any music on the soundtrack, whether it is part of the diegesis or not, risks spilling over and creating residual emotions. This helps to explain why *Conte d'automne* met with such warm public response. Magali's realisation that Gérald is not such a bad match for her after all, and Isabelle's pride at having found Magali a companion, find expression in the rootsy, jubilant sounds of a *langue d'oc* number, performed outside on the lawn by a live band. Placed high up in the mix, the music, coupled with the tale's happy end, elicits an impression of levity greater than any film in Rohmer's œuvre.

All things considered, if he acknowledges the presence of music in the everyday life of his characters, Rohmer has been steadfast in refusing non-diegetic music. This is not simply a question of personal taste but of knowing how to respect and to savour the world around us. As Rohmer remarks in *De Mozart en Beethoven*,

> Je n'aime pas *la* musique. Je m'applique à l'éliminer de ma vie et de mes films. Elle m'agace, me gêne, me fatigue ... Je me trouve tout à fait à l'aise dans le silence. Il ne me *pèse* nullement. Car ce silence, celui des champs ou de la rue lointaine, offre un tissu sonore d'une richesse *sui generis*, révélatrice du lieu, au même titre que l'odeur qui en émane.[7] (Rohmer 1998: 15)

It is fitting that the most 'talkative' of French filmmakers should also be the one to alert us to this inherent musicality and order of the silent world.

7 'I don't like *music*. I take pains to eliminate it from my life and films. I find it annoying, bothersome, tiresome [...]. I'm completely at ease in silence. It doesn't weigh me down a bit. Silence, whether that of the countryside or of the faraway street, provides a sonic texture rich in and of itself that reveals a place in the same way as the odour that issues from it.'

Methods

Style is the product not simply of technical decisions taken during the shoot or in the editing room, but also of the work habits and collaborative spirit uniting director, cast, and crew. The creative methods that Rohmer has consistently employed since the late 1960s strike a felicitous balance between constraint and freedom, bridging the ideals of the classic cinema and those of the New Wave and encouraging novel forms of interaction between director and actor.

Critic François Vanoye usefully distinguishes two basic models in film production. While the 'scénario-programme' or programmatic model presents a story ready for production, usually in the form of a screenplay, shooting script, and/or storyboard, the 'scénario-dispositif' may consist merely in a loose set of guidelines that leave open to the shoot decisions as to *mise en scène*, the shape and content of dialogue, character development, and even the course of the action (Marie 1997: 69–71). Among the cohort of *Cahiers du cinéma* critics-turned-filmmakers, Godard and Rivette clearly favour this second model, radicalising the role of chance and day-to-day inspiration, sometimes to the extreme. Rohmer, together with Chabrol and Truffaut, would seem to espouse the first, programmatic method: tightly scripted dialogues, predetermined plot, taught scene transitions, consistent style – all these suggest significant levels of preparation in the interest of artistic control. Shooting would be more a matter of getting a clean take than of eliciting a spontaneous performance, as is the case with a John Cassavetes or a Philippe Garrel, the noted defender of one-take filmmaking. Yet Rohmer's *modus operandi* is more open to exchange and to chance than one might surmise.

The search for a 'subject' and a recognisable genre that so obsesses commercial directors is, to begin with, irrelevant to Rohmer. His primary concern in the drafting phases is with working out plot solutions from basic dramatic and characterological premises. As we will see in Chapter 4, his 'original' screenplays, the length of which varies little from film to film, are in a way profoundly unoriginal when considered as a group. They embody recurrent patterns, a narrow range of character types, and a tone that informed spectators will readily identify as Rohmerian. At the same time, within this set of constants each picture allows for privileged encounters between actors and their roles.

Though Rohmer does not qualify as an 'actor's director' in the conventional sense, those professionals and amateurs to have worked with him are near-unanimous in their support, particularly because of the formative role they are allowed to play in role construction. Adapting to his own designs ideas from the *cinéma vérité* of Jean Rouch, the director regularly asks his actors to lend elements of their private persona to their screen characters. These may include professional knowledge, expressions, hobbies, habits and gestures, and ways of reacting to a given situation or dilemma. On the release of *La Collectionneuse*, Rohmer noted that he would never make out someone to be a painter who wasn't one, nor would he have his actors read books they wouldn't read themselves (Baby 1967). The art objects that Daniel discusses with noted art critic Alain Jouffroy in one of *La Collectionneuse*'s three prologues are the real-life creations of actor/artist Daniel Pommereulle. Language too must be tailored to real-life personae. In strong contrast to Rohmer's own chiselled prose, actor Patrick Bauchau supplies his character, Adrien, with a relaxed syntax:

> Je crois qu'on pense beaucoup trop. L'important c'est pas de penser, mais de participer. Un bouquin, ça me fait penser dans une certaine direction qui est celle du bouquin. Ce que je ne veux pas, c'est penser dans ma direction à moi.[8]

The presence in *La Collectionneuse* of words and expressions like 'infect', 'collant', 'sauteuse', 'petite conne', 'plein le cul', and the very 1960s 'définitivement irrécupérable'[9] can surely be attributed to actors' input in pre-production meetings, which Rohmer tape-recorded, transcribed, and selectively wove into his screenplay. This continuity between private persona and screen role complicates the idea that actors must either identify with or distance themselves from a character. The role is theirs, but once written, it is not theirs to change. If collaborative techniques gave *La Collectionneuse* contemporary immediacy, they also alienated its actors, who considered that the director had mocked their personality and mannerisms (Walker 1998: 42). Significantly, Rohmer did not try out his techniques on seasoned professionals like Jean-Louis Trintignant, Françoise Fabian,

8 'I think people think too much. What's important isn't thinking, but participating. A book, well, makes me think in a certain way that is the book's. What I don't want is to think in my own direction.'

9 Roughly, 'stinking', 'clinging', 'slut', 'little bitch', 'up the arse', 'absolutely hopeless'.

or Jean-Claude Brialy, though other principals of the *Contes moraux*, like the noted theatre director Antoine Vitez, who plays the Marxist philosopher Vidal of *Ma Nuit chez Maud*, or Zouzou, the rough-edged Chloé of *L'Amour l'après-midi*, helped to fashion their roles.

Following his experiments in direct *mise en scène* and theatre in the 1970s, Rohmer returned to collaborative techniques for the *Comédies et proverbes* cycle. As André S. Labarthe's documentary *Eric Rohmer: Preuves à l'appui* shows in fascinating detail, once casting decisions were made for each film, Rohmer would schedule frequent one-on-one interviews with his players. From his office desk at Les Films du Losange, he would explain the basic idea behind the character and solicit input by asking questions like, 'what would you do (or say) in the following situation?' In cases where a draft of a screenplay was already in place, it was a question of revising dialogues based on actors' reactions, recorded on audio tape or on Super-8; in others, when the director knew only with which players he wished to work, the storyline and dialogues evolved out of the weekly conversations themselves. Such was the case of both *Le Rayon vert* and *4 Aventures de Reinette et Mirabelle*, films which, though often referred to as 'improvisations', are better described as collaborative works.

This interactive process allowed Rohmer to particularise the dramatis personae and to bring young, often inexperienced actors into a zone of relative comfort. Early on in preproduction of the *Comédies et proverbes*, he would accompany his actors, individually or more rarely as a group, to the film's locations to perform screen tests and to expose them to their character's milieu. His wager is that a substantive connection between actor, character, and location will produce more convincing results than will an actor's attempts to 'incarnate' a role foreign to him or her. Through a give-and-take process, each role becomes an original creation even as it remains an interlocking element in the screenplay. Once dialogues are fully scripted, however, the collaborative phase ends. The shoot is an occasion for refining and implementing ideas rather than inventing them. Actors are required to memorise their lines weeks in advance of reporting to work, for once on the set they are not allowed to improvise; what's more, they may have only a half-line of dialogue as lead-in to a given take (Hertay 1998: 113; 134). Each shot is copiously rehearsed – ten to twenty times – such that one or two takes usually suffices; if a third take is unsuccessful, the shot may be discarded altogether, since its spontaneity is lost (Hertay 1998: 132). Actors are discouraged from viewing the rushes, over which director and cinematographer have exclusive judgement (since many shots are finished in one or two takes, little is left to decide). Whenever possible, Rohmer has chosen to shoot chronologically, in dramatic continuity, rather than divide up shots by location. This arrangement, more common to the 'scénario-dispositif' model than to the 'scénario-programme', is made possible by the decision to employ reduced crews with a minimum of equipment – the kind of gear that fits in an oversize gym bag, as Rohmer shows his interviewer, Jean Douchet, in *Preuves à l'appui*.

Rohmer's work owes its consistency to what technicians and actors have described as the director's near total mastery over the shoot, from the selection of locations and wardrobe to camera angles, light, and especially sound. This rigour should not be confused with excessive professionalism. As actor Pascal Greggory has noted, Rohmer perceives himself as 'un grand amateur et non comme "un professionnel de la profession"' (a serious amateur and not a 'professional among professionnals') (Hertay 1998: 128). This appreciation for the medium in its craft-like simplicity means that the secondary pleasures often associated with the cinema have no place here. And yet, for all their budgetary restraint, Rohmer's productions are as luxurious as any. For as sound engineer Georges Prat puts it, 'le luxe, dans le métier, c'est le temps' (the real luxury in the business is time) (Hertay 1998: 114). This means having ample time to set up and rehearse shots properly, and above all, being able to wait for the precise moment at which natural light, ambient sound, and performance come together in an instant of grace.

Conclusion

The ontological realist position defended by Rohmer in his critical writings finds clear expression in the means of recording adopted throughout his directing career. 'Objective' rendering of events in conformity to human vision and from a distance conducive to spectatorial empathy and critical judgement alike tempers the artifice of his screenplays. In a sense, it does not matter how much Rohmer's characters talk, so grounded is their activity in the phenomenal reality that surrounds them. At the same time, the transparent mode of representation practised by Rohmer never naturalises its objects to the point at which we confuse them with an unmediated reality. Through its sense of composition (the framing of shots), of syntax (the linkage of shots), and *mise en scène* (staging) each film signals its identity as a fiction whose means are proper to the cinema. Rohmer's approach to dialogue editing and to sound in particular reminds us that film can be self-aware without being meta-critical or iconoclastic. If nothing in Rohmer's pictures strikes our eye or ear initially, it is likely because we are looking and listening in the wrong places. This 'prose' that results from an unwillingness to flaunt the camera, or to drown out the sounds of the world in strains of music, is surely not without its poetry.

References

Adair, Gilbert (1997), *Surfing the Zeitgeist*, London, Faber and Faber.

Almendros, Nestor (1984), *A Man with a Camera*, tr. Rachel Phillips Belash, New York, Farrar, Straus, Giroux.

Aumont, Jacques (1992), *Du visage au cinéma*, Paris, Cahiers du cinéma/ Editions de l'Etoile.

Baby, Yvonne (1967), '"La Collectionneuse", c'est l'histoire d'une pensée', *Le Monde*, 3 March.

Barthes, Roland (1957), *Mythologies*, Paris, Seuil.

Bazin, André (1967), *What is Cinéma?*, vol. 1, tr. Hugh Gray, Berkeley, University of California Press.

Bazin, André (1975), *Qu'est-ce que le cinéma?*, Paris, Editions du Cerf.

Biette, Jean-Claude, Jacques Bontemps and Jean-Louis Comolli (1965), 'L'ancien et le nouveau', *Cahiers du cinéma* 172, November: 32–42; 56–9.

Bordwell, David (1997), *On the History of Film Style*, Cambridge, MA, and London, Harvard University Press.

Chion, Michel (1994), *Audio-vision: Sound on Screen*, tr. Claudia Gorbman, New York, Columbia University Press.

Chion, Michel (1995), *La Musique au cinéma*, Paris, Fayard.

Gorbman, Claudia (1987), *Unheard Melodies: Narrative Film Music*, London, British Film Institute/Bloomington, University of Indiana Press.

Hertay, Alain (1998), *Eric Rohmer: Comédies et proverbes*, Liège, Editions de Céfal.

Legrand, Gérard (1971), 'Un genou ... et un autre genou', *Positif* 125, March: 54–6.

Magny, Joël (1995), *Eric Rohmer*, 2nd ed., Paris, Rivages.

Marie, Michel (1997), *La Nouvelle Vague: une école artistique*, Paris, Nathan.

Revault d'Allones, Fabrice (1991), *La Lumière au cinéma*, Paris, Cahiers du cinéma/Editions de l'Etoile.

Rohmer, Eric (1984), *Le Goût de la beauté*, Paris, Cahiers du cinéma (reprinted 2004).
Rohmer, Eric (1989), *The Taste for Beauty*, tr. Carol Volk, New York and Cambridge, Cambridge University Press.
Rohmer, Eric (1998), *De Mozart en Beethoven*, Arles, Actes Sud.
Russell, Sharon A. (1981), *Semiotics and Lighting: A Study of Six Modern French Cinematographers*, Ann Arbor, MI, UMI Research Press.
Schaefer, Dennis, and Larry Salvato (1984), *Masters of Light: Conversations with Contemporary Cinematographers*, Berkeley and Los Angeles, University of California Press.
Schérer, Maurice (1954a), 'Vertus cardinales du Cinémascope', *Cahiers du cinéma* 31, January: 36–40.
Séailles, André (1985), 'Entretien avec Eric Rohmer', *Etudes cinématographiques* 146/148, *Eric Rohmer* I, Paris, Minard: 5–17.
Vilain, Dominique (1991), *Le Montage au cinéma*, Paris, Cahiers du cinéma/ Editions de l'Etoile.
Walker, Beverly (1998), 'Secrets at Play: Patrick Bauchau', *Film Comment* 34.4, July/August: 38–43.

4

Seriality and theme

Serial filmmaking emerged on the eve of the First World War as the culmination of two decades of efforts to overcome the cinema's temporal limits, initially fixed by the single shot. Just as the film splice and use of multiple reels had allowed directors to move beyond the models of the vignette and short story to that of the five-part play (Abel 1994: 299–300), so too did multiple-feature serials extend fiction's imaginative scope. If creative interest in the serial genre, burdened by its dependence on an indomitable hero or villain, tapered off by the 1920s (Williams 1992: 71), seriality as an organising principle would resurface in the work of French New Wave directors, for whom multi-episode formats were less a commercial ploy than a means to assert film authorship in a personal key. Such was clearly the view of Truffaut, whose semi-autobiographical Antoine Doinel cycle captures the wayward character played by Jean-Pierre Léaud at five stages in life, from his troubled adolescence in *Les 400 coups* (1959) to his post-divorce malaise in the wistful *L'Amour en fuite* (1978); such was also the case of Chabrol, who at the turn of the 1970s brought actress (and spouse) Stéphane Audran to the screen in the four-part 'Hélène cycle' on changing sexual mores.

The sole filmmaker of his generation in France to have consistently grouped his work by cycles, Eric Rohmer has arguably approached serial form in less conventional fashion than his peers. He has all but rejected the continuity provided by recurrent characters – nominally present in the *Charlotte et Véronique* cycle co-authored with Godard (1951–58) – in favour of shared thematic and dramatic motifs. For all their formal rigour, his *Contes moraux* (1962–72), *Comédies et proverbes* (1981–87), and *Contes des quatre saisons* (1990–98) are unburdened by programmatic constraints of the kind that Krzysztof Kieslowski, a self-declared admirer of Rohmer, employs in his ten-part *Dekalog* (1988), inspired by the Holy Commandments (Amiel 1997: 100). Rohmer's series titles themselves are inviting and capacious: in place of the restrictive genres preferred by the industry ('epic', 'thriller', 'biopic'), they set up broad discursive horizons – namely the tale (*conte*) the comedy (*comédie*) – against which to interpret member films. The six *Contes moraux* thus highlight the disjunction between storytelling and action; the six women-centred *Comédies et proverbes* view contemporary situations through the double lens of stage comedy and popular sayings; and the *Contes des quatre saisons* seek inspiration in the fairy tale (*conte de fées*). Auteur theory reaches its logical conclusion in this explicit comparison of filmmaking to the writer's craft.

Under what conditions, one might ask, does a set of films become a series? What distinguishes Rohmer's thematic cycles from trilogies, tetralogies, and other multi-episode formats? Surely it is not a question of quantity alone. More relevant is the issue of diegetic continuity: whether key elements of the story-world carry over from film to film. In Marcel Pagnol's trilogy *Marius/Fanny/César* (various directors, 1931–36), for instance, it is hard to grasp the stakes of the last two pictures without knowing the back-story provided by the first; plot extends across all three films, whose characters continue to inhabit the diegesis even after they have deserted the screen. By contrast, in thematic groupings like Rohmer's or in the comparable 'contes de L'Estaque', which the Marseilles-based Robert Guédiguian has been shooting with a core of actors since 1980 (Cohen 1997: 59), each film is a self-contained fiction. As we move from one feature to the next, we ask not, 'what new adventures have befallen the characters?', but rather, the cast of characters (if not of actors) having changed in its entirety, 'how does the present film illuminate the themes, situations, and texture of its predecessors?' Whatever connections the spectator makes are paradigmatic, founded on resemblance or opposition among elements of the series, rather than syntagmatic, that is, placed on a cause–effect chain.

Rohmer's cycles do present nonetheless a temporal aspect, in that the two sets of *Contes* each took nearly ten years to complete, and the *Comédies et proverbes*, seven. Given the filmmaker's commitment to photographic realism and to the *in situ* representation of contemporary lifestyles, this means, first, that each series registers changing trends in material culture from fashion and interior decoration to architecture. Second, it means that each cycle is vectorised, moving towards an endpoint that may or may not be fixed from the start. So long as the series is a work in progress, its shape is provisional. Yet once it reaches completion, our perspective changes: films which first appeared as successive but independent statements now compose a closed architectural form. The effect is similar to what occurs when an author collects under a single cover short stories or poems first published separately, with the similarity that Rohmer has rectified after the fact the sequencing of two series – both the *Contes moraux* and *Contes des quatre saisons* were shot 'out of order' – and the difference that his serial intentions are, in all three cases, announced at the outset.

The inspiration for what follows is Rohmer's provocative suggestion that the six *Contes moraux* compose in reality a single film. Should we take this idea seriously and extend it to the *Comédies et proverbes* and *Contes des quatre saisons*, it would mean that *Le Genou de Claire*, *Pauline à la plage*, or *Conte d'hiver* – whatever their individual merits – are what they are because they belong to a group; far from an accident, their inclusion in a series is constitutive of their identity. The subject of Rohmer's cycles, then, can be seen as the return and rearrangement of dramatic and stylistic motifs, or the controlled play of difference across an interlocking whole. This may be a source for complaint for some viewers who, as Dominique Païni has written, are tempted 'de ne voir que répétitions ou "broderie" sur un même thème' [to see only repetition or an 'embroidering' on a single theme]. But the turning-over of similar contents is precisely what makes Rohmer's a singularly coherent body of work. Each new film becomes 'un commentaire, un prolongement et un "grossissement" ... de ce qui était resté en suspens dans [l]es films antérieurs' (a commentary, prolongation, and 'enlargement' of what was left unresolved in the previous films) (Païni 1997: 70). Seriality forces the viewer to adopt a self-critical attitude and to refuse absorption in favour of active comparison – precisely the kind of work we most often associate with literary reading.

As it examines the internal dynamics and discursive model(s) of each of Rohmer's three major series, the present chapter aims to problematise the notion that a classically inspired cinema of psychological refinements must be anti-modern or, worse, reactionary. Admittedly, Rohmer's universe is a closed one, restricted to a privileged social set with more than enough time on its hands to expatiate on topics like commitment, seduction, and contentment. But it is the ideological closure ensured by a relatively unchanging subject matter and, as we have seen, audiovisual style that has allowed the director to explore the tension that exists in film between narrative and theatre, between the desire to tell stories and the desire to act them out, between telling (Aristotle's *diegesis*) and showing (*mimesis*). Cast by some critics as a right-leaning bourgeois humanist, Rohmer can also be viewed, on the basis of his cycles, as the same manner of formalist that he and Chabrol considered Alfred Hitchcock to be: a consummate 'inventor of forms' (Rohmer and Chabrol 1957: 159).

Mediated desire and the first-person film: *Contes moraux*

Responding, in 1971, to a critic who disapproved his penchant for 'literary' filmmaking, Rohmer compared his *Contes moraux* to the work of a musician. On the model of symphonic theme and variation, he noted, each of the tales develops a core statement: a male protagonist who is committed to one woman is tempted by another, before returning to the first (Rohmer 1984: 128). The dramatic premise, needless to say, is unremarkable. If it has given rise to such poetic masterworks as Murnau's *Sunrise* (1927), which portrays desire as a battle between the corrupt, licentious city and the simple countryside, it has also engendered countless melodramas, bedroom farces, and second-rate tragedies which are best left in the vaults. Rohmer takes interest not in the subject of infidelity per se but in the dynamic and tonal contrasts enabled by its repeated treatment. While the most visible variations from film to film, like the choice of film stock (following Rohmer's official sequencing, tales one to three in black and white, four to six in Eastmancolor), locale, or season, patently reflect the filmmaker's commitment to recording the world's manifold beauty, these remain secondary to variations in dramatic content and audio-visual form.

The male leads of the *Contes moraux* all bear a family resemblance. Educated, white students and professionals in their twenties to mid-thirties, they are concerned less with realising personal goals in the world of things than with manipulating appearances. They invent moral principles to legitimate, before or after the fact, a chosen line of conduct, so as to appear at an advantage over those around them even should their plans fail. As Pascal Bonitzer notes, these non-heroic characters fashion themselves as heroes 'en imagination, par la puissance de leur rêverie' (via the imagination, by the sheer power of daydreaming) (Bonitzer 1991: 44); each analyses his position as a desiring and potentially desired individual in a loosely defined game of 'seduction'. Spontaneity is for Rohmer's male protagonists inconceivable, as their actions are part of a strategy whose goal is, in the end, egocentric.

The title *Contes moraux* itself has raised eyebrows. Understandably so, for the 'moral' standpoint of its protagonists may bear only a distant relation to what is commonly understood by morality, even as it falls well short of the depravity later showcased by Polish-born surrealist Walerian Borowzczyk in the very un-Rohmerian *Contes immoraux* (1974), a four-part exploration of sexual taboos. As much for the dandyish Adrien (*La Collectionneuse*) as for the middle-manager Frédéric (*L'Amour l'après-midi*), the resolution to sleep with the second woman, should circumstances permit, is no less moral than the contrary decision *not* to do so. If these tales can be called moral, it is primarily because their focus transcends the physical realm to depict the workings of an ethical consciousness. Libertinage appears abstractly, as a sheer hypothesis, irrespective of its accomplishment in a physical act. Indeed, what matters most to the heroes of the *Contes moraux* is the certainty that their position, which they shore up with rhetorical precautions and argumentative proofs, is impervious to attack. It is surprising to see how effortlessly a pirouette of reasoning can turn into victories their sentimental failures. And yet these heroes *do* desire in spite of themselves, perhaps more than they wish to admit. The tales they tell contain a measure of bad faith even as they correctly recall the Nietzschean inescapability of perspective.

Imagining themselves to be masters over their desire, the heroes each confront a similar dilemma: who, aside from the woman I have already chosen to love, might possibly deserve my affections? The precise terms in which that question is posed vary significantly. To begin with, the chosen woman and temptress, or 'l'élue' and 'la séductrice', as Marion Vidal has called them, display differences in age, status, and appearance that may influence the protagonist's choice (Vidal 1977: 37). Often the two women present opposing characteristics. In *La Boulangère de Monceau*, Sylvie is a tall, elegant blonde of some means, and Jacqueline, a short, dark-haired salesclerk; in *Ma Nuit chez Maud,* the blonde, Françoise, is a reserved Catholic from a modest background, and the brunette, Maud, an extroverted, wealthy free-thinker; in *L'Amour l'après-midi,* Hélène, who spends her time grading papers and tending house, is all practicality and stability, while the seductress Chloé, who works as a barmaid and waitress, is a long-haired, long-legged mess. Preference for the first woman is predicated on compatibility, both moral and physical, just as inclination towards the second suggests that compatibility alone is not enough.

As the cycle develops, the hero's relationship to the first woman seems to reflect increased levels of attachment. When action opens, the protagonist of *La Boulangère de Monceau* has yet to exchange a word with Sylvie, while in the next instalment Bertrand is already part of Suzanne's circle of acquaintances; in *La Collectionneuse,* the third tale in order of production (but labelled fourth by Rohmer), Adrien is dating Mijanou, while the engineer of *Ma Nuit chez Maud* seeks, and finds, the young Françoise whom he later will marry; in *Le Genou de Claire,* the vacationing diplomat Jérôme is shortly to wed Lucinde (shown in a photograph), and in *L'Amour l'après-midi* Frédéric and his spouse Hélène, comfortably set up in their suburban apartment, await their second child. Relations between protagonist and temptress are similarly varied, if their gradation is less stark. After a protracted courtship ritual, the game-playing law student of the first tale stands up Jacqueline for their first (and only) date. Bertrand, in the second, dances chastely with the upper-class Sophie at the annual business school ball. Adrien, who flatters himself that the 'collectionneuse' Haydée intends to add him to her list of lovers, kisses her as she sunbathes – only to have sand kicked in his face. The principled Catholic engineer of *Ma Nuit chez Maud* reluctantly abandons Maud's armchair for her bed, but when he half-heartedly cedes to temptation at dawn, the divorcee throws him out into the cold. Jérôme arguably comes closer to his object of desire when, rejected by the sixteen-year-old Laura, he schemes his way into caressing her older sister Claire's knee under the lakeside shelter (see figure 4). All these incidents of failed or partial contact with the second woman pale in comparison with the near fall from grace that concludes the series: Frédéric must wrest himself away from Chloé's naked body, fresh out of the shower (see figure 5), then offered up to him on her bed.

In no case does the protagonist consummate what we may assume to be 'his' desire. Again, as Bonitzer notes, Rohmer's characters – the men in particular – are less interested in being loved, in the physical sense, than in knowing that they are 'preferred' (Bonitzer 1991: 47). They believe their restraint to be grander than the heroism of sexual conquest; it is enough to know that one is capable of seducing the other. This can rightly be interpreted as a function of a post-liberation bitterness felt by French men for whom overt misogyny is no longer an option (Reynaud 200: 259). Yet as Maria Tortajada argues, the seduction practised by Rohmer's characters – male and female alike – is based on connivance, or the mutual acceptance of an unwritten rule, instead of the more frank scenario of victimisation (Tortajada 1999: 26). The gender politics of the *Contes moraux* are indeed far more subtle and complex than the images of Haydée's bikini-clad body, fetishistically cut up in the first prologue to *La Collectionneuse*, would suggest; Adrien's muscular midriff will also get its share of exposure.

While it is not inaccurate to describe the *Contes moraux* as following a three-point pattern wherein a man's desire is caught between two women, it is potentially misleading to do so. Only the first and last pictures cohere to this skeletal three-person model. In all other cases, a fourth figure, usually a man, mediates the circulation of a desire that theorist René Girard describes as 'mimetic': by playing the role of counsellor, helper, rival, or any of these in alternation, the fourth figure gives rise to the desire of the hero, which is not really the latter's 'own' but rather a reflection of the social structures in place.

The figure of the mediator appears but fleetingly in *La Boulangère de Monceau*, as if to hint at its future role in the series. The protagonist's diminutive sidekick Schmidt orchestrates a run-in on the sidewalk with Sylvie, whom the duo had observed for some time in the neighbourhood. Once contact is established between the protagonist and Sylvie, Schmidt disappears, leaving his friend to his own devices. In the absence of a mediator, a three-point geography of desire is inscribed on the street corner where most of the short's action unfolds: the bakery on one side of the rue Lebouteux, Sylvie's apartment on the other, and the mobile protagonist in-between.

La Carrière de Suzanne both intensifies and inverts the relationship between hero and mediator posed in the first tale. Now, it is the Don-Juan-like Guillaume who is the desiring subject, while the timid narrator Bertrand is relegated to the role of witness and helper.

Bertrand observes with unhealthy fascination as the more sexually experienced Guillaume courts Suzanne and, to spite her, flirts with Sophie. Rather than feel jealousy toward Guillaume, Bertrand instead aids him in winning the last favours of Suzanne and in shamelessly exploiting the money she earns as a health-care worker. His desire is, in every way, the desire of the other: unable to desire either woman on his own terms or to devise a strategy through which to move from passivity to action, Bertrand would seem most to crave the attentions of Guillaume himself. When some banknotes he has stashed inside an uncut paperback disappear, Bertrand, like a hurt lover, suspects Suzanne, although the likely culprit is the chronically broke and unscrupulous Guillaume. In the end, Suzanne puts both men in their place, demoting them to the rank of mere 'gamins' (kids) by marrying Franck, whose maturity and good looks put them to shame.

La Collectionneuse similarly highlights the ambivalence of male desire, pointing up the strong homosocial bonds that unite Adrien and Daniel against Haydée (see figure 2). The two men, whose sole objective in coming to the country villa is to disconnect, at first see the young woman as unworthy of their attentions and sorely indiscriminate in her choice of sex partners. As Haydée quickly accedes to Adrien and Daniel's demands for peace and quiet, her presence at the villa begins to fluster both men. Their ambiguous posturing is evident when Adrien asks Daniel to do him the 'favour' of sleeping with Haydée – ostensibly to avoid having to do so himself. Each defers to the other in a test of an unwritten homosocial pact:

> DANIEL: Couche avec elle. D'ailleurs, à ta place, je foncerais.
> ADRIEN: Et bien, vas-y..., fonce, toi!
> DANIEL: Oh! non. Je n'ai plus envie de faire le moindre effort.[1]

Amused by Adrien's tactics and convinced that the supreme exploit is to make oneself disliked by a woman (men, however, may be another issue), Daniel closes the conversation with the injunction, 'mais baisez-la, mon vieux!' (just screw her, mate!). The comment is disingenuous, for by the next morning Daniel himself has joined Haydée's collection. Whatever harmony existed among the three characters is broken thereafter, degrading into psychological warfare of the meanest sort. After Daniel's parting diatribe against Haydée, a

1 '–Sleep with her. Say, in your place, I'd go for it. –Well then, *you* go for it. –Oh no, I no longer feel like making the slightest effort.'

second mediator appears in the person of Sam, the American antique dealer for whom Adrien, in need of a financial backer to start an art gallery, procures a ninth-century Song vase. To ensure the deal's success, Adrien convinces Haydée to stay overnight at Sam's home. But she remains playfully indifferent to her elders' high-cultural pursuits, causing the precious Chinese vase to fall to the floor, as if to remind those present that she is no empty vessel to be exchanged between men. Indeed, after leading Adrien into thinking that he will be her next acquisition, Haydée abruptly leaves town. Mediators, rivals, and that obscure object of desire now absent, Adrien has no choice but to join his girlfriend Mijanou in London, bringing the narrative back to square one. His vacation is but a moral parenthesis, a testing ground for self-imposed rules.

Ma Nuit chez Maud features a more conventional mediator in the philosopher Vidal, an old friend of the protagonist and, importantly, Maud's former lover. Vidal's initial role in the café discussion of Pascal's wager is to bring the protagonist to explain his moral position. But Vidal also takes up one classic function of the confidant by introducing the protagonist to Maud, who has recently divorced. Drunk and mischievous after a long evening at the table, and dejected as he knows his one-time mistress will not have him back, he tricks his friend into spending the snowbound night with Maud (there is no 'guest room' in her apartment). Since the protagonist's sights are already set on Françoise, however, the mimetic desire triangulated by Vidal does not take hold, and Maud's bedside overtures go nowhere. Even if the hero consorts with Maud after their 'night' together, taking hikes in the snow-covered mountains or cooking dinner in her flat, their relationship falls short of the full spiritual commitment he seeks. A chance encounter and inclement weather force the hero to spend a second night out, this time at the modest boarding house where Françoise lives. But Françoise is not, he soon discovers, the ideal churchgoer he thought her to be: 'J'ai un amant. Enfin, j'ai eu, ce n'est pas tellement loin' (I have a lover. Or I had one, not so long ago), she confesses in the memorable hilltop scene (see figure 3). In response, the hero evokes his own 'infidelity' with Maud, uttering what is at best a half-truth. Attentive spectators may have guessed, based on a knowing glance Françoise exchanged with Vidal one evening in Clermont, that Françoise's lover was none other than Maud's husband – something the hero realises only five years later when the two women cross paths at the beach. Vidal, we assume, kept silent so that his friend could follow through in good faith on his 'moral' resolve. If the lead character's credo is never to say black, after having said white ('[ne pas] dire blanc, après avoir dit noir'), the narrative itself points to myriad shades of grey.

It is telling that the chief interlocutor of Jérôme, the hero of *Le Genou de Claire*, is a novelist and a woman. Aurora, whom the diplomat had met in Bucharest six years earlier, has put relationships with men on hold, preferring to study those around her as inspiration for her fiction. Jérôme, who has come to Tailloires to spend his final weeks as an unmarried man, has nothing but time on his hands, and before long finds himself wrapped up in Aurora's fanciful constructions, halfway between fiction and reality. Rarely has Rohmer given more insight into his poetics than in Aurora's conversations with Jérôme, which point to a theory of literary and, by implication, cinematic creation. When Jérôme states that, Aurora's hopes to the contrary, there will be no 'story' to tell at vacation's end, the novelist retorts: 'Il se passera toujours quelque chose, ne fût-ce que ton refus que quelque chose se passe' (Something will happen all the same, if only your refusal that anything happen) – an apt characterisation of the *Contes moraux* themselves. The course of events suggests that Jérôme, an eighteenth-century libertine in contemporary dress, wished for nothing more than a respectable pretext for playing games with adolescents half his age. When he has finished toying with the ingénue Laura, he is all too happy to assail her older sister Claire, whose boyfriend, the haughty but fashionable Gilles, he wholly disapproves of. But when he recounts to Aurora his triumph – having avenged Gilles's mindless gesture of placing his hand on Claire's knee – the novelist laughs, deflating Jérôme's pseudo-heroic posture: 'Je pense que c'est très bien raconté... C'est dommage que je ne sache pas la sténo' (I think you told it very well. It's a pity I don't know shorthand). To save face, Jérôme claims that he acted only out of friendship for Aurora – a claim little substantiated by the facts. Indeed, the film's closing shot, which shows, from Jérôme's point of view, lovers Gilles and Claire on a bench overlooking the lake, intimates that it is the younger generation that makes out best in the end. While Jérôme has resigned himself to a marriage of convenience and habit – 'Si je l'épouse, c'est que je sais par expérience que je peux vivre avec elle' (If I'm marrying her, it's because I know from experience that I can live with her), he says of Lucinde – the youth he envies cling to an idea of uncomplicated, romantic love that the spectator cannot dismiss out of hand.

Like the opening short of the series, the concluding feature, *L'Amour l'après-midi*, lacks a strong fourth character. Frédéric's conviction that all women are all equally receptive to his charms dispels the need for a mediator, now supplanted by the erotic imaginary. 'En étreignant Hélène, j'étreins toutes les femmes' (When I embrace Hélène, I'm embracing all women), the hero affirms, reconciling the bourgeois principle of monogamy with the virile fantasy of unbridled possession. In the epilogue's concluding sequence, Frédéric imagines himself the bearer of a magical amulet which dismantles the willpower of all women who fall in its range. The actresses of *La Collectionneuse*, *Ma Nuit chez Maud*, and *Le Genou de Claire* one by one submit to his desires. A streetwalker, played by Aurora Cornu, instead of accepting money for her services, pays Frédéric for his, exclaiming that his price is a bargain; only the feisty Laura/Béatrice Romand resists the necklace's power. This fantasmatic mode of desire is undone when, in Part One, Chloé appears unannounced in the hero's office. A vague acquaintance from a distant past, Chloé progresses from being a thorn in Frédéric's side to an intimate friend whose entrances and exits leave the hero jittery and his secretaries in giggles. With time, Frédéric discovers that his rivals are not Chloé's occasional boyfriends, but his own demons: if he were to assent to Chloé's wish to make him the father of her child, it would mean that his love for his spouse Hélène was not absolute. The comic image, glimpsed in Chloé's bathroom mirror, of his turtleneck pulled halfway over his head sends Frédéric running back to Hélène. In the final scene, the title *L'Amour l'après-midi* changes from an antiphrasis – Frédéric never makes love to Chloé, in the afternoon or at any other hour – to a just description of the narrator's petty-bourgeois apotheosis: after his wife breaks down and cries in his arms, the couple steals off to the bedroom, reunited like the couple of Murnau's *Sunrise*.

Rohmer once remarked that the screenplays of the *Contes moraux* might well have been written by a computer (Simsolo 1970: 88). If relations among characters do indeed have a combinatoric air about them, they nonetheless display all the nuances proper to art, less precise in its representations than mathematics. These variations extend to audiovisual form itself, unusual in that each film adapts a first-person tale. As Marion Vidal writes,

> l'œuvre de Rohmer-écrivain, est ... adaptée par Rohmer-cinéaste avec autant de respect et de fidélité que s'il s'agissait d'un classique de la littérature.[2] (Vidal 1977: 11)

The choice of first-person source texts poses a key question: how to film from the perspective of a given character while making that character's actions visible onscreen? Unlike Robert Montgomery's *The Lady in the Lake* (1946), which takes point of view to the brink of self-contradiction by attributing every shot to its roaming hero, the *Contes moraux* avoid subjective camera and limit point-of-view shots primarily to eyeline matches of an informational sort. A true first-person cinema, suggests Rohmer, cannot hope to collapse primary (spectator-to-camera) and secondary (spectator-to-character) identification. The solution lies rather in the mediating power of language, or more precisely 'le contrepoint du texte et de la pellicule' (the counterpoint of text and filmstrip) (Rohmer 1984: 61).

Le Genou de Claire excepted, each moral tale conjoins a source of selective authority – the offscreen voice of the narrator-protagonist – and a focalised, but more 'objective' audiovisual rendering of events. Actions are experienced doubly, as they are lived in the (edited) present of their unfolding, and as they are interpreted or glossed by the narrator in hindsight. The film's content becomes not a set of events but an individual's point of view on those events (Rohmer 1998: 10). The presence of the storyteller on the soundtrack tempers the effects of photographic illusion, preventing the spectator from becoming absorbed in the story-world. Caught between subjective and objective modes of presentation, the image thus takes on qualities similar to those of 'free indirect' literary discourse (Deleuze 1983: 110).

Variations in the use of audiovisual counterpoint arise from film to film. *La Boulangère de Monceau* tightly links offscreen utterance and image, making it impossible to decide whether the commentary explains the diegetic sounds and images or whether the latter illustrate the former. *La Carrière de Suzanne* favours voiceover in transitional moments or when the protagonist is alone, while Adrien's perfect-tense commentary in *La Collectionneuse* records key incidents and thoughts as a diarist might in his journal. The ascetic *Ma Nuit chez Maud* pares down the protagonist's interior remarks to two critical moments: first, his realisation, while following Françoise on

2 'the work of Rohmer the writer is adapted by Rohmer the filmmaker with as much respect and fidelity as if it were a literary classic.'

her motorbike through lamp-lit Clermont, that she would one day be his wife; and second, after his seaside meeting with Maud in the epilogue, his understanding that Maud's husband's mistress was none other than Françoise, now his wife. Less talkative than its predecessors – Rohmer surmised that a second layer of discourse would have made his hero unbearable (Simsolo 1970: 89) –, the 1969 film remains functionally no less 'narrated' than they, since the hero's two offscreen interventions suffice to drive an ironic wedge between text and filmstrip. In *Le Genou de Claire*, by contrast, the director eliminates offscreen voiceover altogether. Yet by recounting his exploits to Aurora, Jérôme asserts his authority as storyteller all the same: the oral 'tale' is simply folded into the diegesis, instead of superimposed on the soundtrack. The result is a back-and-forth movement between declared intention and act, between the event and its recapitulation. To bring the series full circle, *L'Amour l'après-midi* gives ample space to the narrator's reveries in voiceover. The commentary, much of it disarmingly personal – 'Je rêve d'une vie qui ne soit faite que de premières amours – et d'amours durables: c'est dire que je veux l'impossible' (I dream of a life made only of first loves – and loves that last. That's to say I want the impossible) – intervenes especially in those segments where the protagonist is shown to be lost in thought, staring out a café window or standing on a commuter train. Each step in his loss of self-mastery brought about by Chloé becomes the occasion for such reflections.

Audio-visual form in the *Contes moraux* is, is sum, anything but monolithic. If, in the abstract, one can dissociate the present tense of story events from the perfect tense of the commentary, constant slippage occurs between these two lines of flight. The truth of each tale ultimately lies neither in its telling by the protagonist–narrator, nor in the 'objective' succession of diegetic events and sounds, but in the dialogic interaction of the two. This is a formal, rather than moral truth, one that engages spectators' freedom by inviting them to contrast observed behaviours and *a posteriori* interpretations. Do the heroes' declarations and self-descriptions conform to the visual record, or are their verbal strategies mere smokescreens designed to hide from view compromising intersubjective facts? Whether under any circumstances language allows for an authentic rapport with other individuals is, Rohmer's first series suggests, anything but certain. Offscreen narration seems above all to exemplify the need for self-justification shared by these 'moral' heroes, unable as they are to live with the idea of their own insignificance.

A discreet theatricality: *Comédies et proverbes*

For Rohmer, the ironic confrontation of thought and action in the *Contes moraux* was inseparable from the novel: 'Je suis plus proche du roman, d'une certaine forme de roman classique ... que du spectacle, du théâtre' (I'm closer to the novel – to a certain classic novel form – than to spectacle, to theatre), he stated confidently in a 1970 interview (Nogueira 1971: 45). Ten years later, after *Perceval le Gallois* and *Catherine de Heilbronn*, no doubt the director could have claimed the inverse to be true. His second cycle, launched in 1981 with *La Femme de l'aviateur*, explicitly sets out to reconcile theatre and film – long seen as mortal enemies by the likes of Robert Bresson (Bresson 1988: 21) – in a pointed exploration of the contemporary cult of appearances, where artifice and naturalness meet.

Since Rohmer did not assign himself a core theme upon which to perform variations, the narrative premises and complications, if not the outcomes, of the six films are less predictable than in the *Contes moraux*. Lighter in tone than the previous series, the *Comédies et proverbes* focus on young women and men in their twenties whose sentimental ups and downs are tinged by pragmatic rather than ethical concerns (Rohmer 1999: I, 8). The absence of voiceover narration reminds us that we are no longer in the space of the tale; storytelling has given way to theatrical enactment. With the exception of *Le Rayon vert*, the films are scripted in a brisk manner reminiscent of Hollywood's sophisticated comedies of the 1940s, Hitchcock's droll *The Trouble with Harry* (1955), or the late period Jean Renoir. Consistent pacing lends them significant homogeneity despite the use of four different cinematographers and two formats (two pictures were shot in 16mm), as does the attribution to each of an assertive colour scheme, usually two or three dominant tones that tie together wardrobe, decors, and seasons.

But it is to the group title that we must turn if we are to grasp the series' specific character. The title directly references the work of dramatist Alfred de Musset (1810–1857), a late romantic noted for his love of exotic settings and historical themes who first collected his plays in 1840 under the title *Comédies et proverbes*. Some works, like *Les Caprices de Marianne*, Musset labelled 'comedies', while others, the titles of which are themselves popular sayings – *On ne badine pas avec l'amour, Il ne faut jurer de rien* – he classified as 'proverbs'. Rohmer makes no equivalent distinction among his six films, to the effect that we must look simultaneously to both registers, the theatrical and the proverbial.

Theatricality in the *Comédies et proverbes* is not primarily a question of performance style, the precious diction of players like Fabrice Luchini or Arielle Dombasle notwithstanding. At issue is rather a debt to classical, romantic, and even vaudeville dramaturgy. Save the loosely episodic *Le Rayon vert*, series instalments obey a scenic logic, predicated on characters' entrances and exits, rather than a sequential one, in which the camera would possess independent narrative authority. Dialogue is the prime motor of action; as in stage comedy, events become meaningful because characters talk about them (they need not be shown). Verbal exchanges are linked through rapid descriptions of character trajectories – from suburb to city (*Les Nuits de la pleine lune*), from Paris to Le Mans (*Le Beau Mariage*), from summer house to beach (*Pauline à la plage*). These intermediary sequences situate action geographically and sociologically with a precision that goes well beyond the simplified 'côté cour/côté jardin' (stage right/stage left) of classical theatre. Within limits, no digressions or secondary lines of action are permitted; all plot ramifications must arise out of the film's exposition, though on occasion a secondary character may be introduced later in the film, like Lucie, the raincoat-wearing high-school student of *La Femme de l'aviateur*, or Louisette, the candy seller in *Pauline à la plage*. The series' dramatic economy is thus wholly distinct from the Hollywood screenwriters' model, in which the successive challenges faced by the hero need not all be contained in the initial premise. This does not mean, however, that the *Comédies et proverbes* do not hold their share of surprises: to the contrary, revelations, chance encounters, and misunderstandings abound.

Beyond the scenic level, dramatic structure may recall the acts of a stage play. *La Femme de l'aviateur* features a prologue (François chats with his co-worker in the postal sorting centre), a first act (François tries to convince Anne that he is a worthier suitor than the aviator), a second act (François meets Lucie in the park and spies on the aviator), a third act (François presents Anne with the 'proof' of the aviator's worthlessness), and an epilogue (François is in for a surprise). In *Le Beau Mariage*, Sabine resolves to leave her lover and get married (Act I), encounters with the help of Clarisse a worthy candidate (Act II), begins courting Edmond (Act III), mounts an offensive at her birthday party, covering herself in ridicule (Act IV), and is rebuffed after a final hearing (Act V). In *Pauline à la plage*, it is not difficult to identify an exposition (four adults and two teenagers meet up at the beach, each in search of a partner), a complication (Marion, who sleeps with Henri, encourages Pierre to indoctrinate her cousin Pauline in love), a dramatic *nœud* or knot (Pierre spies Louisette making love to a man), a *dénouement* (Henri confesses to Pierre that he, not Pauline's boyfriend Sylvain, was with Louisette), and what seems to be a suitably happy end (Pauline and Sylvain are reconciled). *Les Nuits de la pleine lune* and *L'Ami de mon amie* similarly present act-like divisions, where individual confrontations create tension, suspense, and release. In none of the *Comédies et proverbes* do these divisions announce themselves as such; whatever title cards there are signal the passing of calendar time.

Control over the range of information suggests a compromise between the stage, in which point of view is partly at the spectator's discretion, and narrative cinema, where the camera may single out one or more characters for our attention. In four films point of view stays on a single character, present in nearly every scene: the postal clerk François in *La Femme de l'aviateur*, the art history student Sabine in *Le Beau mariage*, the interior designer Louise in *Les Nuits de la pleine lune*, and the secretary Delphine in *Le Rayon vert*. *Pauline à la plage*, contrary to what the title suggests, gives no more screen time to Pauline's adventures that to those of her cousin Marion and the windsurfer Pierre. The camera in *L'Ami de mon amie* initially stays with Blanche, but once the game of musical chairs gets rolling, perspective occasionally shifts to her friend and rival Léa.

By placing the spectator at an informational advantage over his characters or on a par with them, Rohmer envelops actions and declarations with situational irony. This is critical to the success of a dramatic staple of the series, namely the vaudeville conceit of mistaken identity or *quid pro quo*. Four films feature the motif: in *La Femme de l'aviateur*, under dispute is the identity of the mysterious blonde who accompanies the pilot to the park and a law office nearby; in *Pauline à la plage*, that of Louisette's lover, hidden from Pierre's view behind the bedroom window; in *Les Nuits de la pleine lune*, that of a hat-wearing woman whom Octave spots with Louise's boyfriend Rémi in a Paris café; in *L'Ami de mon amie*, that of Blanche's partner in the love affair which took place during Léa's absence. The solution of the *quid pro quo* may work to the satisfaction of all parties, as in the comic conclusion to *L'Ami de mon amie*, when the two couples are rearranged in keeping with their perfectly matched green and blue outfits. It may also yield mixed results, as in the concluding break-up scene of *Les Nuits de la pleine lune*, where Rémi's ecstasy at having found a new girlfriend magnifies Louise's dejection at having lost the man she only now thinks she should love.

Rohmer's characters sport contemporary fashions, from blouses and scarves to wetsuits, and inhabit contemporary decors, like the suburban new towns of Marne-la-Vallée and Cergy-Pontoise, with their postmodern estates and neatly kept public spaces. But even as they wear 1980s style on their sleeve, they remain very much the descendants of La Bruyère, Molière, and Musset. Several characters bear first names that have all but fallen into disuse (Octave, Clarisse, Blanche) and many, following the stage convention, do not even have a surname. Their existence as individuals is further mitigated by their conformity to classical type. So in *Pauline à la plage*, the title character is a young *ingénue*, Marion a self-absorbed *précieuse*, Pierre a *soupirant* turned *jaloux*, and Henri a disabused *séducteur*; this coterie of masters is rounded out by the two servants, the candy-seller Louisette as the *soubrette* and Sylvain as the feisty *valet*; all that is missing in Rohmer's impossibly youthful world is an aged *barbon*, the gruff *pater familias* who most often in the French theatrical tradition gets his come-uppance. In *L'Ami de mon amie*, the individuality of any given character disappears behind the role: Blanche is a timid and painfully honest *soupirante*, Léa her all too trustworthy *confidente*, and Adrienne a *rivale* and counsellor of sorts; on the side of the *jeunes premiers* there is the talented playboy Alexandre and the affable yet insecure Fabien. Rohmer's sleight of hand consists in letting the spectator believe in the real-world existence of each character while suppressing those traits we consider to be constitutive of identity. While we get brief descriptive shots of characters in their place of work, like Sabine in the antique shop, Louise in her design studio, or Fabien in his chemistry laboratory, little information about their origins, personal histories, or family ties is forthcoming. Like their elusive creator Rohmer/Schérer himself, these are characters without a biography or even a rudimentary back-story, so many echoes of a classical pantheon of human types that stand paradoxically outside of history even as they inhabit the most real of worlds, surrounded by pedestrians who, in most cases, are not paid extras but, in photographer's lingo, 'real people' through and through.

We saw earlier how the *Contes moraux* depict desire as an either/or alternative. In that first series, the male hero's position of moral retreat arises from the fact that any admission on his part of the reality of his desire for the second woman would prove his earlier choice – to love one woman exclusively – to have been in error. Throughout the *Contes moraux*, it is assumed that the second woman, who is usually young and always unmarried, is free to choose her partner; she more or less overtly solicits and puts to the test the male hero's desire, if only to obtain narcissistic satisfaction. The women protagonists of the *Comédies et proverbes* are similarly free to make their own decisions in matters of love. The conflict they experience, however, is no longer one of being the object of an unresolved, ambivalent desire. It is rather that they want to be loved by a person whose attentions are already invested in another object.

The individual *Comédies et proverbes* can thus be read as variations on the motif of non-reciprocated love, in which the wish formulated by the protagonist – and often by other characters – fails to elicit a satisfactory response. In *La Femme de l'aviateur*, desire resembles a broken chain: François pines after Anne, who is in love with the aviator; the aviator himself has lost interest in Anne and may have a new mistress or perhaps, as he claims, have returned to his wife. *Le Beau Mariage* simplifies this pattern by cutting off the flow of desire: Sabine, who has left her married lover Simon, decides that Edmond will marry her 'de gré ou de force', willing or not. Though mildly curious and amused by her entreaties, Edmond prefers to devote his energies to his law career, leaving the single-minded Sabine in the lurch. Complexity returns with *Pauline à la plage*: Pierre wants Marion, an old friend who has recently divorced, to love him as he loves her; Marion, who has only amicable thoughts for Pierre, desires the mature Henri. If Henri sleeps with Marion, it is only to add another woman to his collection (it's not for nothing that this Don Juan is an ethnographer); the same goes for his fling with Louisette. The only authentic relationship – as bland as it is simple – is that of adolescents Pauline and Sylvain, which the cynical Henri all but destroys through his libertine scheming.

In *Les Nuits de la pleine lune*, the heroine's choice of object is less at issue than is the precise timing of her desire. Louise is uncertain of her love for Rémi, who appears more dedicated to urban planning and fitness than to their relationship. She seeks independence and, feeling like a new town animal in a furnished cage, decides to redecorate a flat of her own in central Paris where she can spend weekends. Subjected time and again to the overtures of the self-absorbed writer Octave, to whom she is not attracted, she ends up sleeping with a virtual stranger one night after a party. Sleepless and heavy with regret, she returns to the suburbs at dawn to make amends with Rémi, only to discover that he has since met another woman. If the aleatory nature of desire ruins Louise's chances for fulfilment, it works to more positive ends in *Le Rayon vert*. Delphine, who wants companionship but is armed with only vague ideas about how to achieve it, skits about from place to place during a summer vacation that is going nowhere; a chance encounter with a handsome man in the Biarritz train station revives her hopes, which are confirmed by the near-miraculous appearance of the green ray as the sun recedes on the horizon. Delphine's desire for love, in a moment of unhoped-for plenitude that can be described as 'grace' (Reynaud 2000: 259), manifests itself at the same time as does its object. To close the series, *L'Ami de mon amie*'s game of musical chairs reintroduces ambiguity and failed reciprocity: Blanche is attracted to Léa's ex-boyfriend Alexandre, whose feelings are not mutual; Léa is in a hot-and-cold relationship with Fabien, who readily admits that she is not his type; Léa is attracted to Alexandre (both enjoy seduction) but does not wish to hurt Blanche's feelings; Blanche is inclined towards Fabien (both enjoy water sports) but has qualms about stealing her best friend's boyfriend (she sleeps with him anyway, just once, 'pour que cela reste merveilleux' [to keep it magical]). The permutations of the film's love plot are as diabolical as those of any of Marivaux's comedies. In the end, the disorder of conflicting and indifferent desires is reorganised into the fiction of all too perfectly matched pairs, who for all their 'differences' seem indistinguishable in the end, so many reflections of an identikit era. As Alain Hertay has written, the surface appearances of modernity, exemplified by the narcissistic cult of the 'standardised' body, hide an underlying malaise in Rohmer's universe – the notion that something resembling identity has been lost (Hertay 1998: 90–2).

Even in those *Comédies et proverbes* which end on a sardonic note, like *Le Beau Mariage* or *Les Nuits de la pleine lune*, the comic register can be felt in the inadequacy of characters' amorous strategies. In keeping with the French expression 'se jouer la comédie' (to trick oneself), the series title alludes to the way characters lure themselves into believing one version of events instead of another, or how they put themselves on stage at their own expense (Rohmer 1999: I, 8). François's detective work in the Buttes-Chaumont does little to help his cause with Anne, for whom being loved by someone willing to find a handyman to fix a broken kitchen pipe is an insufficient reason to love in return. Sabine's insistence that the respectably bourgeois Edmond be her husband within thirty days is folly of the sort that directors like Howard Hawks turned into screwball, with a race to the finish. Louise's belief that Rémi will put up indefinitely with her wish to spend her weekends in Paris attending trendy *soirées* and to live the steely life of a suburban couple weeknights is wishful thinking. Marion likewise deludes herself in believing that Henri slept with her out of love, just as Léa fools herself in assuming that Blanche, less pure than her name suggests, will keep her hands off Fabien. All things considered, Rohmer's view of such self-deluding female characters lies on the tender side of irony: losing out on a fine catch is no great tragedy, for there will always be another round in the game of love and chance.

Not unlike Marivaux or late-nineteenth-century dramatist Georges Courteline, Rohmer understands comedy to mean something other than conflicts with positive outcomes. To the principle 'all's well that ends well' he opposes the notion that all may not end so well as it seems, if indeed it has ended at all. Endings in *Comédies et proverbes* invariably steer us back to beginnings, specifically to the proverb whose spirit presides over each film. How is our appreciation of the proverb's meaning transformed by the narrative we have just witnessed? To what extent does the proverb invite competing or divergent readings, in keeping with the director's remark that 'on pourra, comme dans les *Fables* de La Fontaine, trouver à la même pièce plusieurs moralités' (as in La Fontaine's *Fables*, one can find several morals for the same text)? (Rohmer 1999: I, 7)

While Rohmer has sought to downplay the influence that Musset exerted on the series' conception, his practice nevertheless invites comparison with the dramatist's, not least because the saying which fronts *La Femme de l'aviateur*, 'On ne saurait penser à rien' (One can't think of nothing), explicitly rewrites Musset's *On ne saurait penser à tout* (One can't think of everything). In other works of Musset's like *On ne badine pas avec l'amour* (Love's no joking matter) and *Il ne faut jurer de rien* (Never say never), the title proverb may be present in the dialogues or dramatic premises. In the latter play, for example, the nephew of a rich textile merchant swears that never will he marry the woman his uncle has picked for him, celibacy being a sure-fire prevention against becoming a cuckold (the nephew, aptly named Valentin, of course falls in love with that very woman).

La Femme de l'aviateur works in more subtle manner than this. Not until the next-to-last sequence does the proverb come into focus. Lying in bed in her aqua-blue studio apartment, Anne converses with François, who paces nervously about. After telling François that the aeroplane pilot has just dumped her, she produces a photograph showing her former lover flanked by two women. One of these catches François's eye: it is the blonde whom he and Lucie, playing Sherlock Holmes, had trailed earlier that day in the park. When Anne reveals the blonde to be the aviator's sister, François can barely contain himself:

> ANNE: A quoi tu penses?
> FRANÇOIS: A rien.
> ANNE: Si. Il y a quelque chose. Tu as l'air perdu dans tes pensées.
> FRANÇOIS: C'est sans importance.
> ANNE: Qu'est-ce que c'est?
> FRANÇOIS: Rien. Ça ne t'arrive jamais de ne penser à rien?
> ANNE: Ben non, justement. Moi, je pense toujours à quelque chose.
> FRANÇOIS: Oui, mais à quelque chose qui n'est rien.
> ANNE: Allez! c'est quoi?[3]

This is typical Rohmerian banter. One character clearly has something on his mind, and the other character knows it; by claiming that a matter is unimportant, the first character piques the curiosity of the second the better to establish an upper hand – and perhaps to attain something in the process. With prodding, François tells Anne the story of his afternoon, speaking not of the pilot and the blonde

3 'Whatcha thinking about? –Nothing. –No. Something's up. You look lost in your thoughts. –It's not important. –What is it? –Nothing. Don't you ever think about nothing? –Well, no, not really. I'm always thinking about something. –Yes, but something that isn't anything. –So out with it!'

(that mystery is now solved), but of his encounter with Lucie, whose mystery remains. In spite of himself, he lets on his elation at having struck up conversation with the fifteen-year-old *lycéenne*, now very much on his mind. He will have a good bit more to ponder later that evening, when, on his way to post a letter informing Lucie of his discovery, he spies his co-worker embracing the very person he was looking for... The film's proverb remains a general comment on the human condition, pointing to the fact that in Rohmer's world, most everyone is preoccupied with his or her standing: Am I preferred? Am I as present in the other's thoughts as I hope to be?

In three films of the cycle, the proverb directly describes the protagonist's plight. *Le Beau Mariage* quotes from La Fontaine: 'Quel esprit ne bat la campagne/Qui ne fait château en Espagne'. Two figurative expressions are conjoined here, 'battre la campagne' (to daydream) and 'faire des châteaux en Espagne' (to build castles in the air). Those who let their mind wander and hatch farfetched plans, in other words, are in for a surprise when reality comes rolling in. Such is the predicament of Sabine. In chasing after Edmond, she makes a few right moves, like helping him find a nineteenth-century Jersey porcelain vase for his mother, and several wrong ones, chief among them insisting that he attend her teeny-bopper birthday party, at which she dons a white princess dress suited for a ten-year-old. Sabine's noble intentions do nothing to change the fact that she is pursuing a pipe dream. The same goes for Louise in *Les Nuits de la pleine lune*, who is patently the 'Qui' of the second half of the rhymed couplet 'Qui a deux femmes perd son âme/Qui a deux maisons perd la raison' (Who has two women loses his soul/Who has two homes loses his mind). Infidelity, this part-invented proverb suggests, may be less of a handicap in the modern age than wanting to lead two lifestyles simultaneously – in Louise's case, those of city dweller and suburbanite. The proverb to *Le Rayon vert*, 'Ah, que les temps viennent/Où les cœurs s'éprennent' (May the time come/When hearts catch aflame), a slightly modified quotation from poet Arthur Rimbaud, is arguably more encouraging. One the one hand, it calls for romantic rebirth, cheering on Delphine in her efforts to rise out of the doldrums; on the other, it ironically describes the lassitude and impatience that Delphine's voyage cannot but arouse in the spectator (will she ever dry her tears and get on with it?).

In a distinct vein, the proverbs to *Pauline à la plage* and *L'Ami de mon amie* apply to a wider cast of characters. In the first film, Marion and Pierre, and perhaps too Henri, hinder their chances at success by saying too much too soon, echoing the quote 'Qui trop parole, il se mesfait' (He who speaks too much wrongs himself), which Rohmer lifts from Chrétien de Troyes's *Perceval*. In the second, the delightfully perverse proverb 'Les amis de mes amis sont mes amis' (My friend's friends are my friends) would seems to border on tautology. Yet the meaning of the noun 'ami', in context, changes from one iteration to the next. The consensual reading of the phrase is that the romantic partners of one's close friends ('Les amis de mes amis' = my friends' boyfriends or girlfriends) must remain one's platonic friends ('amis'), and nothing more. With its non-gendered plural forms, the proverb diverges from the film's title, *L'Ami de mon amie*, which reintroduces the feminine and the singular. The tension between the two forms suggests that if the film's characters are theoretically disposed to the idea of fraternity, there may nonetheless be singular cases in which the rules of collegiality no longer apply. The title speaks for Blanche – her friend Léa's boyfriend, Fabien, will become her own lover for a night – but can also be read from Léa's own perspective, interrogatively, as 'who did my friend Blanche sleep with, my ex-boyfriend, Fabien, or my current one, Alexandre?' Any of these readings will confirm the key place given in the film to rivalry and complicity between women.

On account of their structure and tone, the *Comédies et proverbes* have understandably drawn numerous comparisons to the plays of Marivaux, Musset, or Feydeau. To judge the cycle solely on plot and character or on its 'proverbial' content, however, is to underestimate what is truly original in Rohmer's cinema, namely the cognitive dissonance that results from staging fictional events in a world we recognise as real. By projecting dramatic content onto precisely observed contemporary locations, from the seaside resorts of Normandy and the provincial streets of Le Mans to the new towns of suburban Paris, the filmmaker makes us reconsider theatricality not as value-added artistry or artifice, but as the product of necessity and chance in everyday life. Aesthetic qualities of plot can thus be attributed, via a double reading, both to the guiding hand of the author and to the capacities for theatrical expression latent in the social world. In the end, there is nothing implausible about the scenarios of non-reciprocated desire and sentimental defeat that the *Comédies et proverbes* present. Theirs is a discreet theatricality which, unlike the assertive off-screen narration of the *Contes moraux*, supports film form as if from underneath, rather than lays itself out on the surface.

Rhyme schemes: *Contes des quatre saisons*

That Rohmer should have turned to the season cycle for inspiration in his third film series, completed between 1990 and 1998, is unsurprising. The quest to capture the world's ever-changing beauty in relation to transitional moments in the lives of fictional characters fits comfortably in the seasonal framework. Nature's elemental order replaces the arbitrary divisions that art imposes on experience, such that the project takes on an all but universal dimension. At the same time, Rohmer's choice is somewhat perverse, so worked-over is the seasonal trope in domains ranging from program music and poetry to decorative panels and sculptural allegory. Whereas in the *Contes moraux* and *Comédies et proverbes* the director clearly breaks new ground, here the danger of triviality and academicism is real.

True to classical form, Rohmer seeks neither to celebrate uncritically nor to demystify the four seasons conceit. Following the rules of the genre, each tale, limited to a few days' or weeks' time, unfolds when signs of a change in the weather are apparent: potted flowers in window-boxes and blossoming cherry trees in *Conte de printemps*; sandy beaches crowded with sunbathers in *Conte d'été*; grapevines heavy with ripe fruit in *Conte d'automne*; festive holiday lights in the steel-blue December of *Conte d'hiver*. The situations that Rohmer's characters face likewise reflect the time of year. The philosophy teacher Jeanne, who in the opening scene of *Conte de printemps* returns to her boyfriend's flat to find a vase of wilted yellow tulips alongside hunks of stale baguette and piles of rumpled clothes, finds a welcome change of air in the company of Natacha, an adolescent with a wild imagination. The vacationing Gaspard of *Conte d'été*, though physically in the prime of youth, is emotionally unsure; unable to figure out whether any of the three women he frequents is truly interested in him, he looks at his sentimental ups and downs as a chance to gain experience. In *Conte d'automne*, the fall harvest is metaphorically linked to the predicament of winemaker Magali, a hard-working widow in her forties who is mature enough to accept that she may need some help to find a new companion for the years to come. Finally, *Conte d'hiver*, focusing on Félicie's belief that the man of her dreams (and real-life father of her child) may some day materialise on the streets of Paris, plays on both pagan and Christian themes of steadfastness, death, and rebirth. These seasonal connotations are bolstered by colour-coding, as each title sequence features a dominant hue (bright green for spring, golden yellow for summer, burnt orange for fall, grey for winter).

Were we to attend exclusively to seasonal references and motifs, however, we would miss out on the series' uniqueness. For if the season cycle naturalises art by linking its products to the world's beauty, Rohmer's film cycle formalises nature in turn. Once again, the interplay of motifs across the series becomes the director's proper subject, loosely informed in this instance by the *conte de fées* or fairy tale, a genre rich in coincidences, repeated events, and mythical contents. Like the *Contes moraux* and the *Comédies et proverbes*, this third series presents a dense web of internal echoes, contrasts, and oppositions; more aggressively than they, it contains reminiscences of previous films in Rohmer's œuvre.

No artwork based on the season cycle can neglect the conventional poetic analogy between nature's changing visage and the stages of human life. To the extent that humans find in the seasons an objective correlative of the physical and spiritual journey from birth to death, they impose linear time upon cyclical rhythms which in principle lack either beginning or end. In light of film's own linearity and of the peculiarities of serial film production, the *Contes des quatre saisons* raise a key interpretive question: in what sequence should the four films be viewed? Their production history breaks with the natural order: springtime (1990) was followed by the chill of winter (1992), with summer (1996) and autumn (1998) closing out the cycle. To follow this sequencing is to reveal how the director plays with audience expectations in real time, eliciting curiosity, sustaining ambiguity, and resolving tensions from one picture to the next. A second solution, the one adopted by Rohmer in his published screenplays and self-curated DVD releases, is to restore nature's privilege over the accidents of history, such that *Conte d'hiver* replaces *Conte d'automne* as the capstone of the series. Either of these two readings gives the cycle a comic outcome, though the precise effect obtained differs significantly. A third answer might also be considered, namely, that by grafting itself on the rhythms of nature, the series becomes a 'cycle' in the fullest sense of the word; by this logic, one could enter the series at any given point and then follow the natural order of the seasons. This last solution is the least satisfying of the three, for if nothing prevents us from treating the pictures as if they were a continuous loop, nothing instructs us to do so either. It seems reasonable to accept that *Conte de printemps* opens the series – 'On commence toujours par le printemps', quipped the director (De Baecque *et al.* 1990: 24) – and that either *Conte d'automne* or *Conte d'hiver* may close it. This latter alternative governs the precise nature of the parallelisms and oppositions among the *Contes des quatre saisons*, relationships that Rohmer has suggestively compared to poetic rhyme schemes (Amiel and Vassé 1998: 11).

Such rhyming effects are first apparent in dramatic construction. Both *Conte de printemps* and *Conte d'automne* turn on matchmaking plots in which women scheme to pair off friends or family members with new partners. The matchmakers' motivations are often far from altruistic. When the conservatory student Natacha discovers that Jeanne, whom she befriends at a drop-dead boring party in the suburbs, has no place to stay, she invites her to spend the weekend in her father's Paris apartment and country home. Jeanne is quick to grasp the mercurial Natacha's ulterior motive: the adolescent desires nothing so much as to separate her father Igor from his vampire-like girlfriend Eve, a svelte journalist half his age whom Natacha accuses of all the ills of the world, including stealing a precious necklace. Though the mystery of the lost necklace activates a detective-like plot (is Eve guilty, as her name suggests?), the narrative of *Conte de printemps* resembles even more so a fairy tale, in which Natacha plays the role of the jealous princess wishing to save her adored father from an evil stepmother. The necklace becomes a Hitchcockian Macguffin, for the true dramatic motor is the characters' dissatisfaction or, as David Heinemann writes, 'a feeling of being out of kilter' which 'leaves them open to adventures, to taking risks' (Heinemann 2000: 54).

The matchmaking plot that Natacha engineers as much by omission as through deliberate intervention nearly succeeds. Conversing alone in the sitting room of the family's country house after Eve and Natacha's sudden departure, Jeanne and Igor discuss their preferences and conditions for romantic involvement. The fact that Natacha stands between them, notes Jeanne, means that they can speak to each other 'sans arrière-fond de séduction' (without the subtext of seduction).

But, as always in Rohmer's world, adults will be adults, full of desires and insecurities, and soon an intellectual exchange metamorphoses into a prelude to a kiss. Letting down her guard, Jeanne assents to the three questions that the mannered seducer Igor puts to her:

> IGOR: Je peux m'asseoir à côté de vous?
> JEANNE: Oui.
> IGOR: Je peux vous prendre la main?
> JEANNE: Oui.
> IGOR: Je peux vous embrasser?
> JEANNE: Oui.[4]

When he tries to press further, however, Jeanne announces that his three wishes are up. Having squandered his requests, Igor is thrown back onto the classic position of disavowal, claiming: 'Je ne suis pas amoureux de vous; je pourrais l'être' (I'm not in love with you, though I could be). The ordinarily placid Jeanne, ever willing to discuss in philosophical terms *how* she thinks, discovers that for once she has acted without thinking: 'Je pense surtout que je ne pensais à rien' (I think mostly that I wasn't thinking of anything), she says, echoing the proverb of *La Femme de l'aviateur*. After the incident, Jeanne confronts Natacha, whose manoeuvring has compromised their relationship. It takes the chance discovery of the lost necklace for them to make peace. But as the film comes to a close on this inconsequential note, it seems that Jeanne, who finds her boyfriend's flat in the same state of disarray as before, may be looking to change partners after all. What Antoine de Baecque calls the film's 'maieutics', or the obstetrics of truth, works in both ways (De Baecque 1990: 23). Not only does the philosophy professor pull a truth out of Natacha, who all but admits the puerility of her hatred for Eve, but the pupil forces Jeanne to confront her own feelings.

The matchmaking plot of *Conte d'automne* is both more complex and prosaic – more theatrical, in short – than in *Conte de printemps*. The bookstore manager Isabelle is preoccupied less with her daughter's fast-approaching wedding than with finding a man for her winemaker friend Magali, whose sentimental life, as critic Jean-Marc Lalanne remarks, resembles her vineyards, which have been left to grow untended under the Rhône valley sun to the point of becoming

4 '–May I sit down next to you? –Yes. –May I take your hand? –Yes. –May I kiss you? –Yes.'

luxuriant with weeds (Lalanne 1998: 43). To remedy the situation, Isabelle places a personal advertisement in the local paper and elicits an encouraging response from the sales representative Gérald. Posing as her widowed friend, she nervously fibs her way through a series of lunches, giving increasingly evasive answers to Gérald's straightforward questions before coming clean. At the same time, the student Rosine schemes to introduce her former philosophy professor and lover, Etienne, to Magali, whose son Léo she is dating. The premise again recalls a fairy tale: to free herself from an insatiable lover who routinely devours women half his age, a pretty young woman tries to pair him off with her would-be mother-in-law, hoping that all can remain friends... Even the oafish Léo is not too thick-headed to understand that Rosine's stratagem is 'monstrous'.

At the garden party scene which comprises the final third of the film, Magali, unaware that she is being set up, easily strikes up conversation with Gérald but falters when she is introduced to a diffident Etienne. Inside the house, Isabelle corners Gérald and asks for his frank opinion of her proposed match: 'Disons qu'elle est possible. Et même très possible' (Let's say she's a possibility. Very possible, even). The hostess nearly undoes her own handiwork when she giddily embraces Gérald, for the two are surprised arm-in-arm in high vaudeville fashion by Magali, who scurries off like some hurt animal. Thereafter, Magali must rid herself of the idea that Gérald might be her best friend's mistress – a hypothesis supported by Rosine, who had spotted the two adults together in town a few days earlier. Renewed attempts to unite Gérald with Magali, this time by introducing them properly, lead only to further misunderstandings, and the winemaker, as headstrong as the Sabine of *Le Beau Mariage* (also played by Béatrice Romand), prefers to go her own way. Chance reunites the two adults whom everything seems comically to drive apart, and the two childhood friends make up (see figure 9). Yet as in *Conte de printemps*, the film's closing shot casts doubt on the outcome: spinning about on the lawn with her husband amid other dancing couples, Isabelle gazes dreamily at the camera, perhaps regretful that she did not choose to live an amorous adventure of her own, with Gérald or some other suitor. The bookstore manager reveals herself a descendant of Emma Bovary, dreaming of another life.

In both *Conte de printemps* and *Conte d'automne*, it is the matchmakers who push the drama forward. Much as in the plays of

Marivaux, the 'matched', once she has consented to play by the rules, need only approve or disapprove of the proposed partner. Her answer will bear not only on the qualities of the partner (Igor, Gérald) but even more so on the acumen of the matchmaker (Natacha, Isabelle), who wants also to be 'preferred' as a competent judge of the heart, if not loved (the homosocial subtext is notably weaker here than in the male-centred *Contes moraux*).

Strong dramatic parallels similarly link *Conte d'hiver* and *Conte d'été*. The protagonists are caught up in sentimental quandaries that neatly mirror each other across the gender divide: one woman and three men in the first film, one man and three women in the second. The man whom Félicie has always loved, Charles, who unknowingly fathered her child five years before the main action begins, is absent, likely working in a restaurant in America. Save the fleeting images of the prologue, his existence is reduced to a series of colour snapshots displayed in the bedroom of Félicie's daughter, Elise. While Félicie continues to hope for Charles's return, she lives off and on with the librarian Loïc, with whom her relationship has turned platonic, and pursues an affair with her employer, the physically dominating Maxence, whom she finds to be more her 'type'. Neither partner is wholly satisfactory: Loïc is sensitive but unromantic; Maxence is passionate but irascible. Loïc's apartment, crammed with books, exudes learning and culture but little else, while Maxence's half-furnished, bookless flat above his hair salon in Nevers symbolises its occupant's modest means and dubious petty-bourgeois taste. Neither Loïc nor Maxence makes any great effort to keep Félicie when she gives them notice. She has made her suitors abundantly aware of their failings, and since each is too much of this or too much of that, we presume that only the third bed, which belongs to the absent Charles, can be just right.

Like Félicie, Gaspard of *Conte d'été* patiently awaits his would-be beloved, Léna, whose feelings for him, one suspects, are tepid at best. Her communication skills, at any rate, are nil, since she neglects to inform Gaspard that she will arrive in Dinard a week later than promised. When he is not composing music, Gaspard exchanges with the waitress Margot his views on love and friendship, as well as a kiss or two, which the young woman, herself committed to a man now living in the southern hemisphere, may wish to see as not merely symbolic. Almost in spite of himself, Gaspard becomes involved with Solène, the high-maintenance Breton woman to whom he dedicates his sea shanty and who gives him in return an impressive list of demands. Gaspard's mind, like that of the heroes of the *Contes moraux*, seems to be made up: only Léna would correspond to his 'type' of woman, and he is willing to wait as long as necessary for her to come around.

Plot in both films turns on a splitting of desire between the 'preferred' but absent individual and his or her temporary substitutes, whom the hero or heroine plays off one another in an effort to pass the time and to receive symbolic gratification. But the two films diverge significantly when the absent character finally materialises. Léna proves herself to be inconstant, egotistical, and little appreciative of Gaspard's attention, whereas Charles remains Félicie's unwavering ideal even after the couple's improbable but providential reunion. In what is *Conte d'été*'s parting homage to the Hollywood comedy of Hawks and Capra, Gaspard becomes the victim of his own indecision, receiving three successive telephone calls, each of which upsets the plans he has just made. The first caller, Léna, announces that she wishes to make up with Gaspard and accompany him to Ouessant after all; they agree to meet that evening. The second, Solène, insists that Gaspard join her for a party that same evening and then spend the night at her uncle's before embarking for Ouessant; she does not give him time to respond. A third call from the seller of a multi-track tape recorder, who wants to close a deal, is the *deus ex machina* that rescues Gaspard from an impossibly entangled fate. Gaspard leaves Dinard with few regrets, having promised little to the three women – a boat trip to Ouessant does not a marriage make – and with the certainty that making music is more worthwhile than chasing after chimera on the beach.

Félicie of *Conte d'hiver* is also aided by happenstance. Like the resurrection of the Queen in Shakespeare's *A Winter's Tale*, which she watches with rapt delight, her encounter with the long-lost Charles is magical to behold. Yet it is also humbly quotidian, for their reunion takes place on a public transit bus, then on the sidewalk amid loud traffic. This de-romanticised fairy-tale ending is one compelling reason to treat *Conte d'hiver* as the final instalment of the series. For like *Die Marquise von O...*, but with an emphasis on providence rather than honour and pardon, *Conte d'hiver* stages *in fine* an unorthodox family reunion. Father, mother, and child compose a Holy Family of sorts for the modern age. It is left to the spectator to decide whether the event is a miraculous one pointing to God's handiwork (Rothman 2004) or just an incredible stroke of luck.

Rohmer's comparison of parallels among the *Contes des quatre saisons* to poetic rhyme enables us better to grasp the series' unique form. If, following the analogy, we consider pairs of films to be couplets and the four-part series as a quatrain, it becomes apparent that the rhyme scheme obtained will differ according to viewing order. Assuming A is the matchmaking plot and B the plot of amorous indecision, the series' dramatic structure would read ABBA following the order of production, but ABAB according to the 'natural' order of the seasons. Should different criteria be invoked, new patterns will arise. For instance, the characters of *Conte de printemps* and *Conte d'hiver* engage in philosophical discussions – Gyges's ring as recounted in Plato and Kantian transcendental idealism in the former, and Plato's theory of metempsychosis and Pascal's wager in the latter –, whereas those of *Conte d'été* and *Conte d'automne* seem to be preoccupied solely with matters of the heart; this opposition yields either two successive couplets of CCDD (production history) or the 'rime embrassée' CDDC (the seasons). If we look to the variable of narrative closure, the rhyme changes yet again. *Conte de printemps* and *Conte d'été* end on open notes (we know not what is next for Jeanne and Gaspard), whereas the dramatic lines are tightly drawn in the other two pictures (both Félicie and Magali have found a soul mate); the result is either EFEF (production) or EEFF (the seasons). The prevalence of fixed camera and shot–countershot set-ups in *Conte de printemps* and *Conte d'automne*, and of mobile framings, tracking shots, and even subjective camera in *Conte d'hiver* and *Conte d'été* suggests patterns of GHHG (production) or GHGH (the seasons). There is no need to labour the point: rhyming patterns are distributed in such a way that between any two films in the series, parallelisms and oppositions can both be found. Even more strongly than the *Contes moraux*, based on theme and variation, then, the *Contes des quatre saisons* aspire to the musical language of counterpoint. However light or inconsequential its content, the series represents in this respect the quintessence of Rohmer's classicism, a homage to composers and filmmakers from Mozart and Beethoven to Renoir and Hitchcock.

One could argue that one potential consequence of this formal rigour is that the series become frozen, turning in on itself. If this does not come to pass, it is in part due to the numerous allusions the

Contes des quatre saisons make to other films in the director's œuvre. When we see Natacha/Florence Darel standing on a ladder, her leg bent, as her father repaints the garden trellis, we cannot but think of a similar shot in *Le Genou de Claire*, where the title character played by Laurence de Monaghan, also perched on a ladder, picks cherries as Jérôme looks on. In *Conte d'été*, a shot of Gaspard sitting on the rocks across from Margot isolates the actress's knee – a knee all the more interesting for the fact that it belongs to Amanda Langlet, who played the Pauline of *Pauline à la plage* ten years earlier. In another scene of *Conte d'été* Margot describes Gaspard's predicament of having not two but three girls to choose from as similar to that of 'un clochard qui se réveille milliardaire' (a bum who wakes up a millionaire) – an allusion to *Le Signe du Lion*, in which Pierre Wesserlin is saved from his misery by an inheritance, and, indirectly, to Murnau's *The Last Laugh*. Vaudeville motifs in *Conte d'automne* recall the earlier *Comédies et proverbes*, where characters busily work at cross-purposes and instances of *quid pro quo* are common. And, finally, *Conte d'hiver* is littered with references to *Ma Nuit chez Maud*: as Tom Ennis has shown, most every sequence alludes to one aspect or another of the 1969 film of which *Conte d'hiver* is the after-image. It is Christmastime and the streets are lit with decorations; Loïc, like the engineer protagonist played by Trintignant, is a practising Catholic; there are long tracking shots from inside cars; the characters attend a performance, and so on (Ennis 1996). Most importantly, in both films faith is cast in terms of the Pascalian 'infinite gain', the notion that the perspective of eternal life justifies the individual's belief in a higher power capable of grace. Together, these references remind us that a series, even as it aspires to internal coherence and beauty, opens up onto the whole of cinema, and to the whole of the world.

Conclusion

Spanning more than three decades and comprising sixteen films all told, Rohmer's three series are certain to go down as his signal contribution to the French cinema. His tales and comedies of infidelity, inconstancy, and yearning suppose a particular intelligence and complicity on the part of spectators, who are asked to consider each film as part of a larger whole and who acquire, over time, a filmic 'memory' of each series indispensable to the comprehension of that whole. Allegations that Rohmer's cinema is literary reflect perhaps nothing other than the interdependence of its parts, which present themselves both historically, as successive elements in a series, and, once each series is completed, in relation to an arrested but dynamic whole.

To the extent that these fictions work through a limited number of motifs, they pointedly critique the notion according to which true filmmakers are those who refuse to repeat themselves. For Rohmer, the art of the film director lies not in the search for new subjects, genres, or tones but in orchestrating now subtle, now overt effects of similarity and difference. The challenge is to find an equilibrium between content and form such that the return of motifs is not confused with sterile repetition or the mere application of a rule along neo-classical lines. As the director remarked upon completing *Contes des quatre saisons*,

> Ce qu'il ne faut pas, c'est s'enfermer dans une manière. Et travailler au sein d'une série, paradoxalement, empêche de s'enfermer dans une manière. Du moment où mes histoires sont assez semblables, je suis obligé de chercher la variété ailleurs.[5] (Amiel and Vassé 1998: 15)

In all three series, narrative similarities are constantly offset by changes in situation, character types, locales, and seasons. Whether the variety achieved prevents Rohmer's films from falling into mannerism is a matter for debate, and to some extent a question of taste: at what threshold, indeed, does similarity become mere repetition? As such, the director's serial work stands as an invitation to reflect on the fraught workings of spectatorial desire itself, which, even as it renews in front of the screen its demands for something different, asks for more of the same, namely, the experience of moving from a state of disorder to one of order, from uncertainty to relative closure. The dialectic of sameness and difference to which the *Contes moraux*, *Comédies et proverbes*, and *Contes des quatre saisons* give expression is unique in that, far from an empty, abstract form turning on itself, it seems to arise out of the concrete, sensuous world of human interactions that the film apparatus seeks dutifully to capture.

5 'What's to be avoided is confining oneself to any one manner. And paradoxically, working within a series keeps that from happening. Since my stories are more or less alike, I have to seek variety elsewhere.'

References

Abel, Richard (1994), *The Ciné Goes to Town: French Cinéma 1896–1914*, Berkeley and Los Angeles, University of California Press.

Amiel, Vincent, ed. (1997), *Krzysztof Kieslowski*, Paris, Jean-Michel Place.

Amiel, Vincent and Claire Vassé (1998), 'Eric Rohmer: des gestes proches du dessin', *Positif* 452, October: 11–15.

Bonitzer, Pascal (1991), *Eric Rohmer*, Paris, Editions de l'Etoile/Cahiers du cinéma.

Bresson, Robert (1988), *Notes sur le cinématographe* [1975], Paris, Gallimard.

Cohen, Clélia (1997), 'Le goût de l'Estaque', *Cahiers du cinéma* 518, November: 58–61.

De Baecque, Antoine (1990), 'Jeanne, ou l'idée d'enseigner', *Cahiers du cinéma* 430, April: 22–3.

De Baecque, Antoine, Thierry Jousse and Serge Toubiana (1990), 'Entretien avec Eric Rohmer', *Cahiers du cinéma* 430, April: 24–31.

Deleuze, Gilles (1983), *L'Image-mouvement*, Paris, Minuit.

Ennis, Tom (1996), 'Textual Interplay: The Case of Rohmer's *Ma Nuit chez Maud* and *Conte d'hiver*', *French Cultural Studies* 7.3: 309–19.

Heinemann, David (2000), 'Reinventing Romance: Eric Rohmer's *Tales of the Four Seasons*: Freedom, Faith, and the Search for the Grail', *Film Comment* 36.6, November–December: 50–4.

Hertay, Alain (1998), *Eric Rohmer: Comédies et proverbes*, Liège, Editions de Céfal.

Lalanne, Jean-Marc (1998), 'L'annonce faite à Magali', *Cahiers du cinéma* 428, October: 43–4.

Nogueira, Rui (1971), 'Entretien avec Eric Rohmer', *Cinéma 71* 153, February: 42–58.

Païni, Dominique (1997), *Le Cinéma, un art moderne*, Paris, Cahiers du cinéma.

Reynaud, Béatrice (2000), 'Representing the Sexual Impasse: Eric Rohmer's *Les Nuits de la pleine lune*', in *French Film: Texts and Contexts*, ed. Susan Hayward and Ginette Vincendeau, 2nd ed., London, Routledge: 253–68.

Rohmer, Eric (1984), *Le Goût de la beauté*, Paris, Editions de l'Etoile/Cahiers du cinéma (reprinted 2004).

Rohmer, Eric (1998), *Six contes moraux*, Paris, Cahiers du cinéma.

Rohmer, Eric (1999), *Comédies et proverbes*, 2 vols, Paris, Cahiers du cinéma.

Rohmer, Eric, and Claude Chabrol (1957), *Hitchcock*, Paris, Editions universitaires.

Rothman, William (2004), '*Tale of Winter*: Philosophical Thought in the Films of Eric Rohmer', in *The "I" of the Camera*, 2nd ed., Cambridge, Cambridge University Press: 325–39.

Simsolo, Noël (1970), 'Entretien avec Eric Rohmer', *Image et son* 235, January: 88–92.

Tortajada, Maria (1999), *Le Spectateur séduit: le libertinage dans le cinéma d'Eric Rohmer*, Paris, Kimé.

Vidal, Marion (1977), *Les* Contes moraux *d'Eric Rohmer*, Paris, Pierre Lherminier Editeur.

Williams, Alan (1992), *Republic of Images: A History of French Filmmaking*, London and Cambridge, MA, Harvard University Press.

5

Literature and history

On the surface, the period film is a losing proposition. If, as an extension of photography, the cinema is by definition the art of mechanically rendering a present reality, then any attempt to recreate past epochs onscreen must fail to attain its object, however 'authentic' the costumes, props, dialogues, or locations. Marc Ferro, breaking with historians' traditional concern with veracity when it comes to film, argues to this effect that

> paradoxalement, ce sont seulement les films sur le passé, les reconstitutions historiques, qui sont incapables de dépasser le témoignage sur le présent.[1] (Ferro 1993: 74)

Admittedly, no film fully transcends its moment, lavish costume pictures certainly less so than others. Yet as Rohmer, convinced of the medium's ability to enchant and instruct, cautiously puts it in his production notes to *Die Marquise von O...*,

> il n'est peut-être pas impossible, par le truchement du film, de mieux percevoir les moeurs et la sensibilité d'une époque passée[2] (Rohmer 1976: 5)

If the cinema can play a formative role in transmitting historical knowledge, it is because *mise en scène* brings with it the understanding that our relation to the past is imaginary to begin with. 'Objective' retrieval of the past is no longer at issue; awareness of our historical perspective, and of the cinema's own place in history, is what counts.

1 'paradoxically, the only films that are unable to go beyond an account of the present are films about the past, that is, historical reconstructions.'
2 'it may not be impossible by means of film to better perceive what the mores and the sensibility of a past epoch might have been.' (Rohmer and Kleist 1985: 7)

As we have seen, the bulk of Rohmer's fictions feature contemporary characters who lead modern lifestyles and use up-to-date language. On several occasions, the director has turned the clocks backward, looking to moments as remote as the high Middle Ages and Revolutionary and Napoleonic Europe, and as recent as the 1930s and 1940s. *Die Marquise von O...* (1976) and *Perceval le Gallois* (1979), shot in the interim between the *Contes moraux* and *Comédies et proverbes*, are versions of literary classics, by Heinrich von Kleist and Chrétien de Troyes respectively; *L'Anglaise et le Duc* (2001), produced after the *Contes des quatre saisons*, brings to the screen a nineteenth-century memoir by Scottish aristocrat Lady Grace Elliott, while *Triple agent* (2004) draws on historians' narratives, newspaper articles, and legal documents related to a little-known espionage case of 1937, the Miller–Skobline Affair. Though these pictures do not officially compose a cycle, they reflect a common vision as to film's power and limits in opening up the past. The *film en costumes* need not, Rohmer suggests, partake of an illusionism that would equate period 'authenticity' with objective historical truth. Instead of directly reconstructing past events in a realist vein, the filmmaker turns to pre-cinematic ways of seeing – from manuscript illumination and sculpture to easel painting – which reshape our perception of film's ontology. What kind of works for the cinema, he asks, might one have imagined before that medium properly came into being, two hundred or seven hundred years ago (Rohmer 2004)? The four analyses to follow of what are arguably the director's most original, if not the most representative contributions to the contemporary French cinema, will address that question.

Angels and devils

Of Robert Bresson's *Journal d'un curé de campagne* (1950), André Bazin writes that the director, rather than 'ransack' or 'pillage' Bernanos's novel, 'se propose de transcrire pour l'écran, dans une quasi-identité, une œuvre dont il reconnaît *a priori* la transcendance' (sets out to transcribe virtually unaltered for the screen a work whose transcendence he acknowledges *a priori*) (Bazin 1975: 82/1967: 54; tr. mod.). Free of the cumbersome 'equivalents' and 'useless liberties' that characterised literature-to-film adaptations, Bresson's film strikes Bazin as so unswervingly faithful that it becomes an independent creation which bears little comparison to its source. The same could be said of Rohmer's achievement with respect to Kleist's *Die Marquise von O...* of 1811. Like Bresson, the filmmaker ascribes total authority to the source text, subordinating his designs to Kleist's narrator's indications of mood, action, and speech. The novella becomes, in Rohmer's words,

> un véritable 'scénario', sur lequel le travail de mise en scène peut s'appuyer directement, sans l'intermédiaire de ce que l'on appelle une 'adaptation'.[3] (Rohmer 1976: 5)

Insofar as it privileges dialogue and gesture over inner thoughts and emotional states, Kleist's story, a model of detachment and efficiency, is cinematic *avant la lettre*. Whence Rohmer's paradoxical claim that the work of a writer who knew nothing of film is 'techniquement un aussi bon scénario qu'un scénario écrit pour le cinéma' (technically as good a film script as one written for the cinema) (Fieschi 1976: 9). This principle the director obeyed to the letter: a cut-up German-language paperback edition with hand-written annotations served as his shooting script (Braucourt 1976: 20).

The search for fidelity begins for Rohmer with the respect for language. Suggestions from his German collaborator that Kleist's antiquated syntax and vocabulary be updated in keeping with current usage were rejected: 'Ein Wort verändern, ist für mich ein Verbrechen' (To change a single word is in my view a crime), exclaimed Rohmer, who reasoned that had he staged the works of Marivaux, Diderot, or Stendhal, he would have proceeded no differently (Von Berthel 1979: 115). Together with Kleist's own dialogues, passages of indirect discourse in the novella furnish the material for nearly all of the film's speaking parts, while bits of narration copied onto black title cards provide scene transitions and temporal indications, in the spirit of D.W. Griffith. Minor changes in plot occur in instances where Kleist's story pushes the limits of verisimilitude for today's readers. These alterations serve principally to deflect attention from the circumstances of the Marquise's rape, the invisible, non-representable event around which the plot turns (Rohmer 1976: 6).

The film opens with a framing device that both recalls the tale's literary origins and signals the extended flashback to follow. A group

3 'a veritable "scenario" on which a *mise en scène* can directly be based without the intermediary stage of an "adaptation".' (Rohmer and Kleist 1985: 7)

of pipe-smoking bourgeois in a tavern read an announcement from the local gazette: the Marquise of O... lets it be known that 'without her knowing how, she has become pregnant' and asks that the presumptive father present himself. The patrons laugh at the unlikely predicament of the Marquise, whom they identify as a widow and mother of 'unblemished reputation'. Point of view enjoins spectators to reject the attitude of the bourgeois – should we laugh at the Marquise, we will appear as churlish and petty as they – and to side with the sullen, red-haired individual seated several tables away, who turns his ears toward the gossiping town-folk before the fade to black. We will later recognise this man as the Marquise's brother.

Action commences as a Russian battalion, under cover of night, attacks the citadel commanded by the Marquise's father, a middle-aged Colonel concerned less with military valour than with his family's well-being. Rather than render the battle scene from the outside – for example, by cross-cutting between enemy camps – Rohmer uses a single deep-focus shot of a spacious interior hall – now filled with puffs of smoke – to show the panicked reactions of the Marquise, her mother, children, and domestic servants. When the women flee unarmed through the courtyard, they are surrounded by riflemen who seize the underdressed Marquise and throw her to the ground. As if to hide from view the act of violation they are about to accomplish, a cloud of mist reminiscent of Murnau's effect-heavy *Faust* envelops the predators. The bellowing offscreen cry 'Ihr Hünde' (Dogs!) justifies the cut to the low-angle countershot of a Russian officer perched on a wall, his white uniform luminous against the sky. In this figure who descends from on high, the Marquise finds her saviour and guardian angel. Intoxicated by his power, and swayed by the Marquise's beauty, the Count will prove himself to be quite the opposite.

Few ellipses in literary history are as legendary as Kleist's dash, which stands in for the Marquise's rape. And what cannot be said cannot be shown. Each shot preceding the ellipsis hence will become a potential clue to an enigma that the Marquise, who is sedated during the rape, will struggle to comprehend. Two symmetric shots foment uncertainty as to the author of the crime. First, when the Count exits the fortress cellar to which he has escorted the Marquise, the camera holds frame on the servant Leopardo, who gazes at the Marquise as she weeps on a bed of hay in offscreen space. Only when a chambermaid insists that he fetch a sleeping potion for their mistress does

Leopardo wrest his eyes from the spectacle; the shot fades to black. Some time thereafter, the Count, who has obtained the Colonel's surrender, returns to the cellar, halting before he enters, perhaps to whisper a word to the sentinel. We cut to a low-angle view of the Count descending the staircase, lantern in hand. Passing by Leopardo, the chambermaid, and the Marquise's children – all fast asleep – he reaches a chamber brightly lit by a single candle (Almendros seems deliberately to transgress his principle of justified illumination). Within, the Marquise, in a cream-coloured satin gown, lies on a bed draped in lavish red cloth (see figure 5).

This highly stylised shot is, as commentators have noted, a quotation of Henry Fuseli's *The Nightmare* of 1781 (Dalle Vacche 2002: 89–90; Damisch 2004). Like the model of that celebrated canvas, the Marquise's supine body extends across the frame, her head to the right, eyes closed and lips open, and her legs, slightly parted, pointing left; her left arm cascades down the side of the bed on a near-vertical line. While Rohmer's tableau strongly resembles Fuseli's own, it presents an essential difference in that the grotesque horse and incubus which visit the painting's dreamer are absent. More precisely, these allegorical figures are displaced metonymically, first onto the Marquise, who stirs in her drug-induced torpor as the Count looks on, then, in the countershot, onto the gaze of the Count, who stands transfixed in an eroticised atmosphere of shadow and light. And where the shot of Leopardo in the earlier scene remained at a fixed distance connoting either voyeuristic pleasure or empathy or both, here the camera tracks in from medium close-up to close-up, as if to register the mounting intensity of the Count's illicit desires.

By effacing the fantastic elements that Fuseli's painting borrows from Christian allegory, Rohmer suggests that in the enlightened world-view espoused by the Marquise's entourage (and by cinema in its claim to photographic objectivity), there are no such things as demonic spirits, only more or less moral forms of conduct. Indeed, in a disenchanted era in which religious truths are no longer absolute, the agonistic forces of Good and Evil that a metaphysical view would hold apart are endlessly confused, such that a single being may unite contrary traits. Pascal Bonitzer argues along these lines that the constitutive rhetorical figure of *Die Marquise von O...* is the oxymoron (Bonitzer 1976). The Count, angelic and diabolical at once, embodies this figure. The day after storming the citadel – doubly so – he displays a gaucherie that contradicts his noble mien. To repair a crime no one yet suspects, he precipitously asks for the Marquise's hand in marriage, refusing to leave town until he receives a response. These discussions are laden with situational irony, generated by camera distance and point of view.

The Colonel's family is also prey to contradictions and faced with a conflict that surpasses the ordinary opposition between inclination and reason. The mother is compassionate, even indulgent towards her daughter who speaks frankly of her mysterious 'condition'. Yet she curses the Marquise when doctor and midwife confirm what the widow herself has suspected from the start: in the new age of science, no one believes for a minute that the widow might have conceived immaculately. The father is rational but given to fits of rage. He at first allows her daughter to choose her own future – the decision to break her vow of celibacy is hers alone – but reasserts the patriarchal order once the truth is out, firing a comical gunshot into the ceiling to chase the sinful Marquise from his household. The red-haired brother meekly seconds his father's initiatives; his disapproval of his sibling may betray little more than unspoken incestuous desire.

The many dialogue scenes that unfold in the family's living quarters break with Rohmer's habitually restrained *mise en scène*. Taking cues from Kleist's text with respect to posture and gestures, the director encourages dynamic compositions which exude picturality without taking on the frozen quality of a *tableau vivant*. In a given shot, spatial relationships may shift several times as actors throw themselves to the ground, bury their heads in their hands, turn their backs to their interlocutors, or storm out of the room. While some of these gestures might be considered histrionic, they are tagged as culturally accepted behaviours shared by men and women alike. Witness the scene of reconciliation between father and daughter, when the Colonel, having accepted his wife's word that their daughter is innocent, takes the Marquise into his lap and smothers her with long kisses on the mouth. Our reaction may be one of bemusement or of mild disgust; more appropriate would be to realise the sentimental poverty of our own age (Vitoux 1976: 111). The censorship that bourgeois society would put on the human body has not yet taken hold in the Marquise's world – though one suspects that the majority of the attitudes on display are learned, rather than spontaneous outpourings of emotion.

On another level of film meaning, *Die Marquise von O...* recalls a collective European artistic heritage. Allusions abound to French and German paintings with which Kleist's contemporaries and fictional characters (the Marquise herself paints in her spare time) would have been familiar. These range from the candle-lit genre scenes of Georges de la Tour to the dramatic canvases of a Greuze or a Fragonard (Dalle Vacche 1996: 94–101). The neo-classical decorative style of Napoleonic Europe permeates production design, from the Marquise's high-waisted dresses to the Greco-Roman busts and furniture that grace the citadel's living quarters. To his German critics, who claimed that these sparse decors à la Jacques-Louis David contradicted Kleist's own pre-Romantic sensibility, the director responded that in the absence of precise descriptions of the characters' surroundings (Kleist is no Balzac) it was only logical to employ the period style which then dominated Europe. As Dalle Vacche points out, neo-classical decor corresponds to the ideal of civic and military virtue upheld by the Colonel and his family (Dalle Vacche 1996: 94) – to which one must add religious piety, suggested by the several crucifixes that can be spotted on the wall or on side tables.

But virtue is precisely what the Marquise lacks in the eyes of her parents, reluctant as they are to see in the Count anything other than a hurried but meretricious suitor. The Marquise's spiritual trajectory describes a fall from grace, followed by an equally painful struggle to reassert her moral rectitude. By moving with her children to her country estate and by resolving to give her child a father, however modest his rank, she proves to her family that she is beyond reproach. When, on the day of reckoning, the Count himself, and not some sorry lout, throws himself at her feet asking for her pardon, the Marquise is overwhelmed, unable to accept the impossible. Her more worldly mother, by contrast, remarks on the family's blindness: 'Who else? We are such idiots ... who else but he?' (Rohmer and Kleist 1985: 72). As the Marquise runs off down the hallways, throwing holy water upon those present as if to dispel the diabolical spirit that has returned to haunt the citadel, the camera holds position in the salon, accentuating the scene's ambivalence.

Neither tragic nor fully comic, *Die Marquise von O...* qualifies as what Rohmer calls a 'comédie larmoyante' (tear-filled comedy) (Rohmer 1976: 5). Its conclusion shares with other films by the director a deep ambiguity. The marriage to be celebrated is of purely formal intent, for the Colonel has requested that the Count relinquish his conjugal rights while retaining his responsibilities. At the ceremony, not a single glance is exchanged by the betrothed, united in shame. The camera isolates the Marquise's face, directed towards the altar, then cuts to the matching point-of-view shot. In the immense altar panel of a Saint casting an angel out of heaven, the Marquise finds a description of her own spiritual battle. She must now acknowledge the duplicitous nature of her desire: the man for whom she feels both gratitude and inclination is the very person who defiled her. In the epilogue, the Count concludes his tale of the swan Thinka, which he had begun to tell months earlier. As a child, he recalls having covered the bird in mud, only to see it emerge from cleansing waters, its feathers an immaculate white. The screen kiss and title card that close the film confirm the Marquise's acceptance of this allegory of ambiguity and the necessity of pardon.

Never falling into the excesses of comedy or pathos, *Die Marquise von O...* stages an encounter with the past which succeeds not in spite of its theatricality but because of it. Acting codes and speech patterns are not our own – but nor do they conform to a stereotypical vision of the period enforced by the industry standard. While photography and editing remain realist at base, art-historical allusions situate the film in relation to a broad history of representation in the West which partly transcends Kleist's story. On an intimate scale, *Die Marquise von O...* is arguably no less a model – if not a monument – of period adaptation than Visconti's *The Leopard* (1963), with the important difference that Rohmer's actors – unlike Burt Lancaster and Alain Delon, whose well-established screen personas sometimes get in the way – were all but unknown to cinema-goers (the film launched Bruno Ganz's film career). And, to be sure, in his respect for classical decorum, Rohmer spares us the politics and the chamber pots.

The Grail and the cross

Perceval le Gallois has been described as a 'rêve pédagogique' (pedagogical dream), an idealistic attempt to rescue a twelfth-century literary monument from indifference in the age of punk rock (Dubroux 1979: 42). Composed in verse circa 1180, Chrétien de Troyes's *Perceval* is one of the earliest extant French sources to relate the legend of the Holy Grail. Like *Lancelot*, *Cligès*, and *Erec et Enide*, the courtly romance, in which pagan (Celtic or Breton) and Christian elements exist side by side, laid the groundwork for modern European literatures, including the picaresque novel and novel of education. In adapting Chrétien's text, which he first brought to the French public in the educational short *Perceval ou le Conte du graal* (1964), Rohmer again valorises linguistic authenticity, if to a lesser extent than in *Die Marquise von O....* Whereas most translations available at the time of production turned Chrétien's octosyllabic verse into prose and modernised it beyond recognition, Rohmer's own verse translation preserves something of the original's musicality and even of its lexicon. Peppered with well-known archaisms like 'occire' (to kill) and 'ouïr' (to listen), the film's neo-medieval lingua franca is meant to be accessible to contemporary viewers – there are no subtitles for the French audience – who need only overcome the barrier of listening to verse. But language is arguably the least of the challenges posed to the director by Chrétien's expansive and often cryptic work. Indeed, the source text calls for a new film language capable of rendering not the Middle Ages themselves, but those elements of the medieval imaginary that can be recovered in contemporary times. The film thus breaks with the topographical realism still present in *Die Marquise von O...* to invent an abstract, heavily symbolic *mise en scène*, one which takes its inspiration from the reigning art forms of Chrétien's own time, namely miniature illustration, sculpture, and music.

The episodic *Perceval le Gallois* traces the eponymous hero's journey from innocence to knowledge and, in Rohmer's strongly religious reading, from sin to redemption. Sheltered from the ways of chivalry by his mother, whose two sons and husband died in combat, Perceval mistakes a group of knights in shining armour first for devils, then for angels, and blasphemes when he confuses their leader with God himself. Astonished by these beings' other-worldly appearance, he resolves to become like them and leaves home on horseback armed only with his throwing spears and his mother's counsel: he must be courteous with damsels, learn from those whom he encounters, and pray in church. Despite this, Perceval constantly misinterprets signs along his path and behaves impetuously, often to comic effect. He forces kisses upon a damsel and steals her ring; when he reaches King Arthur's court, he insists on being knighted despite his questionable valour. Counselled by a master of arms, he nevertheless proves worthy in combat (the undersized Perceval, played by Fabrice Luchini, dismounts all his opponents on the first pass). At the request of the comely Lady Blanchefleur, with whom he chastely spends the night, he saves from a siege the fortified city over which she reigns.

The centrepiece of Perceval's journey is his visit to the crippled Fisher King's castle, where during a banquet a cortege of youth parade a silver-tipped spear from which flow drops of blood, followed by the luminous Grail. In keeping with the master of arms' warning that 'qui trop parle commet mesfait' (he who speaks too much does wrong), Perceval remains silent before these mysterious objects. He later learns from a hideous, fantastic lady that had he spoken up at the banquet, the Fisher King would have been cured; to pay for his silence, never again will Perceval see his mother alive. He crosses paths with the damsel whose ring he had stolen, her dress in tatters, and defeats her burly protector. Winter arrives, and on the pristine snow a wounded bird (rendered in animation) leaves three drops of blood that remind Perceval of Blanchefleur (actress Arielle Dombasle's face appears in a process shot). The knight then meets up with Arthur's men and vanquishes the Senechal Ké, who had offended him in his first visit to the court.

Narrative perspective next shifts from Perceval, left to wander about the plain, to the good-natured Gauvain. Accused of treason by a peer, Gauvain reserves his forces for their upcoming combat, yet when he is spotted at a joust by a bevy of impertinent demoiselles, he consents to fight all the same. In a second episode, he accepts hospitality in a bustling city, only to be recognised as the murderer of his hostess's father, King Escalavon. We return to Perceval, who has wandered for five years. A group of Christian pilgrims stops the knight, who is unaware that it is Good Friday. They direct him to a hermit, who confirms that Perceval's mother has died from grief and who asks him to repent. A vision of the bed-ridden Fisher King, whose sole nourishment comes from a host dipped in a chalice, reveals to the knight the true meaning of the Grail. Perceval then goes to a chapel where a Passion play is being staged by costumed believers while officiants in flowing robes chant Latin liturgy. Having fallen from a state of innocence into error, the character finds redemption in the body of Christ in most literal fashion, for a well-disguised Fabrice Luchini plays the martyred saviour, while the Virgin Mary, dressed in blue, and Mary Magdalene, in red, are incarnated by the same actresses who play Perceval's mother and Lady Blanchefleur respectively.

The most explicitly religious scene in Rohmer's œuvre, this twelve-minute concluding sequence reveals the director's interpretive agenda with respect to his source text, the Christian contents of which continue to fuel debate among medieval scholars. Extrapolating from a brief reference to the Passion in *Perceval* (Chrétien de Troyes 1994: 1132, ll. 6413–38), Rohmer makes clear that the medieval author is, for him, every bit the believer his name suggests. The fact that the film's final shot shows not Jesus on the cross, but Perceval roaming the countryside to the sung couplet 'le chevalier sans nul arrêt/va chevauchant par la forêt' (the knight, with nary a pause/rides on through the forest), does little to relativise the narrative's evangelical message. Now armed with the truth of Christianity and having expiated his sins, Perceval continues his journey on this earth anew.

If the Passion-play sequence makes us consider the knight's adventures in the here-and-now as subordinate to his spiritual quest, it also signals the attitude viewers must adopt toward *Perceval le Gallois* as a whole. What we witness onscreen is not Christ's arrest, flagellation, bearing of the cross, and crucifixion (a mytho-historical event) but a conventional representation thereof (the medieval Passion play). This mimetic logic informs Rohmer's *mise en scène* throughout. Rather than feign the possibility of representing the events recounted in Chrétien's romance, the director films individuals who are engaged in an enactment of a story. Even as that enactment draws on period sources like illuminated manuscripts, costume, and song, it makes no claim to historical veracity. The fact that musicians and chorus share the soundstage with the actors alerts us to the fact that we are always already in the space of performance.

The film's sparse set design reflects the abstract symbolic register of Chrétien's text (see figure 7). To summon up a field of wildflowers, it is enough to paint the floor green with white floral motifs; paint the floor white and all is covered in snow. To show that the castle Perceval now visits is not the one he just left, it suffices to change the insignia hung at its entrance, from a stag, to a rose, to a lion. By the same token, a lone grove of trees, their branches shooting rigidly upward in flame-like arabesques, can figure any number of forests. Rohmer's debt to the 'primitive' vocabulary of Romanesque painting and sculpture is evident. Flats of castles and cities which rise up against a painted backdrop of mountains and sky at the stage's perimeter flaunt their disregard for correct perspective, while gold-leaf interiors, always generously lit, and crimson and azure costumes evoke the limited colour palette and clean volumes of manuscript illuminations.

More difficult to seize perhaps is the peculiar geometry that links actor movement and ocular perspective. In Jean Douchet's 'making-of' entitled *En répétant Perceval* (1979), Rohmer claims that just as the curved edges of a church tympanum force the artist to 'bend' objects to fit the frame, so too does the film's self-enclosed stage, a trapezoid with rounded edges, alter our ordinary Euclidean sense of space. Perceval's 'linear' journey must be rendered through a curved trajectory, not a straight line. As in *Die Marquise von O...*, then, the goal is not to imitate painting, but to film a decor which distils the architectural and pictorial spirit of a period.

The danger of this enterprise is that spectators take the film's abstract symbolism as an end in itself, such that the chivalric narrative becomes a mere pretext for a one-off experiment in *mise en scène*. *New Republic* critic Stanley Hoffmann found the result unsatisfactory: '*Perceval* remains outside the [film] medium, its presentational devices unabsorbed and uncommunicated. Rohmer's serious religious-historical purpose is reduced to a series of tasteful Christmas Cards' (Hoffmann 1980: 263). For the picture's magic to work, we must be willing to adopt, as does Danièle Dubroux, the position of 'l'enfant spectateur (ébahi par la réalité qui l'entoure)' (the child-spectator, astonished by the reality that surrounds him) and take the film as an exercise in make-believe (Dubroux 1979: 43). Arguably, the most successful aspect of *Perceval le Gallois* is its integration of dialogue, narration, and musical accompaniment on the model of musical theatre. In any given scene, actors or musicians may become narrators who comment on the progress of the romance; in several instances characters deliver their lines in the third person, creating a gap between action and word. If this technique recalls Brecht's critique of character-role identification through distantiation, it also points to the collective mythical heritage of the medieval *gestus*, as if the characters themselves, in this second-degree representation, possessed a heroic consciousness of the roles they are playing. In such a world of symbol and convention, spectators must shed the realist prejudice to which Rohmer's own cinema has accustomed them and surrender to a naive poetry. This is perhaps much to ask, for even the most artistically inclined directors of 'medieval' period films, like Bergman in *The Virgin Spring* or Bresson in *Lancelot du lac*, are not above showing knights riding on horseback through the woods. If Rohmer's most ambitious film is also his most imperfect, it is perhaps because we cannot see the forest for the trees.

The digital revolution

As literary adaptations, *Die Marquise von O...* and *Perceval le Gallois* typify an apolitical trend in the European art cinema. Even as these pictures evoke the values, material life, and artistic vision of past epochs, they remain divorced from historical discourse proper. The case of *L'Anglaise et le Duc* (2001), adapted from Lady Grace Elliott's all-but-forgotten *Journal of My Life during the French Revolution*, is quite different. By taking as its object a foreign aristocrat's intimate view of events culminating in the 1793 execution of Louis XVI and Robespierre's Reign of Terror, the film enters the volatile terrain where politics, ideology, and the history of cinema collide.

In light of Elliott's anti-Jacobin reading of French political history, Rohmer's decision to stage a revolution of his own, namely by mounting the first all-digital French production, is particularly significant. Indeed, so heavily does the 1789 Revolution weigh on French national consciousness that no screen representation thereof can hope to be judged on aesthetic or technical merits alone. It must stand before a tribunal juried by viewers whom French Republican schools have equipped with firm convictions about the shape and meaning of Revolutionary events. As directors like Abel Gance, whose monumental *Napoléon* (1927–29) was considered an apology for fascism and individualism, and Jean Renoir, whose Popular-Frontist *La Marseillaise* (1937) sang the collective heroic actions of the people, were well aware, to film the French Revolution is to perform a historiographical act.

In its focus on a victimised female subject, *L'Anglaise et le Duc* shares a number of traits with historical melodrama, a genre well-represented in the Revolutionary canon since D.W. Griffith's *Orphans of the Storm*. In that feature of 1921, two adoptive sisters (played by Lilian and Dorothy Gish) are thrown into the 'storm' of the Old Regime's final days and persecuted by the expeditious justice of the Terror. Political events, which Griffith treats with little concern for veracity (Danton personally leads the assault on the Bastille), appear in relation to individual destinies. Rohmer's picture of 2001 similarly portrays in a sympathetic light its aristocratic heroine, who is victim to historical circumstance. It differs from most historical melodrama, however, in that the sentiment it expresses stems not from the imagination of screenwriters, but from the descriptive abilities of the witness herself. A Scottish Catholic, Grace Dalrymple Elliott (c. 1755–1823) enjoyed no small notoriety in courtly circles of her time. After her disastrous marriage to the aged Sir John Elliott, she became the mistress of the future George IV, with whom she bore an illegitimate daughter in 1782. Her liaison with the anglophile Duke of Orléans brought her to Paris in 1786, where sources corroborate her presence from 1789 to 1794, the years recounted in *Journal of My Life during the French Revolution*. Ostensibly written beginning in 1801 at the request of the King of England, the memoir was printed in Britain only in 1859, suggesting that Elliott's narrative and language may have been reworked to satisfy contemporary tastes (Elliott 2001: 8).

For Rohmer, authenticity was of secondary concern, for the memoir relates with the skill of a novelist

> l'histoire, non seulement des épreuves d'une femme, mais de son *regard*, regard dont le point d'émission dans l'espace et dans le temps est constamment précisé.[4] (Elliott 2001: 5)

The same logic that informs gesture and language in *Die Marquise von O...* thus applies to episodes to which Elliott was witness and party. Insofar as it highlights her friendship with the Duke of Orléans, the screenplay is nonetheless an independent artistic construct. Crucially, however, its first-person voice obviates the question of historical objectivity. For a spectator inured to 'les mensonges de l'écran' (the lies of the screen), writes Rohmer in his programme notes, 'l'objectivité du regard ne peut être atteinte que par le filtre d'une première subjectivité' (an objective outlook can be achieved only through the filter of an initial subjectivity). Our duty as spectators, then, is to forget what we 'know' of the French Revolution the better to see how events might have been perceived. Point of view supplies the filmmaker with a convenient alibi. Once the colour of the source text is made known, the question of the film's politics is partly resolved; whatever 'monarchist sympathies' the director would express are prima facie Elliott's own.

4 'the story, not only of a woman's ordeals, but of her *vision*, the spatial and temporal point of origin of which is constantly specified.'

Again, as with *Die Marquise von O...* and *Perceval le Gallois*, fidelity to source means fidelity to the spirit of an age, to be captured by reference to pre-cinematic visual culture. After the opening credits roll to a harpsichord version of Claude Balbastre's 'Carillon national', best known as the air to which 'Ça ira' is set, a watercolour painting of a semi-rural Paris street fills the screen. An offscreen male voice situates the action: in the rue de Miromesnil, near the Champs-Elysées, lies Lady Grace Elliott's *hôtel particulier*. The carriage entrance, courtyard, and porch of the Lady's residence appear in three further painted stills, followed by photographic views of a sitting room and bedroom. The transition between painted exterior and filmed interior is made nearly seamless by a unified decorative style and colour palette. As the commentator introduces the drama's protagonists, the camera singles out two wall-hung portraits executed in late eighteenth-century style and modelled on lead actors Lucy Russel and Jean-Claude Dreyfus, rather than their historical counterparts. Painted views of the Duke's own residences at the Palais Royal and on the Monceau Plain conclude the prologue.

The stage now set, a title card reading '1790' appears and we return to the painting of the Palais Royal. As if by magic, the diminutive human figures assembled on the city square set slowly into motion, walking about within a painted decor now animated by the noises of the city. This odd synthesis of painterly and photographic perspective, where actors and real-life horses and carriages disappear into *trompe-l'œil* backdrops, elicits a naive wonderment more reminiscent of Méliès than of the erstwhile twenty-first-century 'pioneers' who put digital imaging techniques to the ends of fantasy, science fiction, and horror. Rohmer's gesture – to move back in time the better to move forward – surpasses the qualification of technical exploit and points to a theory of cinema itself. In recalling painting's historical priority over photography, *L'Anglaise et le Duc* rewrites the birth of the moving image to suggest that in a pre-photographic era, the only 'cinema' imaginable is one in which the painter's mimetic art overcomes its fixity and embraces the movement characteristic of real life. The ancient principle *ut pictura poesis* is thus updated to read, 'out of a painting, cinema'. At the same time, Rohmer reminds us that this archaic moving image, like the two-dimensional canvas, is bounded by the frame. All shots in the film featuring Jean-Baptiste Marot's painted exteriors are taken from a fixed angle, with changes in scale permitted only along the camera's axis. This was not simply a cost-saving measure but an esthetic *parti pris* that Rohmer adopted from Griffith's *Orphans of the Storm*, which likewise employs an immobile camera for its exteriors (Blouin *et al.* 2001: 57). But where Griffith's studio-built Paris often looked like a small village, with much of the action clustering in a narrow street of half-timbered houses, Rohmer's own recreation of the Revolutionary capital suggests monumentality and openness, combining deep corridor-streets and broad panoramic vistas. To render the topography of 1790s Paris, Marot consulted architectural drawings, maps, and registers of city buildings; cityscapes from the likes of Boilly, de Machy, and Hubert Robert provided stylistic models (Kaganski 2001). The viewer's experience of Revolutionary space becomes inseparable from an aesthetic experience that is itself not without revolutionary qualities.

Rohmer's presentation of historical context through title cards – often copied directly from Elliott's *Journal* – and dialogue cues is gently didactic, such that viewers lacking extensive knowledge of the period can appreciate the drama's historical stakes (compare with the historical telefilms of the late Rossellini, like *La Prise de pouvoir par Louis XIV* or *Blaise Pascal*). When action begins on the eve of the July 1790 Fête de la Fédération, order reigns in the capital. Passers-by huddle around a street singer intoning 'Ça ira', the original lyrics of which hail the new regime's achievements and recall the need for virtuous conduct as the world looks to France for Enlightenment:

> Ah, ça ira, ça ira, ça ira,
> Nous l'avons juré nous serons tous fidèles.
> Dans tout l'univers tout le monde parlera
> De ce beau serment que le cœur tiendra.[5]

As the Duke of Orléans' carriage crosses the square, shouts of 'Vive Orléans!' and 'Vive la Nation!' are heard from all sides, proving the good graces in which the pro-revolutionary Duke, renamed Philippe Egalité, is held by his fellow citizens. Yet as we learn from the opening parlour-room discussion between the Lady and the Duke, all is not so calm as it appears. Assailed by rumours that tie him to the conspiring émigrés, Orléans has returned from England to make a public appearance at the Revolutionary festival. Though he makes no secret

5 'Ah ça ira.../We have sworn that we will all be faithful/Across the universe everyone will speak/Of this fine oath that our hearts will keep.'

of his scorn for his cousin Louis XVI, his lineage requires that he prove his Republican virtue – this in spite of his preference for the gentle ways of English reformers. Lady Elliott, loyal to monarchic principle and personally devoted to the French Queen, roundly disapproves her former lover's enthusiasm for the Revolution, though she too has learned to live with the times. In the course of these exchanges, filmed largely in shot–countershot, Elliott's refusal to leave politics to the stronger sex is apparent, confirming her status as a modern Rohmerian heroine. The Duke comes across as well-meaning, if somewhat paternalistic in begging the Lady to return to her home country while there is still time.

A title card reading 1792 puts history on fast-forward. Against the Duke's admonitions, Grace Elliott has remained in Paris even as the rift between monarch and Nation has deepened and revolutionary order has yielded to mass violence. The Lady's household is abuzz with news that the Tuileries palace has been sacked by Revolutionary troops. It is surely no accident that *L'Anglaise et le Duc* picks up chronologically where Renoir's *La Marseillaise* left off, on 10 August 1792. The culminating sequence of the 1937 film follows the Revolutionary columns as they storm the royal palace and defeat the Swiss guards. Shooting in the real exteriors of Fontainebleau with hundreds of extras, Renoir ushers the spectator into the fray, adopting multiple camera angles, rhythmic editing, and cross-cutting to heighten the scene's impact. The contrast with Rohmer's portrayal of this turning point in Revolutionary chronology is stark. All we see from Elliott's point of view, as she and her chambermaid peer out a minuscule staircase window, are wisps of smoke in the distance; the Revolutionary violence remains at a comfortable remove. Yet anti-aristocratic sentiment has long since infiltrated Elliott's household. Upon learning the rout of the Swiss guards, the Jacobin cook Pulchérie breaks into the bloodthirsty, *sans-culotte* version of 'Ça ira':

> Ah! Ça ira, ça ira, ça ira
> Les aristocrates à la lanterne
> Ah! Ça ira, ça ira, ça ira
> Les aristocrates on les aura[6]

Skipping about the courtyard, the pugnacious Pulchérie remarks to her fellow servants that their mistress would best not to show herself

6 'Ah ça ira.../Aristocrats to the gallows!/Ah ça ira.../The aristocrats are done for!'

in public. The subsequent shot of Lady Elliott, hidden behind a windowpane as if imprisoned in her own home, foretells the nobles' retreat into private spaces, and their inability to keep separate 'la rue et la chambre, le tribunal populaire et le boudoir rhétorique' (the street and the bedroom, the people's court and the boudoir of rhetoric) (Béghin 2004: 38).

The sack of the Tuileries prepares the first in a series of suspenseful encounters through which Lady Elliott reveals herself to be an authentic action heroine, arguably the only character in Rohmer's œuvre of either sex to merit the qualification. Recognising that the time for enlightened political debate is over, Elliott resolves to leave for her country residence at Meudon. Her chambermaid informs her that although the capital has been ordered shut, a breach in the city wall near the Invalides should afford passage outside. En route for the Left Bank, the two women in disguise cross the place Louis-XV (now place de la Concorde), strewn with cadavers. A Swiss guard is stabbed to death before their eyes, provoking wide-mouthed expressions of horror worthy of silent-era heroines. The remainder of Elliott's journey to Meudon capitalises on the muted blue-and-grey hues of Marot's moonlit paintings to create a storybook atmosphere. Its symbolic centre is a close-up of Grace, seated on a log, who removes her ruined white shoe to reveal a bloodied, dirt-stained foot. This de-eroticised appendage reminds the spectator that the aristocratic body cannot be reduced to a pure culture of appearances: it is similarly subject to suffering and to defilement.

And suffer it will, with the phantasm of dismemberment scaling up the body from foot to head, pointing inexorably toward what Charles Tesson, playing on the French homonym *cou/coup* ('neck'/'blow'), calls 'le cou de Grace' (Tesson 2001). When she decides to help save the protégé of a friend and, like the Chevalier de Varnaye in Griffith's *Orphans of the Storm*, enters Paris over the sentinels' warnings that the city is no place for aristocrats, Elliott soon finds herself face-to-face with death itself: like a stagecoach out of a western, her carriage is surrounded by a cockade-wearing mob of *sans-culottes*, one of whom shoves into her window, mounted on a pike, the bloodied head of the King's mistress, the Princesse de Lamballe. The camera registers only Elliott's horror as she turns away in disgust, as if to suggest that no shot–countershot exchange were possible between the dead and the living.

On her arrival at her friend's home, Elliott learns that she is to save the Marquis de Champcenetz, Governor of the Tuileries Palace and one of the Duke's sworn enemies. Out of obligation to a fellow nobleman, she consents to escort the fugitive Marquis, his leg injured, to Meudon. Like most of the 'exterior' scenes in the film, their journey brims with suspense. Barred from exiting Paris and abandoned by their coachman at curfew, Elliott and her feverish companion are left to cross the city on foot while battalions of soldiers patrol the streets, much like the Gabin and Bourvil characters in Claude Autant-Lara's *La Traversée de Paris* (1956). When they reach Elliott's Miromesnil estate on the Right Bank, Elliott must quell her vindictive cook's suspicions through play-acting and ruse. But just when this internal danger seems to have been averted, the local Republican Section arrives with a warrant to search. We watch in anticipation as valet and chambermaid hurriedly improvise a hiding place for Champcenetz amid their mistress' bedding. A psychological showdown ensues between Elliott, who lies in her bed just inches from Champcenetz, and the rifle-toting guards who turn the house upside down but neglect to undo the bedclothes. Suspected as an *ennemie de la liberté*, Elliott weathers the ordeal with poise: clearly, she is not called Grace for nothing.

This first house visit signals an erosion of the divide between public and private realms that culminates in the 1793 Terror, covered in the film's second half. Political debate returns to the fore with the impending trial of Louis XVI. Rallied by competing factions, the Duke of Orléans, who is a member of the legislative Convention, finds himself in a double bind: as Louis's cousin, he cannot reasonably vote *la mort inconditionnelle* (unconditional death), but as Philippe Egalité, a Republican who believes the King to be in league with foreign powers and inept to boot, he must show Revolutionary resolve. Charles Tesson has compared the scene in which Elliott and fellow aristocrats, gathered around the hearth, await the results of the vote to election-night coverage, 'avec ses estimations, ses résultats définitifs, et les commentaires des spécialistes' (with its predictions, its final tallies, and commentary from experts) (Tesson 2001: 41). When Elliott learns that the Duke, despite his earlier promise, has gone to the Convention and will cast a vote after all, she is shaken; when the final tally comes in, with a majority – Orléans among them – voting for the King's death, the uncomprehending Lady breaks down. The next day, her tears having yielded to indignant anger, she condemns the treacherous Duke, whom she beheads after a fashion by removing his portrait from her bedroom wall.

The scene of Louis XVI's execution sheds light on Rohmer's implicit position as storyteller and historiographer. Refusing the demands of spectacle – a gleaming guillotine, a rapt crowd, a brute of an executioner –, the camera scarcely ventures any closer to the scene than did the memoirist herself. An establishing shot shows the Lady and her servant at a lookout point in the heights of Meudon, southwest of Paris; the meanders of the Seine below lead toward the spires of the capital. We cut in to medium shot. The Lady, her alabaster complexion set off against a black hood with crimson lining, faces the camera, while her chambermaid, back to camera, points a spyglass toward the place Louis-XV off in the distance. Actress Lucy Russel runs through a range of expressions from Elliott's initial dread (the king is about to die) and the fleeting hope that the people revolt (the king will be saved), to the realisation upon hearing a cannonade that an era has ended: 'Ne restons pas là' (let's not stay here). As filmed by Rohmer, the scene departs significantly from Elliott's memoir, in which the Lady stays inside her house at the hour of the King's execution and later, on the road, greets a peasant bearing a handkerchief – soaked, he claims, in the monarch's blood. Had Rohmer filmed this 'relic' of the fallen monarchy, no doubt the controversy around his picture would have been even greater.

Thereafter, the mood turns increasingly black. Fearing for her life as Robespierre's Law of Suspects sweeps France, the Lady asks the regicide Duke to atone for his 'crime' by securing her passage to England. A handsome bribe notwithstanding, the passport is denied, the Duke having lost his influence with a radicalised Jacobin leadership. In the Lady's presence, Orléans becomes irascible and authoritarian, requesting that she keep her politics to herself; abandoned by family, peers, and nation, he resigns himself to a premature death while urging his friend to lay low. Heedless of these warnings, the Lady is visited by the Committee of Public Safety. The duo of inspectors who seize her correspondence, the one diminutive and outspoken, the other lanky and timid, resemble third-rate detectives out of a B-movie. After struggling to open a simple writing case, the chief inspector gloats in his discovery of a sealed letter addressed to Englishman Charles Fox – irrefutable proof, he believes, of the *citoyenne*'s treachery. Elliott's explanation that the addressee is a friend of the Revolution not to be confused with William Pitt, the noted Tory, is too much for the inspectors to handle, and after fumbling about for their tricolour sashes, they emphatically arrest the Lady in the name of the Republic.

Even as it provides comic relief, the search scene raises a question asked by many reviewers of *L'Anglaise et le Duc*: is not Rohmer's portrayal of the Revolutionaries unnecessarily harsh? Earlier images of the Parisian populace in revolt are unflattering at best; from afar, the people are an indistinct mass; from up close, they are dirty, misshapen, and inarticulate. Take the lubricious, winesoaked guards who corner Elliott in a holding cell and torture her with the guillotine's 'jolie musique' (pretty music): 'clic, clac, boum! clic, clac, boum!'. The further one moves up in the Revolutionary hierarchy, however, the more forgiving are the portraits. During Elliott's trial, rational debate wins the day – the 'suspect' letter intended for Charles Fox contains only praises for the Revolution –, and the overzealous juror who hounds the Lady after her acquittal is put in his place by a stately, dispassionate Robespierre. That said, it is the aristocrats who receive the most ennobling treatment in *L'Anglaise et le Duc*, nowhere more so than in its final sequence. Lined up against the walls of a dank cell, still wearing formal attire and powdered wigs, the noblemen march forward one by one, their gaze directed to the camera. In this boldly frontal *mise en scène* coloured by Gossec's stately 'Marche lubugre', the camera takes the place of the (unrepresentable) guillotine whose mechanism the camera shutter curiously resembles. As her peers, like the Duke before them, walk to their death, Lady Elliott stands fast in the background against the cell wall. A title card informs us in the soberest of tones that Robespierre's fall on 9 Thermidor led to her release.

Unorthodox by dint of its very faithfulness to source, *L'Anglaise et le Duc* reawakens historical consciousness by exposing the traumatic kernel of the 1789 Revolution as experienced by a social class that many history books, defending Republican tradition, continue to demonise. If Rohmer's film broadly falls within the camp of historiographers who, at the time of the 1989 Bicentennial, emphasised the continuity between democratic Revolution and Terror ('no 1789 without 1793'), it cannot, for several reasons, be reduced to a revisionist history lesson – even if it does, to all intents and purposes, dispense with 1789 altogether. The fact that there is no Fall of the Bastille, no Declaration of the Rights of Man and Citizen, no Tennis Court Oath, no Night of 4 August – so many events that brought down the Old Regime and opened the way to formal equality among citizens – points merely to the memoirist's prerogative as historical witness. *Mise en scène* corresponds to a subjective viewpoint on events and in no way attempts to narrate the Revolution as such. Such epic designs lie outside of the filmmaker's set of concerns, which extend primarily to the possibility of capturing local truths from an individual's perspective. Far from an edifying lesson on tyranny meant to spurn the Revolutionary establishment, *L'Anglaise et le Duc* can be said to exemplify – however perversely – the exercise of artistic freedom and liberty of conscience that the Revolution itself strove to protect. Responsibility for critical judgement lies ultimately with spectators themselves, who can emend Grace Elliott's faulty recollections and ideological bias to intuit a more comprehensive view of events. The French Communist Party daily *L'Humanité* perhaps best understood the value of Rohmer's pedagogical enterprise as an enticement to critical understanding when it entitled its review of the picture 'Votons la grâce' (let us vote for pardon).

Its political charge aside, *L'Anglaise et le Duc* is an artfully rendered double-portrait. But its most lasting impressions are perhaps those created by Marot's paintings of landscapes and cityscapes, which suspend Rohmer's fiction between the silent cinema of yesteryear and an incipient all-digital age. In the end, the film raises the question of the currency of Bazinian realism: after the digital revolution has dethroned celluloid, can the truth of the image still be said to derive from the truth of the world? The director of *L'Anglaise et le Duc* seemed to think that little, in sum, had changed:

> j'aime prendre la réalité telle qu'elle est, même si ... c'est moi qui la produisais par le tableau. La vérité vient du tableau et pas du montage.[7] (Ferenczi 2002)

Conservative as it may appear in an increasingly 'virtual' age, this view of the cinema as ontologically bound to a filmed reality is anything but counter-revolutionary.

7 'I like to take reality as it is, even if in this case I myself created it, through the paintings. The truth comes from the painting, not from editing.'

Anatomy of a marriage

Against the illusions of period reconstruction, Rohmer's first three costume films seek historical authenticity through dialogue with pre-cinematic art forms capable of enriching the medium's expressive range. *Triple agent* (2004) continues this search for a critical authenticity in a new key, since its action is set at a time when motion pictures are themselves woven into the fabric of daily life. After the credit sequence, over which we hear a recording of Dimitri Shostakovich's 'Chanson des Jeunes Travailleurs' ('Youth Workers' Song') of 1932, black-and-white newsreel footage takes the screen. It is 1936, and at a polling place in the tenth district of Paris a Communist has just won a legislative seat in one of many victories for the unified Left. Archival excerpts such as these, which recur throughout *Triple agent*, embody the collective time of history – here, 1936 to 1943 – against which the destinies of Rohmer's characters play out. Grainy yet concrete, they recall film's role in disseminating information to ordinary citizens before images of current events became ubiquitous. As the past flickers across the screen, we are reminded of the camera's vocation as a device for recording what once was: Popular Front leader Léon Blum speaking before a sea of workers' faces, Franco's guns pummelling the Spanish sierra, the gaze of a young amputee hobbling down a country road after the May 1940 Nazi invasion of France.

In counterpoint to archival footage, pristine 35mm colour stock relates *Triple agent*'s story proper, based on a September 1937 affair implicating an exiled Czarist general, Nicolas Skobline, in the abduction of his superior, the General Miller. Rather than recreate the event as the spy genre would require, Rohmer's original screenplay, which transposes the original names and changes the heroine's nationality (from Russian to Greek) to justify its French dialogue, explores instead how an international climate of secrecy and mistrust comes to unravel a couple's relationship. Despite its historico-political subtext, the central issue in this domestic tragedy remains, as elsewhere in Rohmer's *cinéma de chambre*, the circulation of language: how saying too much, or asking too little, foments ignorance, jealousy, and suspicion.

Rohmer hoped initially to integrate archival and fictional materials using techniques similar to those of *L'Anglaise et le Duc*. The actors, he surmised, could be filmed on a sound stage and then be digitally embedded in decors selected from stock film footage of the 1930s and 40s. This *Zelig*-like idea was jettisoned for want of shots of sufficient length and proper composition (Azoury and Lefort 2004). As it stands, *Triple agent* pushes the viewer imaginatively to breach the gap between the two filmic registers and to recognise the newsreel images as belonging simultaneously to a collective historical past and to the fictional present in which the characters dwell. Comparison with *L'Anglaise et le Duc* is instructive. If in the latter film the photographed interiors and painted exteriors of Revolutionary Paris form two communicating vessels, in *Triple agent* the exterior world of politics and violence (black-and-white) and the interior one of love and rhetoric (colour) are held fast apart. Unlike the Lady, who moves from her boudoir to the street and back again, heroine Arsinoé, whose point of view *Triple agent* adopts, is all but trapped in her apartment and other enclosed spaces (restaurants, chapels, hotel rooms), where she attempts to pierce the mystery behind the silences of her husband Fiodor Voronine, the well-heeled 'triple agent' of the title (see figure 10). The near total lack of exteriors in this largely studio-shot film gives a claustrophobic impression particularly conducive to its Hitchcockian programme: how to create suspense solely out of the gaps and omissions that inhabit language.

The first third of *Triple agent* dutifully creates portraits of its two lead characters against the backdrop of Popular-Front-led France. Childless after twelve years of marriage, the Voronines live comfortably at the edge of Paris in a modern social housing unit (HBM), its shelves lined with books in Greek and Russian. Fiodor drives each morning to the White Russian Army Veterans' Association Bureau, where he manages officers' pensions and reviews intelligence reports, while Arsinoé, in poor health, rarely strays from her easel and teapot. Her paintings of market scenes and sunbathers that enliven the apartment walls lead Arsinoé to befriend her neighbour Janine, a classics teacher married to a Communist Party member, André. Exchanges between Fiodor and his would-be ideological rival from upstairs point up Rohmer's penchant for paradox: the anti-Bolshevik White Russian approves the conservative canons of Soviet Realism, whereas the pro-Soviet Frenchman prefers painterly abstraction, the official party line notwithstanding. Fiodor's deflationary rhetoric – 'Picasso? Horrible. Et les autres connais pas' (Picasso? Horrid. Never heard of the others) – contrasts with André's looping dialectics and revolutionary commonplaces on bourgeois society and the march of socialism.

If these scenes, which include numerous inserts of paintings and drawings, underscore the inseparability of aesthetics and politics in 1930s Europe, they recall above all the dangers of talk. When asked by Janine about her husband's activities, the protective Arsinoé holds her tongue. Yet Fiodor himself is curiously forthcoming with his Red neighbours, making no secret of his trade. 'Il est parfois plus habile de dire le vrai que de mentir, car alors on ne vous croit pas' (It is sometimes more clever to tell the truth than to lie, because then no one believes you), he later remarks. We are left wondering whether Fiodor is as committed to the Czarist cause as his White Russian associates think.

A series of encounters with family and friends fuels Arsinoé's doubts as to Fiodor's allegiances. Through Fiodor's cousin, the ruined Prince Alexis Tcherepnine, now a Paris cab driver, Arsinoé learns that her husband has turned down an invitation to join Franco's ranks in Salamanca. Furious at having being left in the dark, she lashes out at Fiodor, who hides from his own wife information he routinely shares with strangers. The situation recalls Hitchcock's *Suspicion* (1941), in which the timid Lina (Joan Fontaine) elopes with playboy Johnny Aysgarth (Cary Grant) without doing the requisite background check. Upon returning from their honeymoon, Lina discovers that her husband has never held down a job and is a gambler and thief to boot. Put on her guard by third parties, she begins to suspect her husband, who is an avid reader of detective stories, of plotting to murder his friend and business partner Beaky, and to do her in as well. By adopting Lina's perspective throughout, Hitchcock leaves Johnny's presumptive guilt open to question. As Rohmer wrote of the film in his 1957 study, 'Nous restons dans le doute, comme y reste l'héroïne. Nous pourrions même dire: comme elle *veut* y rester' (We remain in doubt, as does the heroine. Or even: as the heroine *wants* to be) (Rohmer and Chabrol 1957: 72).

Like *Suspicion*, *Triple agent* describes the corrosive effects of failed communication, exposing how 'la vrille du soupçon perfore l'unité d'un couple' (the drill of suspicion bores through a couple's unity) (Rohmer and Chabrol 1957: 72). Just as Beaky unintentionally clues in Lina to her husband's dubious activities, so too does Maguy, the wife of the wealthy industrialist Boris, tip off Arsinoé: Fiodor has recently been spotted with government officials in Berlin. Unwilling to accept that her husband may have lied to her (he had spoken only of going to Belgium) and, worse, that he consorts with Nazi party members, Arsinoé confronts Fiodor just as he is about to leave for Brussels: 'En passant par Berlin?' (via Berlin?), she asks. Outraged that his cover has been blown, Voronine launches into a diabolically effusive monologue on the ins and outs of the spy trade. Pacing about the winter garden of their suburban villa, his wife silent in offscreen space, he compares his work to a military battle, to a chess match, and to stage-managing history from behind the scenes. Actor Serge Renko's spiralling delivery and penetrating gaze convey the exalted state of a man who suspects that his own decisions might affect 'l'avenir des puissances européennes, pour ne pas dire mondiales' (future relations among European or even world powers).

Since Rohmer's camera never accompanies Voronine on his missions outside the home, nothing prevents us from believing this to be so. The monologue leaves Arsinoé reassured that her spouse harbours nothing but ill will for the Nazis. But when news of Stalin's purges reaches France, she again finds herself the victim of Fiodor's pathological reticence. Citing the excellence of Soviet medicine and the Black Sea's salubrious climate, Fiodor all but presents Arsinoé with a *fait accompli*, noting that he is in line to accept a high command post in the Soviet army. Again, the revelation elicits from Arsinoé a complex response of incomprehension and grateful recognition: is the White Russian Fiodor a Red in disguise? A shrewd opportunist, or a husband with good intentions but remarkably poor ways of sharing them? Arsinoé's mental and physical fragility is deftly rendered by actress Katerina Didaskalou, with her sunken features, persistent cough, and imploring gaze.

Two-thirds into the film, Rohmer opens up a dramatic black hole of sorts, the effect of which is to plunge his heroine further into doubt – and the spectator with her. Visiting Paris for an official function, the Voronines stop by a dressmaker's shop. Fiodor leaves to make some telephone calls while Arsinoé, seated in the waiting room, nurses her foot, injured the night before at an officers' ball. An iris closes out the image when Fiodor exits the shop; when the cache is lifted, one hour has passed, Fiodor has returned, and Arsinoé's dress is ready. Like the fade to black that precedes the rape in *Die Marquise von O...*, this ellipsis hides from view the unrepresentable event around which everything thereafter turns. Later that evening in their hotel room, a nervous Fiodor opens up to his wife or, rather, briefs her in the fear that she be questioned. A meeting that he and his superior Dobrinski had scheduled with German intelligence operatives that same afternoon – the 'telephone call' he went to make while Arsinoé waited at the dressmaker's – has gone awry, and Dobrinski has disappeared, whisked away by a motorcar before Voronine could join him inside. The 'Germans', it would seem, were Soviet agents in disguise. Tapping his fingers on a leather briefcase to re-enact the episode, Voronine runs through several hypotheses which seem to reflect uncertainty on his part as to who was manipulating whom – though Arsinoé suspects that her husband, too intelligent to have fallen into a simple trap, has double-crossed his White Russian employers. Like Grace Elliott betrayed by the Duke at Louis XVI's trial, she bursts into tears, left alone on the hotel bed while Fiodor asks her to support his alibi. The confrontation is claustrophobic, the framings and dim lighting emphasising the growing distance between husband and wife.

Voronine is escorted to the Veterans' Association for questioning, where White Russian officials produce a warning note left that morning by a prescient Dobrinski. Though Voronine declares the note to be a fake, it is clear that the triple agent's cards are up. In a final *coup de théâtre,* he steals out of the office under cover of darkness just as his colleagues are about to take him to the police station. The dénouement leaves the spectator with more questions than answers: was Voronine aware from the start that the Germans were covert Soviet agents, or were he and Dobrinski both taken in? Did he rather turn coats on the spur of the moment, realising the advantages of compliance with Soviet intelligence for his political future in his homeland? Or were German and Soviet services cooperating to eliminate White Russian agents, in an eerie presentiment of the Hitler–Stalin pact, as Voronine himself would seem to suspect?

The subsequent sequence adopts the tone of history. An offscreen commentator, who notes that Fiodor's trace was never found, relates Arsinoé's arrest and condemnation for conspiracy by the French State. In a shot inspired by a 1940 press photo, Arsinoé appears in a drab courtroom flanked by two French guards, her cheeks hollow and eyes expressionless. The image is followed by a black-and-white still of the prison where, according to the narrator, Arsinoé would die after the unsuccessful amputation of her foot. This quasi-documentary presentation of the heroine's fall creates a melancholy rarely experienced in Rohmer's universe: usually, characters stay with us right to the end.

The sombre tone is prolonged by the laconic title cards that preface newsreel footage from 1939 and 1940: 'The German–Soviet Pact', 'The War', 'Defeat', 'Exodus', 'Occupation'.

A shift in tone and register occurs in the full-colour epilogue, which, like the concluding scenes of many Hitchcock films, provides a possible explanation of Voronine and Dobrinski's disappearance – and by extension of the Skobline/Miller affair. It is 1943, and German occupation officials have just discovered that the offices of the White Russian Army Veterans' Association were bugged from the flat below, occupied by a known Soviet agent. The General Melinski, under whose watch Voronine had escaped, merely smiles at this discovery. But the enterprising French police inspector played by actor Georges Benoit (the fumbling Revolutionary inspector of *L'Anglaise et le Duc*) recalls the details of the unsolved Voronine affair. Putting two and two together, he identifies the electrical box in the Soviet agent's flat that would have enabled Voronine to darken the building's stairway and make his escape. Whether Voronine was sent to Barcelona with the International Brigades and then disposed of along with countless other anti-Stalinists as the inspector thinks, or, following Melinski's hypothesis, sent back to Moscow to be executed is of secondary importance. For both men agree the true victim of the affair was Arsinoé, an innocent woman who, swept up in the throes of interwar history, paid the price of her husband's divided allegiances. Spoken in unison, the final line of the film – 'Elle est morte' (she's dead) – rings with both irony and sympathy.

Interviewed on *Triple agent*'s release, Rohmer noted that in history films,

> on tend vers quelque chose qu'on n'arrive jamais à saisir. C'est pourquoi d'emblée, je préfère montrer un film où on ne saisit pas.[8] (Herpe and Neyrat 2004)

If we never fully understand the facts of the Voronine case, or those of the real-life Skobline Affair which it meticulously transposes, there is one fact we cannot but grasp: Arsinoé is the first, and only, heroine to die in Rohmer's entire œuvre. And she owes that death, as we should perhaps expect from her creator, to the fact that her husband has talked too little, too late – or perhaps simply too much.

8 'you move toward something you can never quite grasp. That's why I'd rather make a film that can't be grasped to begin with.'

In any case, her quiet stoicism in front of a catastrophe that is at once intimate and collective make her every bit a tragic heroine.

Conclusion

It is tempting to reflect on how different a career Rohmer might have led had he and his producers consistently sought the means to bring to the screen other literary classics or episodes from the history books. The pedagogical value of his few costumed enterprises – five features out of twenty-five, counting *Les Amours d'Astrée et de Céladon* (2007) – is undeniable, and their artistic merits no less so. Each encourages an original dialogue with the historical imaginary in lieu of the 'direct' period reconstruction long promoted by the motion-picture industry, often against its best economic interests. In confronting the spectator with authentic language and visual codes from periods past instead of showy 'production values', Rohmer underscores the fact that the cinema, for all its aspiration to an intemporal classical perfection, remains but one instance in a broad history of representation. Motion-picture photography – analogue or digital – unearths new possibilities through contact with pre-photographic forms of expression.

To be sure, the precise choices Rohmer has made as a period filmmaker are as open to criticism as any. A labour of love like *Perceval le Gallois* proves for many viewers the impossibility of retrieving medieval ways of seeing without lapsing into cartoon-like caricature, while *Triple agent*, which simultaneously attempts to elucidate the real-life Skobline affair by fictional means and to pay homage to Hitchcock, may come across as a failed exercise in storytelling, its means ill-suited to its ends. The conviction remains after viewing Rohmer's costume films that only through deference to past instances of the artistic imaginary can the filmmaker arrive at historical and aesthetic truth. The cinema can attain to a measure of authenticity in representing the past only on the condition that it accepts the limited, subjective position implied by all art.

References

Azoury, Philippe, and Gérard Lefort (2004), 'Les mots sont plus importants que les idées', *Libération*, 17 March.

Bazin, André (1967), *What is Cinéma?*, vol. 1, tr. Hugh Gray, Berkeley, University of California Press.

Bazin, André (1975), *Qu'est-ce que le cinéma?*, Paris, Le Cerf.

Béghin, Cyril (2004), 'Le peuple et le boudoir', *Cahiers du cinéma* 588, March: 38–9.

Blouin, Patrice, Stéphane Bouquet and Charles Tesson (2001), 'Je voulais que la réalité devienne tableau', *Cahiers du cinéma* 559, July–August: 50–8.

Bonitzer, Pascal (1976), 'Glorieuses bassesses', *Cahiers du cinéma* 272, December: 26–30.

Braucourt, Guy (1976), 'L'envie de me sentir vraiment metteur en scène', *Ecran* 47, May: 19–23.

Chrétien de Troyes (1994), *Romans*, Paris, Librairie Générale Française.

Dalle Vacche, Angela (1996), 'Eric Rohmer's *The Marquise of O...*: Painting Thoughts, Listening to Images', *Cinema and Painting: How Art is Used in Film*, Austin, University of Texas Press: 81–106.

Damisch, Hubert (2004), 'Le temps de la citation', *Cahiers du cinéma* 558, March: 28–30.

Dubroux, Danièle (1979), 'Le rêve pédagogique', *Cahiers du cinéma* 299, April: 42–3.

Elliott, Grace (2001), *Journal de ma vie durant la Révolution française*, foreword by Eric Rohmer, Paris, Les Editions de Paris.

Ferenczi, Aurélien (2002), 'Entretien avec Eric Rohmer', *L'Anglaise et le Duc*, Paris, Pathé Vidéo DVD.

Ferro, Marc (1993), *Cinéma et histoire*, rev. ed., Paris, Gallimard.

Fieschi, Jacques (1976), 'J'ai voulu mettre en scène un texte', *Cinématographe* 19, June: 9–11.

Herpe, Noël, and Cyril Neyrat (2004), 'Je crois à la litote', *Vertigo* 25, spring: 5–10.

Hoffmann, Stanley (1980), *Before My Eyes: Film Criticism and Comment*, New York, Harper and Row.

Kaganski, Serge (2001), 'La révolution numérique: Eric Rohmer provocateur?', *Les Inrockuptibles*, 4 September.

Rohmer, Eric (1976), 'Notes sur la mise en scène', *L'Avant-scène cinéma*, October: 5–6.

Rohmer, Eric (2004), 'Entretien avec Eric Rohmer', in *Historiens et cinéastes: rencontre de deux écritures*, ed. Priska Morrissey, Paris, L'Harmattan: 207–37.

Rohmer, Eric, and Claude Chabrol (1957), *Hitchcock*, Paris, Editions universitaires.

Rohmer, Eric, and Heinrich von Kleist (1985), *The Marquise of O...*, New York, Ungar.

Tesson, Charles (2001), 'Le cou de Grace', *Cahiers du cinéma* 559, July–August: 48.

Vitoux, Frédéric (1976), '*La Marquise d'O...*', *Positif* 183–4, July: 110–12.

Von Berthel, Werner, ed. (1979), *Heinrich von Kleist: Die Marquise von O...*, Frankfurt, Insel.

6

Conclusion

In a world where gun-slinging, pistol-packing men short on vocabulary and long on machismo have all but defined what it means to be a hero (and even a heroine), the characters whom Eric Rohmer has brought to the screen may come across as impossibly lightweight. Their sole arm for resolving disputes – ones which principally concern their own anxieties in the face of potential sentimental attachment – is, after all, language. But as Rohmer stubbornly shows, talk is of higher dramatic calibre than is usually assumed. A mode of action and a symptom of a desiring consciousness, it is something to be looked at and listened to in its own right. As the director would have it,

> [il] est plus intéressant de montrer un dialogue entre deux personnages que de filmer deux personnes qui se tirent des coups de pistolet. Une fusillade, ça a été vu mille fois. Alors qu'il y aura toujours quelque chose de passionnant à faire avec un dialogue.[1] (Kaganski 2004)

The general viewing public may beg to differ – and, to all appearances, it has indeed done so, even as critics in France have continued to heap largely unqualified praise on this self-professed *auteur*. As a former editor of the esteemed *Cahiers du cinéma*, Rohmer has incontestably received preferential treatment from his peers; with few exceptions, critics in France have seconded the idea that the work of a true film author contains no outright failures, only fresh iterations on core themes and obsessions. If the present study is guilty of the same, it is because Rohmer himself has taken the principle of literary

1 'It's more interesting to show two characters in dialogue than people firing pistol shots at one another. Gunfights have been seen a thousand times. But there will always be something exciting to do with a dialogue.'

auteurism further than most, creating cycles that endlessly rearrange basic motifs in patterns both familiar and unique. While any given series instalment may fall short of what most cinema-goers construe as 'greatness' – a threshold attained perhaps only in *Ma Nuit chez Maud* –, what matters ultimately is its place in an interlocking whole. Consequently, the *Contes moraux*, *Comédies et proverbes*, or *Contes des quatre saisons* are, as cycles, less open to critique than any one of their given parts. Viewers are held to the very moral obligation of reserving final judgement until each series' end.

A keen sense of economy encouraged by Les Films du Losange and his own Compagnie Eric Rohmer has only reinforced the director in his dedication to theme and variation as an enabling artistic and commercial principle. The incomparable *Perceval le Gallois* aside, even the grander statements he has had occasion to make, like *L'Anglaise et le Duc*, are suitably small films that skilfully paint the ever-changing moods of women and men with a limited palette. All things told, however, Rohmer may not have led the career he would have liked most:

> Si j'envisage l'ensemble d'une carrière, à choisir entre celle de quelqu'un comme Renoir, avec ses difficultés, les adaptations qui lui ont parfois été imposées, mais qui ne l'ont pas empêché de faire des sujets qui étaient à lui, et celle plus unie d'un Bergman enfermé dans son univers et reprenant sans arrêt ses propres thèmes, ... la première me conviendrait infiniment mieux.[2] (Braucourt 1976: 23)

This statement dates to 1976. Despite surface resemblance, Rohmer is unlikely to go down as the 'French Bergman': there are too many laughs, too much sun, and altogether too many young people drunk with talk. But it is doubtful that his highly personal craft will ever stand comparison with such giants as Renoir, or his own contemporary Godard; more apt affinities could be found with Marcel Pagnol and, surprisingly, Jean-Pierre Melville, both of whom exerted significant control over production and managed to subsist largely outside the cogs of the industry.

2 'Looking at a career as a whole, if I had to choose between that of someone like Renoir, with his troubles and the adaptations he was sometimes forced to make – but which didn't keeping him from working on subjects of his own – and the more unified one of someone like Bergman, trapped in his universe and endlessly rehearsing his own themes, ... the first one would suit me infinitely better.'

Whether the creator of films as sensually hip as *La Collectionneuse* and as ascetic as *Ma Nuit chez Maud* qualifies as modern or classical, reactionary or innovative, is a question not easily resolved, in either political or aesthetic terms. Rohmer has long maintained that his *mise en scène* is modern precisely because it is avoids modernism's excesses in favour of classical equilibrium, and innovative to the extent that, unlike its competitors, it stakes no claim to revolutionising the medium. This enlightened conservatism, tailored to a limited yet discerning public, looks askance at its historical moment, as if to declare its indifference toward the busier, noisier aesthetic that has become the cinematic norm.

In a hundred years' time, media archaeologists – the descendants of today's film scholars – may look back to Eric Rohmer's œuvre as one of the odder embodiments of a belatedly classical aesthetic, one devoted to clarity of presentation, absence of effects, and to a well-nigh mystical belief in the camera's ability to bring together the material and spiritual realms, directing us to a reality that is meaningful in and of itself. Aside from an idealistic view of the medium's ontology, they will find in Rohmer's work a rarefied description of late-twentieth-century European society in which disarmingly homogenous individuals confront disarmingly similar situations to disarmingly similar results. Yet so indelible is the authorial stamp left by Rohmer on his works that the very representativity of his characters as social beings comes into question. As director Robert Guédiguian notes,

> on ne peut pas dire ... qu'un personnage de Rohmer est un 'jeune Français', car tous, sans exception, sont des 'jeunes Français vus par Rohmer'.[3] (Cohen 1997: 59)

Nor can it quite be said, given this, that what Rohmer's characters speak is French, for each of them without exception speaks 'French as heard by Rohmer'. It is fitting that perhaps the greatest legacy of this former professor of letters should be the creation of a language unto itself: *le rohmérien*, that unfailingly clear, but not always concise tongue that in its immoderate respect for grammar and its melodic intonations seems to chastise and seduce at one and the same time. 'Si parler te soulage, fais-le' (If talking makes you feel better, go right ahead), exclaims Arsinoé to her secretive husband Fiodor in *Triple*

3 'you can't say that a Rohmer character is a "young French person", because all his characters without exception are "young French people viewed by Rohmer".'

agent. By now, Rohmer, the standard-bearer of the modern talking cinema, should be feeling a good bit relieved.

References

Braucourt, Guy (1976), 'L'envie de me sentir vraiment metteur en scène', *Ecran* 47, May: 19–23.

Cohen, Clélia (1997), 'Le goût de l'Estaque', *Cahiers du cinéma* 518, November: 58–61.

Kaganski, Serge (2004), 'Soupçons', *Les Inrockuptibles*, 17 March.

Filmography

Table of viewing figures for features by Eric Rohmer

Year*	Title	Paris**	France***
1962	*Le Signe du Lion*	4,978 / 14,073	16,527
1967	*La Collectionneuse*	52,031 / 156,205	296,504
1969	*Ma Nuit chez Maud*	263,569 / 411,678	1,019,987
1971	*Le Genou de Claire*	205,628 / 277,578	636,013
1972	*L'Amour l'après-midi*	252,020 / 275,241	902,179
1976	*Die Marquise von O...*	135,707 / 158,139	295,144
1978	*Perceval le Gallois*	50,146 / 59,114	144,955
1980	*La Femme de l'aviateur*	44,399 / 66,046	110,989
1982	*Le Beau Mariage*	94,473 / 104,582	202,540
1983	*Pauline à la plage*	125,720 / 139,785	322,928
1984	*Les Nuits de la pleine lune*	303,210 / 310,981	626,461
1986	*Le Rayon vert*	187,648 / 183,457	459,627
1987	*4 Aventures...*	76,172	–
1987	*L'Ami de mon amie*	213,901 / 193,273	494,840
1989	*Conte de printemps*	112,335	–
1992	*Conte d'hiver*	90,413	–
1993	*L'Arbre, le maire...*	70,065 / 70,797	177,767
1995	*Les Rendez-vous de Paris*	36,651	79,329
1996	*Conte d'été*	135,507	318,739
1998	*Conte d'automne*	137,661 / 133,097	369,567
2001	*L'Anglaise et le duc*	119,238	225,000
2004	*Triple agent*	under 100,000	under 100,000

* Indicates year of theatrical release.
** The first figure corresponds to first-run figures for Paris furnished by the Bibliothèque du film as reported in *Le Film français*. When a second figure is given, it reflects box office continuous to the year 2000, based on the CNC data compiled by Simon Simsi in *Ciné-passions: 7e art et industrie de 1945 à 2000*, Paris, Editions Dixit, 2000.
*** Statistics for France during initial run from the databases of the Bibliothèque du film, Paris.

Features

Les Petites Filles modèles 1952–53 (unfinished), 60 min.

Production: Guy de Ray and Joseph Kéké, for the Consortium parisien de production cinématographique (CPPC)
Screenplay: Eric Rohmer, after the Comtesse de Ségur
Technical consultant: Pierre Guilbaud
Assistant director: André Cantenys
Cinematography: Jean-Yves Tierce (35mm b/w)
Sound: Bernard Clarens
Montage: Jean Mitry
Principal actors: Marie-Hélène Mounier, Martine Laisné, Anna Misonzine, Catherine Clément, Josette Sinclair, Josée Doucet, Olga Ken, Jean-Yves Tierce

Le Signe du Lion 1959–62 (***The Sign of Leo***), 100 min.

Production: AJYM Films
Screenplay: Eric Rohmer
Dialogues: Eric Rohmer and Paul Gégauff
Cinematography: Nicolas Hayer (35mm b/w)
Editing: Anne-Marie Cotret
Sound: Jean Labussière
Music: Louis Sauger
Principal actors: Jess Hahn, Van Doude, Michèle Girardon, Jean Le Poulain

La Collectionneuse (***Six contes moraux, IV***) 1967, 90 min.

Production: Les Films du Losange, Rome-Paris Films
Screenplay and dialogues: Eric Rohmer, with the collaboration of Patrick Bauchau, Daniel Pommereulle, and Haydée Politoff

Cinematography: Nestor Almendros (35mm Eastmancolor)
Editing: Jacqueline Raynal
Music: Blossom Toes
Principal actors: Patrick Bauchau, Haydée Politoff, Daniel Pommereulle, Seymour Hertzberg
Silver Bear (Special Jury Prize), Berlin 1967

***Ma Nuit chez Maud* (*Six contes moraux, III*) 1969 (*My Night at Maud's*), 110 min.**

Production: Les Films du Losange, with FFP, Simar Films, Les Films du Carrosse, Les Productions de la Gueville, Renn Productions, Les Films de la Pléiade, Les Films des Deux Mondes
Screenplay and dialogues: Eric Rohmer
Cinematography: Nestor Almendros (35mm b/w)
Editing: Cécile Decugis
Sound: Jean-Pierre Ruh
Principal actors: Jean-Louis Trintignant, Françoise Fabian, Antoine Vitez, Marie-Christine Barrault
Prix Max Ophüls 1970

***Le Genou de Claire* (*Six contes moraux, V*) 1970 (*Claire's Knee*), 105 min.**

Production: Les Films du Losange
Screenplay and dialogues: Eric Rohmer
Cinematography: Nestor Almendros (35mm Eastmancolor)
Editing: Cécile Decugis
Sound: Jean-Pierre Ruh
Principal actors: Jean-Claude Brialy, Aurora Cornu, Béatrice Romand, Laurence de Monaghan, Michèle Montel, Gérard Falconetti, Fabrice Luchini
Prix Méliès 1970, Prix Louis Delluc 1971

***L'Amour l'après-midi* (*Six contes moraux, VI*) 1972 (*Love in the Afternoon/Chloé in the Afternoon*), 98 min.**

Production: Les Films du Losange with Columbia SA
Screenplay and dialogues: Eric Rohmer
Cinematography: Nestor Almendros (35mm Eastmancolor)
Editing: Cécile Decugis
Sound: Jean-Pierre Ruh

Music: Arie Dzierlatka
Principal actors: Bernard Verley, Zouzou, Françoise Verley, Daniel Ceccaldi

Die Marquise von O... 1976 (***La Marquise d'O.../The Marquise of O...***), 102 min.

Production: Les Films du Losange, Janus Film Produktion, Artemis Film, Gaumont, United Artists
Adaptation, screenplay, and dialogues: Eric Rohmer, after Heinrich von Kleist
Cinematography: Nestor Almendros (35mm Eastmancolor)
Editing: Cécile Decugis
Sound: Jean-Pierre Ruh
Artistic design: Roger von Möllendorff
Costumes: Moidele Bickel
Music: Roger Delmotte
Principal actors: Edith Clever, Bruno Ganz, Peter Lühr, Edda Seippel, Otto Sander, Bernhard Frey
Voice actors for French version: Marie-Christine Barrault, Feodor Atkine, Hubert Gignoux, Suzanne Flon
Special Jury Prize, Cannes 1976

Perceval le Gallois 1979 (***Perceval***), 138 min.

Production: Les Films du Losange and FR3, with ARD, SSR, RAI and Gaumont
Production director: Margaret Menegoz
Adaptation, translation, screenplay, and dialogues: Eric Rohmer, after Chrétien de Troyes
Cinematography: Nestor Almendros (35mm Eastmancolor)
Editing: Cécile Decugis
Sound: Jean-Pierre Ruh
Mixing: Dominique Hennequin
Artistic design: Jean-Pierre Kohut Svelko
Principal actors: Fabrice Luchini, André Dussolier, Pascale de Boysson, Clémentine Amouroux, Marc Eyraud, Gérard Falconetti, Arielle Dombasle, Coco Ducados, Marie-Christine Barrault, Anne-Laure Meury
Prix Méliès 1979

La Femme de l'aviateur* (*Comédies et proverbes, I*)** 1981 (The Aviator's Wife***), 104 min.

Production: Les Films du Losange
Screenplay and dialogues: Eric Rohmer
Cinematography: Bernard Lutic (16mm Eastmancolor)
Editing: Cécile Decugis
Sound: Georges Prat
Music: Jean-Louis Valéro
Mixing: Dominique Hennequin
Principal actors: Philippe Marlaud, Marie Rivière, Anne-Laure Meury, Mathieu Carrière, Haydée Caillot, Rosette, Fabrice Luchini

Le Beau Mariage* (*Comédies et proverbes, II*)** 1982 (A Good Marriage***), 97 min.

Production: Les Films du Losage and Les Films du Carrosse
Screenplay and dialogues: Eric Rohmer
Cinematography: Bernard Lutic (35mm Fujicolor)
Sound: Georges Prat
Music: Ronan Girre and Simon des Innocents
Mixing: Dominique Hennequin
Paintings: Alberto Bali
Principal actors: Béatrice Romand, André Dussolier, Feodor Atkine, Arielle Dombasle, Huguette Faget, Pascal Greggory
Prix Louis Lumière 1982
Golden Phoenix (Best Actress, Béatrice Romand), Venice 1982

Pauline à la plage* (*Comédies et proverbes, III*)** 1983 (Pauline at the Beach***) 94 min.

Production: Les Films du Losange, Les Films Ariane
Screenplay and dialogues: Eric Rohmer
Cinematography: Nestor Almendros (35mm Eastmancolor)
Editing: Cécile Decugis
Sound: Georges Prat
Mixing: Dominique Hennequin
Actors: Amanda Langlet, Arielle Dombasle, Pascal Greggory, Feodor Atkine, Simon de la Brosse, Rosette
Golden Bear (Best Director), Berlin

***Les Nuits de la pleine lune* (*Comédies et proverbes, IV*)** 1984 **(*Full Moon in Paris*)**, 102 min.

Production: Les Films du Losange, Les Films Ariane
Screenplay and dialogues: Eric Rohmer
Cinematography: Renato Berta (35mm colour)
Editing: Cécile Decugis
Sound: Georges Prat
Music: Elli et Jacno
Mixing: Dominique Hennequin
Decors: Pascale Ogier
Principal actors: Pascale Ogier, Tcheky Karyo, Fabrice Luchini, Virginie Thévenet, Christian Vadim, Laszlo Szabo
Golden Phoenix (Best Actress, Pascale Ogier), Venice 1984

***Le Rayon vert* (*Comédies et proverbes, V*)** 1986 **(*The Green Ray/ Summer*)**, 98 min.

Production: Les Films du Losange, with Canal Plus
Screenplay: Eric Rohmer
Dialogues: Eric Rohmer, Marie Rivière and the actors
Cinematography: Sophie Maintigneux (16mm colour)
Editing: Maria-Luisa Garcia
Mixing: Dominique Hennequin
Production assistant: Françoise Etchegaray
Green ray photography: Philippe Demard
Principal actors: Marie Rivière, Vincent Gauthier, Béatrice Romand, Rosette, Irène Skobline
Golden Lion (Best Picture), Venice 1986

4 Aventures de Reinette et Mirabelle 1986 **(*Four Adventures of Reinette and Mirabelle*)**, 95 min.

Production: Compagnie Eric Rohmer (CER) and Les Films du Losange
Screenplay and dialogues: Eric Rohmer
Cinematography: Sophie Maintigneux (16mm colour)
Editing: Maria-Luisa Garcia
Sound: Pascal Ribier, Pierre Camus
Music: Jean-Louis Valéro and Ronan Girre
Production assistant: Françoise Etchegaray
Paintings; Joëlle Miquel

Principal actors: Joëlle Miquel, Jessica Forde, Marie Rivière, Béatrice Romand, Haydée Caillot, Fabrice Luchini

L'Ami de mon amie* (*Comédies et proverbes, VI*)** 1987 (Boyfriends and Girlfriends***), 102 min.

Production: Les Films du Losange
Screenplay and dialogues: Eric Rohmer
Cinematography: Bernard Lutic (35mm colour)
Sound: Georges Prat
Music: Jean-Louis Valéro
Mixing: Dominique Hennequin
Principal actors: Emmanuelle Chaulet, Sophie Renoir, Anne-Laure Meury, Eric Viellard, François-Eric Gendron

Conte de printemps* (*Contes des quatre saisons*)** 1990 (A Tale of Springtime***), 108 min.

Production: CER, Les Films du Losange
Screenplay and dialogues: Eric Rohmer
Cinematography: Luc Pagès (35mm colour)
Editing: Maria-Luisa Garcia
Sound: Pascal Ribier
Mixing: Jean-Pierre Laforce
Principal actors: Anne Teyssèdre, Florence Darel, Hughes Quester, Eloïse Bennett

Conte d'hiver* (*Contes des quatre saisons*)** 1992 (A Winter's Tale***), 114 min.

Production: Les Films du Losange, CER, with Soficas Investimage, Sofiarp, and Canal Plus
Screenplay and dialogues: Eric Rohmer
Cinematography: Luc Pagès, and Maurice Girard for Shakespeare's *A Winter's Tale* (35mm colour)
Editing: Mary Stephen
Sound: Pascal Ribier
Mixing: Jean-Pierre Laforce
Principal actors: Charlotte Very, Frédéric Van Den Driessche, Michel Voletti, Hervé Furic, Ava Loraschi, Christiane Desbois

L'Arbre, le Maire et la Médiathèque ou Les sept hasards 1993 (***The Tree, the Mayor and the Leisure Centre of the Seven Fortuities***), 105 min.

Production: Compagnie Eric Rohmer
Screenplay and *mise en scène*: Eric Rohmer
Cinematography: Diane Baratier (16mm colour)
Sound: Pascal Ribier
Montage: Mary Stephen
Music: Sébastien Erms
Principal actors: Pascal Greggory, Arielle Dombasle, Fabrice Luchini, Clémentine Amouroux, François-Marie Banier

Conte d'été (***Contes des quatre saisons***) 1996 (***A Tale of Summer***), 113 min.

Production: Les Films du Losange, La Sept cinéma, Canal Plus
Screenplay and *mise en scène*: Eric Rohmer
Cinematography: Diane Baratier (35mm colour)
Sound: Pascal Ribier
Montage: Mary Stephen
Music: Philippe Eidel, Sébastien Erms
Principal actors: Amanda Langlet, Melvil Poupaud, Gwenaëlle Simon, Aurélia Nolin

Conte d'automne (***Contes des quatre saisons***) 1998 (***A Tale of Autumn***), 110 min.

Production: Les Films du Losange, La Sept cinéma
Screenplay and *mise en scène*: Eric Rohmer
Cinematography: Diane Baratier (35mm colour)
Sound: Pascal Ribier
Montage: Mary Stephen
Principal actors: Marie Rivière, Béatrice Romand, Alain Libolt, Didier Sandre, Alexia Portal, Stéphane Darmon, Aurélia Alcaïs
Best Screenplay, Venice 1998

L'Anglaise et le Duc 2001 (***The Lady and the Duke***), 125 min.

Production: Pathé Image/CER, with France 3
Screenplay and *mise en scène*: Eric Rohmer, based on *Journal of My Life during the French Revolution* by Grace Elliott
Cinematography: Diane Baratier (colour beta DV)

Sound: Pascal Ribier
Montage: Mary Stephen
Historical research: Hervé Grandsart
Artistic director: Antoine Beau
Interior sets: Antoine Fontaine
Exteriors: Jean-Baptiste Marot
Costumes: Pierre-Jean Larroque
Special effects: BUF Compagnie
Principal actors: Jean-Claude Dreyfus, Lucy Russel, François Marthouret, Leonard Cobiant, Caroline Morin, Alain Libolt, Helena Dubel, Georges Benoit, Charlotte Very, Rosette, Marie Rivière, Serge Renko, Christian Ameri, Eric Viellard, François-Marie Banier

Triple agent 2004, 115 min.

Production: CER/Rezo Films, with Bim Distribuzione (Italy), Alta Producción and Tournasol Films (Spain), Strada Productions (Greece), Mentor Cinema Company (Russia)
Screenplay and dialogues: Eric Rohmer
Cinematography: Diane Baratier (35mm colour)
Editing: Mary Stephen
Sound: Pascal Ribier
Costumes: Pierre-Jean Larroque
Sets: Antoine Fontaine
Music: Dimitri Shostakovitch
Paintings and sketches: Pascale Boillot, Charlotte Very
Historical research: Irène Skobline
Principal actors: Katerina Didaskalou, Serge Renko, Amanda Langlet, Emmanuel Salinger, Dimitri Rafalsky, Vitaliy Cheremet, Jorg Schnass, Georges Benoit

Les Amours d'Astrée et de Céladon 2007

Production: CER/Rezo Films with Alta Producción (Spain), BIM Distribuzione (Italy)
Screenplay and dialogues: Eric Rohmer, after the novel by Honoré d'Urfé
Cinematography: Diane Baratier
Costumes: Pierre-Jean Larroque
Principal actors: Stéphane de Cravencourt, Andy Gillet, Cécile Cassel, Serge Renko, Jocelyn Quivrin

Shorts

Journal d'un scélérat 1949–50, 16mm, b/w silent, approx. 30 min.

Screenplay: Eric Rohmer
Editing: Eric Rohmer
Actor: Paul Gégauff

Présentation, ou Charlotte et son steack 1951, 16mm b/w, 12 min.

Production: Guy de Ray
Screenplay and dialogues: Eric Rohmer
Music: Maurice le Roux
Montage: Agnès Guillemot
Actors: Jean-Luc Godard, Andrée Bertrand (voice Anna Karina), Anne Coudret (voice Stéphane Audran)

Bérénice 1954, 15 min.

Screenplay, dialogues, and editing: Eric Rohmer
Cinematography: Jacques Rivette (16mm b/w)
Actors: Eric Rohmer, Teresa Gratia

La Sonate à Kreutzer 1956, 50 min.

Production: Jean-Luc Godard
Screenplay, dialogues, and editing: Eric Rohmer, after Leo Tolstoy
Cinematography: Jacques Rivette (16mm b/w)
Actors: Jean-Claude Brialy, Eric Rohmer, Françoise Martinelli

Véronique et son cancre 1958, 20 min.

Production: AJYM Films
Screenplay, dialogues, and editing: Eric Rohmer
Cinematography: Charles Bitsch (35mm b/w)
Sound: Jean-Claude Marchetti
Principal actors: Nicole Berger, Stella Dassas

La Boulangère de Monceau (***Six contes moraux, I***) 1962 (***The Girl at the Monceau Bakery***), 26 min.

Production: Studios Africa, Les Films du Losange
Screenplay, dialogues, and editing: Eric Rohmer
Cinematography: Jean-Michel Meurice (16mm b/w)
Principal actors: Barbet Schroeder (voice Bertrand Tavernier), Fred Junk, Michèle Girardon, Claudine Soubrier

La Carrière de Suzanne* (*Six contes moraux, II*)** 1963 (Suzanne's Career***), 52 min.

Production: Les Films du Losange
Screenplay, dialogues, and editing: Eric Rohmer
Cinematography: Daniel Lacambre (16mm b/w)
Principal actors: Catherine Sée, Christian Charrière, Philippe Beuzen, Diane Wilkinson, Jean-Claude Biette, Patrick Bauchau, Pierre Cottrell, Jean-Louis Comolli

Nadja à Paris, 1964, 13 min.

Production: Les Films du Losange
Screenplay: Eric Rohmer
Text: Nadja Tesich
Cinematography: Nestor Almendros (16mm b/w)
Editing: Jacqueline Raynal
Actress: Nadja Tesich

Place de l'Etoile, 1965 in ***Paris vu par...*** (***Six in Paris***), 15 min.

Production: Les Films du Losange
Screenplay and dialogues: Eric Rohmer
Voiceover: Eric Rohmer
Cinematography: Alain Levent and Nestor Almendros (16mm Ektachrome)
Editing: Jacqueline Raynal
Principal actors: Jean-Marie Rouzière, Marcel Gallon, Jean Douchet, Philippe Sollers

Une étudiante aujourd'hui, 1966, 13 min.

Production: Les Films du Losange
Screenplay: Eric Rohmer, after an idea by Denise Basdevant
Cinematography: Nestor Almendros (16mm b/w)
Editing: Jacqueline Raynal

Fermière à Montfaucon, 1968, 13 min.

Production: Les Films du Losange
Screenplay: Eric Rohmer, after an idea by Denise Basdevant
Cinematography: Nestor Almendros (16mm colour)
Actress: Monique Sendron

Bois ton café, 1986 (colour video), 3 min.
Music: Jean-Louis Valéro
Continuity: Eric Rohmer
Actors: Rosette, Pascal Greggory

Television

1963: *Paysages urbains*
1964: *Les Cabinets de physique au XVIIIe siècle; Les Métamorphoses du paysage: l'ère industrielle; Les Salons de Diderot; Perceval ou le Conte du Graal*
1965: *Don Quichotte de Cervantes; Histoires extraordinaires d'Edgar Poe; Les 'Caractères' de La Bruyère; Entretien sur Pascal; Carl T. Dreyer* ('Cinéastes de notre temps'); *Post-face à* Boudu sauvé des eaux
1966: *Victor Hugo: les Contemplations; Le Celluloïd et le marbre* ('Cinéastes de notre temps')
1967: *L'Homme et la machine; L'Homme et les images*
1968: *Entretien avec Mallarmé; L'Homme et les frontières; L'Homme et les gouvernements; Nancy au XVIIIe siècle; Postface à* L'Atalante; *Louis Lumière*
1969: *Victor Hugo architecte; La Sorcière de Michelet; Le Béton dans la ville*
1970: *Le Français, langue vivante?*
1975: *Ville nouvelle: 1. L'Enfance d'une ville; 2. La Diversité du paysage urbain; 3. La Forme d'une ville; 4. Logement à la demande*
1980: *Catherine de Heilbronn*
1988: *Trio en mi bémol*
1989: *Jeux de société*

Select bibliography

See also references at the end of each chapter.

Books by Rohmer

With Claude Chabrol, *Hitchcock* (1957), Paris, Editions universitaires; *Hitchcock: The First Forty-Four Films* (1979), tr. Stanley Hochman, New York, Ungar. This film-by-film analysis turns on the idea of 'exchange' or the transfer of guilt in a universe wracked by original sin. Rohmer's contributions on the American period are exacting and anecdote-free. A model monograph in its time, though it lacks the theoretical sophistication of Rohmer's best work.

Le Goût de la beauté (1984, reprinted 2004), Paris, Cahiers du cinéma, ed. Jean Narboni; *The Taste for Beauty* (1989), tr. Carol Volk, Cambridge, Cambridge University Press. Collects Rohmer's major statements on film aesthetics, first published in the late 1940s and 1950s. Also contains reviews of Huston, Hawks, Welles, Bergman, Hitchcock and Renoir among others, and later pieces on the *Contes moraux* and narrative discourse. Indispensable.

L'Organisation de l'espace dans le Faust de Murnau (1977, reprinted 2000), Paris, Cahiers du cinéma. Defended in 1972, Rohmer's doctoral thesis explores pictorial, architectural and filmic space in Murnau's 1926 masterwork and the manner whereby choices in *mise en scène* create dynamic spatial figures of convergence and divergence, expansion and contraction. Compares *Faust* with Murnau's *Nosferatu*, *The Last Laugh*, *Sunrise*, and *City Lights* and with other expressionist works.

Trio en mi bémol (1989), Arles, Actes Sud. The text of the play written and staged between the *Comédies et proverbes* and *Contes des quatre saisons.*

De Mozart en Beethoven: essai sur la notion de profondeur en musique (1998), Arles, Actes Sud. Argues for an attentive, philosophically informed mode of listening to the classical repertoire in a search for depth. Contains brief but revealing passages on the uses and abuses of music in film (on Godard and Duras in particular).

Screenplays of works by Rohmer

The following titles have been published in the series 'Petite bibliothèque des Cahiers du Cinéma': *Six contes moraux* (1998); *Comédies et proverbes* (two volumes, 1999); *Contes des quatre saisons* (1998); *Triple agent: scénario* (2004). By dint of its literary structure and first-person point of view, *Six contes moraux* can be read independently as an intermedial work of art. Shot-by-shot descriptions of many of Rohmer's films can be found in *L'Avant-scène cinéma* (see numbers 69, 98, 173, 221, 293, 310, 336, 355, 366. 392, 414, 429, 455 ...).

In English, two screenplays are available: *The Marquise of O* (1985), including the Kleist novella and an afterward by Alan Spiegel, New York, Ungar; and *My Night at Maud's* (1993), ed. English Showalter, New Brunswick, New Jersey, Rutgers University Press.

Selected books on Rohmer

Bonitzer, Pascal (1991, 2nd ed. 1995), *Eric Rohmer*, Paris, Editions de l'Etoile/Cahiers du cinéma. This investigation of narrative duplicity and narcissistic blindness presents Rohmer as an anti-realist whose films play on mysteries, secrets, and suspense. If the essay focuses on the *Contes moraux*, its hypotheses on the role of the spectator and on narrative desire extend to the entirety of Rohmer's work.

Crisp, Colin (1988), *Eric Rohmer: Realist and Moralist*, Bloomington and Indianapolis, Indiana University Press. The only monograph previously available in English takes Rohmer's Catholic beliefs as its starting point and deftly unravels the workings of grace, redemption, chance and necessity from *Le Signe du Lion* to *Les Nuits de la pleine lune*.

Desbarats, Carole (1990), *'Pauline à la plage' d'Eric Rohmer*, Crisnée (Belgium), Yellow Now. Abundantly illustrated, this single-film analysis includes the text of a 1987 presentation by Rohmer on pictorial quotation in the *Comédies et proverbes*.

Heredero, Carlos F. and Antonio Santamarina (1991), *Eric Rohmer*, Madrid, Cáthedra. The central chapter on style, which unravels the myth of visual transparency with great subtlety, makes this Spanish-language study worth seeking out, as does its comprehensive bibliography.

Hertay, Alain (1998), *Eric Rohmer: Comédies et proverbes*, Liège, Editions de Céfal. Argues for Rohmer's second film cycle as an ironic representation of the inadequacy of social relations and the intermittence of desire in the 1980s. Features unpublished interviews with actors and technicians involved in the films' production.

Magny, Joël (1995), *Eric Rohmer*, Paris, 2nd edn, Payot & Rivages. The best single introduction in French to Rohmer, this comprehensive volume presents a substantive critical essay and film-by-film commentaries which go well beyond ordinary synopses in their attention to theme and style.

Molinier, Philippe (2001), *Ma Nuit chez Maud*, Neuilly, Atlande. Billed as a prep guide for competitive exams, this volume provides close analysis of the 1969 film in relation to the *Contes moraux*.

Serceau, Michel (2000), *Eric Rohmer: les jeux de l'amour du hasard et du discours*. Paris, Editions du Cerf. Underscores the social import of Rohmer's work as a representation of French society, its class and gender distinctions, languages, habitats, and conceptions of love.

Tortajada, Maria (1999), *Le Spectateur séduit: le libertinage dans le cinéma d'Eric Rohmer*, Paris, Kimé. Informed by psychoanalytic apparatus theory, this work underscores structural ambiguities which simultaneously foster spectatorial identification and separation. The relationship of Rohmer's characters to eighteenth-century libertine strategies of seduction (and to their New Wave counterparts) is discussed, as is the instability of desire.

Vidal, Marion (1977), *Les* Contes moraux *d'Eric Rohmer*, Paris, Pierre Lherminier Editeur. Explores the contradictions behind the 'moral' position of Rohmer's heroes. Stresses plot and character typologies, though comments on editing and acting are often insightful.

Interviews with Rohmer

The single best introduction to the working methods of the director – and his sole official television appearance in that capacity – is the two-part documentary *Eric Rohmer: Preuves à l'appui* (AMIP/La Sept ARTE/INA/Les Films du Losange, 1994), directed by André S. Labarthe for the television series 'Cinéma, de notre temps'.

Equally revealing is Françoise Etchegaray and Jean-André Fieschi's *La Fabrique du* Conte d'été (CNDP/SCEREN, 2005), a 'making-of' that redefines the parameters of that now-ubiquitous genre.

Since the 1980s, French-language journals *Cahiers du cinéma* and *Positif* have consistently interviewed the filmmaker with the release of each new feature. Regrettably, English-language interviews remain scarce, though *Sight and Sound, Film Comment*, and, more recently, the on-line journal *Senses of Cinema* have generously covered Rohmer's career.

Index

Note: for references to individual films other than Rohmer's own, see the name of the director. Page listings in *italics* refer to illustrated figures.